European History in Perspective
General Editor: Jeremy Black

European History in Perspective
Series Standing Order
ISBN 0–333–71694–9 hardcover
ISBN 0–333–69336–1 paperback
(*outside North America only*)

You can receive future titles in this series as they are published by placing a standing order. Please contact your bookseller or, in the case of difficulty, write to us at the address below with your name and address, the title of the series and the ISBN quoted above.

Customer Services Department, Palgrave Ltd
Houndmills, Basingstoke, Hampshire RG21 6XS, England

Nazi Germany

TIM KIRK

First published 2007 by
PALGRAVE MACMILLAN
Houndmills, Basingstoke, Hampshire RG21 6XS and
175 Fifth Avenue, New York, N.Y. 10010
Companies and representatives throughout the world

PALGRAVE MACMILLAN is the global academic imprint of the Palgrave Macmillan division of St. Martin's Press, LLC and of Palgrave Macmillan Ltd. Macmillan® is a registered trademark in the United States, United Kingdom and other countries. Palgrave is a registered trademark in the European Union and other countries.

ISBN-13: 978–0–333–60072–6 HB
ISBN-10: 0–333–60072–X HB
ISBN-13: 978–0–333–60073–3 PB
ISBN-10: 0–333–60073–8 PB

This book is printed on paper suitable for recycling and made from fully managed and sustained forest sources.

A catalogue record for this book is available from the British Library.

A catalog record for this book is available from the Library of Congress.

10   9   8   7   6   5   4   3   2   1
16   15   14   13   12   11   10   09   08   07

Printed in China

Contents

Acknowledgements

This book has taken a long time to make its appearance, and I am grateful to a number of people at Macmillan/Palgrave for their support and forbearance, above all Jonathan Reeve, Terka Acton, Beverley Tarquini and Sonya Barker. No book is ever entirely the product of the author alone. Among the many anonymous and unwitting contributors are members of the many cohorts of students over many years at the universities of Northumbria and Newcastle upon Tyne, who helped prevent some of my fixed ideas becoming immovable. I am grateful to the many friends and colleagues who, in one way or another, have helped this one finally see the light of day, including Jeremy Boulton, Malcolm Gee, Jeremy Gregory, Graham Ford, Bridget Leonard, Tony McElligott, Roger Newbrook, Colin Riordan, Patrick Salmon, and Jill Steward, and especially Alan Worsley for his invaluable advice. Special thanks are due to Stephen Salter and David Saunders, both of whom read earlier versions of the manuscript and whose observations were invariably helpful and constructive. Above all, however, thanks are due to Liz Harvey whose careful reading, thoughtful comments and constructive criticism have gone far beyond the assistance that any friend or colleague should be called upon to give, and have undoubtedly made this a better book.

Introduction

Between October 1976 and April 1977 some 3000 pupils from schools across West Germany took part in a revealing exercise. They were all set the same essay title: 'What I have heard about Adolf Hitler.... Most of the students were asked to complete the exercise in one period (45 minutes) in class, but the majority took about half an hour and produced on average three quarters of a page. Extracts from the results were published later the same year, following pre-publication features in *Spiegel* and *Die Zeit*. The widespread confusion, ignorance and even indifference about the history of Nazism and the Second World War revealed by the exercise prompted further headlines in Germany and abroad: few students knew exactly when Hitler had lived or when the Nazi dictatorship had been established, and most had little idea about the nature of the regime, its policies or the experience of those who had been persecuted.[1] Equally revealing were some of the responses received by Dieter Bossmann, the organiser of the exercise and editor of the subsequent book, from teachers. Many were at a loss about how to approach the subject, and felt that they lacked adequate teaching materials or guidelines. The observations ill-informed, but not necessarily untypical, and it should be added that they reflect not so much what children were taught in school, as what they heard from their families or absorbed from popular discussion. At the height of the Cold War, when theories of 'totalitarianism', were popularised in the media, it is not surprising that some two dozen of the students stated emphatically that Hitler was a Communist or a Socialist.

A quarter of a century on, few would argue that a lack of awareness of Hitler and the Nazis is much of a problem; and surveys of the views of university history teachers published annually in the magazine

1

History Today suggest that even fewer would argue the subject is under-represented on school curricula; in fact many would argue excitedly (and mistakenly) that students are only interested in dictators. In addition, this explosion of academic concern has been accompanied by an unflagging popular interest in the events of the period. Hitler, the Nazi regime, the Second World War and the Holocaust are now more than ever ultimate reference points in the public discussion of a range of political issues, and have increasingly dominated 'popular history' as it is understood by the mass media. This impression of abundance is misleading, however, and there remain many aspects of the history of Nazism and the Third Reich where there is relatively little to read, and even less that is readily available in English.

The main reasons for researching and writing about the subject, however, remain the same as they always were: it was one of the most important and revealing episodes in European history. Although Hitler's dictatorship was relatively short-lived, the scale and intensity of the crimes it unleashed was unparalleled, and still remains to be satisfact-orily explained. To that extent the history of Nazi Germany remains the 'past that will not pass away'; and this is not least because interpret-ations and representations of Nazism of all kinds – academic, official or popular – have been determined in part by the political agendas of post-war Europe.

It is not the main purpose of this book to deal with interpretations: there are already several excellent overviews of historiography, which combine a history of the history of Nazism with rigorous analysis and evaluation of changing perspectives.[2] Others, with equal thoroughness, have located specific debates about the meaning of Nazism – above all the *Historikerstreit* of the 1980s – in a broader historiographical context.[3] Nevertheless it is useful at the outset to introduce some of the most important issues that have been raised during the 60 years since the end of the Second World War.

Peculiarities of German Historiography

Although Nazism attracted sympathy, support and imitators from all European societies, and vehement opposition and active resistance on the part of many Germans, one of the most important questions confronting historians is the relationship of Nazism to German history. Leaving aside the anti-German accounts of the immediate post-war years (and the recent recrudescence of national generalisation in Goldhagen's

Hitler's Willing Executioners), the issue of Germany's 'peculiar' or 'exceptional history' remains very much a matter of continuing debate.[4] Put simply, the so-called '*Sonderweg*' thesis suggests that the history of Germany diverged from that of other western countries. The idea that Germany was different was widespread among German academics long before the Second World War, when Germany was compared favourably with the liberal West. The comparison looked less flattering from the post-1945 perspective: the institutional peculiarities of imperial Germany – above all the strength of the monarchy, military and civil service – which had been seen as positive by contemporaries, now served to explain the catastrophe of the Third Reich. Unlike Britain, France and the United States, Germany had not undergone a bourgeois revolution, and this meant that the elites of pre-industrial Prussia retained political power and dominated German institutions, above all the army and the civil service. The middle classes on the other hand, cowed by the failure of the 1848 revolutions, were, according to this argument, compelled to accept the 'feudal' values of the traditional ruling class. When constitutional government and parliamentary democracy were eventually established in Germany after the defeat of 1918 the traditional elites retained their social position and political and economic power. Those most hostile to liberal democracy were over-represented in the country's most important institutions, and their willingness, and in some cases eagerness, to consider authoritarian solutions to the problems of the Weimar Republic contributed to its demise and the eventual triumph of Hitler.

There have been many criticisms of the idea of a German *Sonderweg*. One of the most fundamental objections is to the normative assumptions underpinning the idea of successful and aberrant experiences of 'modernisation'. The notion of 'abnormal' history, defined as deviation from a western model of progress towards liberal democracy not only has a triumphalist ring, but glosses over the myths and misunderstanding about the democracies. Proponents of the *Sonderweg*, it has been argued, have not adequately scrutinised the Anglo-Saxon model against which they went on to measure Germany's deficiencies. In addition, historians of pre-Nazi Germany rightly object to an essentially ahistorical interpretation of German history, which reduces the Weimar Republic to little more than a prelude to Nazism and fails to recognise the many possible outcomes of earlier historical developments, none of them an inevitable or a necessary step on the way to the dictatorship.[5]

We should be sceptical of explanations of the origins of Nazism that emphasise the problematic course of German history, but this does not mean that the Nazis appeared like a bolt from the blue after the First World

War, or were the consequence of short-term factors alone. The discussion in chapter one locates the long-term origins of Nazism in the emergent radical right of the late nineteenth century, and by implication places it alongside other varieties of a broader European fascism with similar ideological and organisational roots. Although there are compelling reasons for emphasising the unique radicalism of Nazi racial policy and genocide, as there are for comparisons between the Nazi police state and that of the Soviet Union, there are – arguably – stronger reasons for seeing Nazism as part of a broader wave of (largely unsuccessful) fascist movements which took hold in much of continental Europe between the wars; movements with similar values, a similar social base and similarly close relations with other extreme nationalist and authoritarian conservative movements. Fascism, as Michael Mann has reiterated, was not 'a mere sideshow', but 'an essential, if predominantly undesirable part of modernity'.[6]

This raises the question of where we locate Nazism among the political ideologies and organisations of the twentieth century. Contemporary commentators, particularly those on the left, observed similarities between Italian fascism and a number of similar radical right-wing populist movements and analysed the new political development as a generic phenomenon.[7] The similarities between Fascism and Nazism were even conceded by Hitler himself:

It is striking, how the development of Germany and Italy proceeds in a related fashion. [. . .] I must say I am always happy to meet Mussolini: he is a great personality altogether . . . In its intellectual fundamentals our doctrine is self-contained, but every person is the product of one's own influences and those of others, and one should not say that events in Italy were without influence on us. The brownshirt would perhaps not have come about without the blackshirt. The march on Rome in 1922 was one of the turning points in history. The fact alone that such a thing could be done gave us impetus.[8]

The ideology and constituency of the two movements (and others beyond them), the similarities in their organisation and tactics, the ritualistic trappings of party and state, the way they came to power, and not least the way in which that power was exercised reinforced the understanding of generic fascism as a broad movement encompassing both Italian Fascism and Nazism, and despite the relative lack of systematic comparative analysis of the two regimes this still seems the most convincing comparative framework within which to locate the NSDAP – but not the only one that historians have found persuasive.

During the Cold War, and particularly during the 1950s, when tension was greatest between the West and the Soviet bloc, western political scientists and popular commentators turned their attention to the similarities between Nazi Germany and the Soviet Union under Stalin, pointing out the structural similarities between the two ideologically opposed regimes: the messianic nature of their respective ideologies, the total claim on the life and mind of the individual in the service of the state and its leader, and not least the power of the secret police. The apparent efficiency of these police states in enforcing their claims suggested a qualitative difference between 'totalitarian' dictatorships such as Nazi Germany and the Soviet Union and less extreme 'authoritarian' states, most of which were not (or had ever been) enemies of the West, and some of which were cold-war allies.[9]

Similarly, when the intellectual climate shifted to the left in the late 1960s there was a renewed emphasis on the generic nature of fascism, which was often no less a product of the political climate of the time than theories of totalitarianism had been in their day.[10] Some of these new studies of fascism have easily withstood the test of time;[11] others increasingly came to reflect the atomisation of the 'new left' itself during the early 1970s. Although there was something of a muted revival of the totalitarianism model during the 1980s, the focus of debate moved on to other issues. It is possible to write about fascism as a generic phenomenon without having to embark on a prolonged theoretical justification, as has been demonstrated by a number of recent collections and comparative studies.[12]

Debates about the nature of Nazism raised the further issue of the role of Hitler. The cult of leadership which the Nazis themselves promoted reinforced the image of a 'strong dictator' that dominated interpretations during the decades that followed the end of the war. Increasingly, however, this interpretation was challenged, and it has become increasingly clear that Nazi Germany was characterised not by strong central government, or by monolithic political discipline in the service of a clear programmatic agenda, but by administrative chaos. The formulation and implementation of policy in the Third Reich proceeded not in accordance with a pre-conceived plan overseen by Hitler himself, but by a process of 'cumulative radicalisation' which rested as much on radical initiatives from below as the straightforward imposition of policy from above. This structuralist' or 'functionalist' explanation of politics in the Third Reich was in turn challenged by 'intentionalist' historians, who reasserted the centrality of Hitler, especially, but by no means only, in the fields of foreign policy and anti-semitism.[13] This fundamental disagreement dominated debates about the nature of the Nazi Germany during the 1970s and early 1980s, and shifted perspectives discernibly onto the structuralists' terrain, albeit with qualifications: Hitler's intentions were not straightforwardly implemented, but shaped the political climate which made possible the unleashing of the radical dynamics of Nazism.[14]

The debate between intentionalists and structuralists was displaced by a much more explicitly political disagreement during the 1980s. Some historians and political commentators, encouraged by the political shift to the right with the formation of the Kohl administration, wanted finally to consign the Third Reich to history and move on. Their critics, mainly on the liberal left, took exception to what they saw as attempts to relativise Nazism (and especially the Holocaust), in order to furnish Germany with a 'usable past'. The 'historians' quarrel' (*Historikerstreit*) as it was termed, was carried on not only in the pages of academic journals, but also in the broadsheet press, primarily in the pages of the conservative *Frankfurter Allgemeine Zeitung* and the more liberal Hamburg weekly *Die Zeit*. This broader discussion was in itself evidence of the continuing importance of the subject to a general public beyond the self-styled 'guild' of academic historians, and the impossibility of 'historicising' an issue which could so readily prompt public controversy.[15]

Even as the *Historikerstreit* was at its height, it was being eclipsed by developments which altered perspectives fundamentally: the collapse of the Soviet bloc, and with it the German Democratic Republic and the re-unification of Germany. The most direct consequences of these events for the historiography of the Third Reich were relatively minor. First there was an end to discussion of the so-called 'Stamokap' theories of fascism, according to which the Nazi party and its leader were tools of big business rather than historical agents in their own right. Although it was universally rejected by Marxists outside the Soviet bloc, and half-heartedly subscribed to by those within it (who were scarcely free to reject it as thoroughly as some of them might have liked), it had been regularly discussed at some length in the West. Another direct consequence was the attempt, less fruitful than some of its proponents would have liked, to suggest parallels between the Nazi regime and the recently defeated 'totalitarian' regime in the GDR.

In the meantime focus on political and institutional studies had given way to a greater emphasis on the social history of Nazi Germany, beginning with the *Alltagsgeschichte* 'everyday history' of the late 1970s and early 1980s. This attempt to write 'history from below' was not without its problems or its critics, but it opened up both new fields of enquiry and new perspectives of interpretation.[16] Where earlier interpretations had all too readily asserted clear categories and black-and-white distinctions between oppressors and resisters, for example, or victims and perpetrators, the new social history showed that the relationship between regime and people was far more complicated: attitudes shifted over time; popular responses to the regime were selective and both consent and dissent were often limited to specific policies; behaviour was determined as much by personal circumstances as by political events. This new approach was epitomised in a large-scale collaborative research project on Bavaria in the Third Reich, and the concept of '*Resistenz*' advanced by Martin Broszat. The term was used to suggest an analogy between resistance in the biological sense and the immunity of certain social groups to Nazism in the context of a nuanced 'social history of political behaviour'.[17] The role of consent in a 'plebiscitary democracy', a political system which employs techniques of mass mobilisation to elicit acclamation and consent without enabling genuine political participation, has been recognised more fully, and historians have looked again at the police state, and in particular the extent of collaboration with the Gestapo. These are themes that are explored more fully in Chapter 6.

As the emphasis shifted from the history of institutions to the history of society new questions were raised about the impact of Nazism. There was a re-emphasis on the singularly racist nature of Nazism and the Nazi regime, articulated perhaps most emphatically in the work of Michael Burleigh.[18] The importance of racial policy also informed a number of works on the history of women's experience and population policy in Nazi Germany. Nazi racism was not merely a question of persecuting 'racial' enemies. It also involved the 'purification' of the German nation itself, through the regulation and policing of reproduction and sexuality, compulsory sterilisation, the mass-murder of the mentally and physically handicapped and the promotion of the 'healthy' German family at the expense of excluded, and often in some cases physically segregated, 'asocial' family.[19] There is now a substantial and sophisticated literature on the subjects of reproduction, the family and racial hygiene, themes that are dealt with more fully in Chapter 7.

The mobilisation of support and the promotion of Nazi racial policy were both reinforced by a range of cultural policies that embraced, with the usual confusion of overlapping jurisdictions, the newly created Propaganda Ministry under Goebbels, the education system and the Hitler Youth, along with a plethora of competing offices and institutions – not least the leisure organisation Strength through Joy, which both encouraged participation in 'healthy' collective activity and simultaneously reinforced an ideology of fitness, achievement, health and hygiene. Approaches to the history of culture under the Nazis have tended to focus on the catastrophic impact on high culture and intellectual life that followed upon the regime's unreflecting anti-Semitism and crude hostility to 'cultural bolshevism'. Without diminishing the irreversible loss to German culture caused by the exodus of intellectuals and the wanton destruction or cynical selling off of important work, more recent research has shown that there were conflicting views of culture, even within the Nazi regime.[20] Culture – variously understood – was important in defining what Germany stood for and was fighting for, from the First World War to the assertion in the last months of the war that Germany was fighting for European civilisation – for Christendom itself – against the threatening hordes of Asiatic Bolshevism. Recent research has demonstrated the extent to which these assumptions were not restricted to an ideologically motivated fringe of Nazi ideologues, but were shared in substantial measure by the country's jobbing intelligentsia, the writers, journalists, scientists, researchers and university teachers, who remained in Germany and for the most part worked uncomplainingly in the service of the new regime. Such research has contributed immensely to our understanding of the role of the educated middle classes in Nazi Germany without distracting attention from the grim realities of everyday life in the manner of recent studies of Italian culture under Fascism.[21] Similarly, so far, historical writing seems to have avoided the dangers of reducing Nazism to 'an account phrased in terms of competing discourses and the like'.[22]

The intention of this book is to provide as comprehensive an overview of Nazi Germany as is possible in such a limited space, and to reflect the emphasis and approaches of recent research, especially research in German whose findings are not otherwise widely available to an English-speaking readership. It is based largely on secondary literature, but where possible and appropriate primary sources have been used in an attempt to give something of a feeling of the experience of Nazi Germany from below. The *Deutschland-Berichte* (Germany Reports) of the SPD in exile (Sopade) are an extensive and still a very much under-used resource, and one which, for all the qualifications that have to be made about the particular concerns and perspectives of underground Social Democrats reporting on the political realities and popular opinion in Germany during the 1930s, provides a largely reliable reflection of everyday life under the Nazis both in peace-time and during the first years of the war.[23] Similarly the published reports of the SD provide important insights into the impact of political developments between 1938 and the end of the war. These reports too are coloured by distinctive perspectives and concerns, but – intended as they were for internal consumption rather than publication as propaganda – they are as reliable, if read correctly, as sources of this kind can be.

Despite these attempts to convey something of the impact of Nazism on the everyday lives of ordinary people, what follows is often characterised by the view from above, from the political consequences of the Nazi takeover of power, the development of the political system and the circumstances surrounding the gestation and implementation of policy to the decision-making that led to war, genocide and ultimately defeat, occupation and the division of Germany. Rightly so: despite the obscure, marginal and lowly origins of the Nazi movement, the Nazi dictatorship was, after all, an initiative from above. Hitler attended his first DAP meeting as a paid agent of the state, the movement he took over was helped over obstructions by rich and powerful backers (albeit ones that were untypical, in their support of Nazism, of Germany's elites), and despite the dramatic increase of support for the party that came with the collapse of Germany's conservative parties during the Depression, the NSDAP came to power through palace intrigue rather than popular election, and only with the eventual and grudging consent of a powerful clique among the country's traditional ruling class. A substantial proportion of the leading figures in the regime – ministers and party plenipotentiaries, generals and senior policeman, intellectuals and senior civil servants – were both well-educated and well-heeled. The myth of a nation hijacked because 'simple people' – *das einfache Volk* – were led astray by a demagogue who hijacked the country's otherwise sound political institutions bears little relation to reality, and is a reminder that threats to democracy do not come so much from political unrest as from those who manipulate it.

Chapter 1: The Origins and Development of Nazism

The long-term origins of Nazism are located in the late nineteenth century, when the advent of popular politics transformed all parts of the political spectrum, and all levels of the political process. Everywhere in Europe the existing order was being contested on an unprecedented scale by new forms of political organisation espousing new ideologies. More people were involved in politics, both as activists in political organisations and as voters. The turnout for elections increased dramatically from just over 50 per cent in the Bismarckian Germany of the 1870s to around 85 per cent in the last Reichstag elections before the First World War.[1] The greatest, most obvious challenge came from workers' movements, which attracted a mass membership – particularly in central Europe – and generated the greatest anxiety among Europe's ruling elites. The Social Democratic Party of Germany (*Sozialdemokratische Partei Deutschlands*, SPD) had a million members and was the largest party in the Reichstag after the 1912 election.

The Radical Right in Central Europe

There was no single political party on the right that could match the SPD in terms of political mobilisation. Political allegiances were spread across a fragmented spectrum of conservative and liberal parties in the Reichstag, and more radical nationalist organisations outside parliament. The mainly small, marginal groups which made up the so-called '*völkisch*' movement espoused a new kind of ethnic nationalist ideology. Membership of a more mainstream conservative or nationalist party was often combined with sympathy for, or involvement with one or other of the more radical groups. Adolf Stöcker, for example, sat in the Prussian House of Representatives with the ostensibly respectable German Conservatives (*Deutsche Konservative*), but was also the co-founder (in 1878) and leader of the Christian Social Workers' Party in Berlin. The 'Stöcker movement', as it was sometimes called, tried to win over workers from the irreligious SPD with a mixture of anti-Semitic agitation and proposals for social welfare. The party failed completely in its first election campaign, and Stöcker subsequently redirected his appeal, under the aegis of the 'Berlin movement' of anti-Semitic splinter groups, towards a more receptive constituency among the lower middle classes and university students.[2]

The experience of the Stöcker movement was not untypical. Radical right-wing politics in imperial Germany was an affair of marginal, ephemeral groups with a high turnover of members. Although they made little inroad into support for more established political parties, however, they exercised a substantial degree of ideological influence on mainstream politics. The Agrarian League – which was vehemently opposed to 'Jewish Liberalism', whether political or economic, and to socialism – had enormous influence on the politics of the Conservative Party. In addition, a range of other ostensibly single-issue pressure groups such as the Navy League, the Army League, the Society for the Eastern Marches (*Ostmarkenverein*), and the Pan-German League (*Alldeutscher Verband*) helped shift the political agenda of imperial Germany firmly to the right.[3] Some historians have found very clear precursors of Nazism in this milieu. For Hans-Jürgen Puhle, for example, the Prussian traditions of German conservatism were displaced by *völkisch* nationalism and conservative politics took on 'clearly pre-fascist characteristics.'[4] Similarly, cultural historians in pursuit of an intellectual lineage for the Third Reich have identified a broader culture of 'irrationalism' and 'illiberalism' among the intelligentsia at the turn of the century.[5]

Many historians, foremost among them Geoff Eley, find this kind of analysis problematic in its 'teleological implication' that Wilhelmine Germany was little more than a staging-post on the way to the Third Reich.[6] Similarly, an insistent focus on the prehistory of Nazism distracts attention from the sneaking 'embourgeoisement' of German society, and undue focus on emblematic proto-Nazi intellectuals such as Langbehn and Lagarde distracts attention from more mainstream developments, such as the burgeoning popular commercial culture that was increasingly complementing – and challenging – the classical culture inculcated in the educated middle class through the curriculum of the humanistic *Gymnasium*.

Although a marginal minority, however, the radical right did not exist in isolation from German society. On a whole range of issues – nationhood and geopolitics; authoritarian alternatives to liberal institutions and democratic politics; ethnology and racial difference; class and criminality – *völkisch* ideologues drew on the more 'mainstream' intellectual currents of the day, and the result was often a crude simplification, albeit one which nevertheless passed easily into common usage. Radical nationalism, authoritarian politics, eugenic ambitions and the 'biologist' assumptions that later characterised Nazi thinking were anticipated in the late nineteenth and early twentieth centuries.[7] The formation of geography as an academic discipline, for example, was influenced by the nationalism of influential scholars such as Alfred Kirchhoff, who saw the subject as a way to reinforce patriotism. Similarly, Friedrich Ratzel emphasised the connection between soil and nation (*Boden und Volk*), and a whole range of terms was generated to emphasise the cultural and political bonds between land and people. The distinguished archaeologist Gustaf Kossina drew on his own research findings when he published *German Prehistory, a Pre-eminently National Discipline* for the popular market in 1912. He explained the superiority of the Nordic race – which had had a decisive influence on history – in terms of physical appearance, a calm but firm character, and intellectual brilliance.[8] Radical anti-Semitism – including proposals for deportation and even genocide – was limited to a tiny minority, but the more muted approval of racism and nationalism by respected figures from the imperial establishment, such as the historian Heinrich von Treitschke, lent respectability to racial ideology and facilitated the easy acceptance of racial prejudice.[9]

Such assumptions about racial hierarchy were not by any means peculiar to Germany. Similar ideas characterised the imperial ideologies of Britain and France, both of which governed multi-ethnic colonies where class and status, wealth and power were determined by race; and similar assumptions were widespread in multinational empires such as Russia, and not least Hitler's native Austria. In Vienna anti-Semitism had been deployed very successfully by the Christian Social Party of Karl Lueger to win elections, uniting the middle classes in a singular popular political party of the right.[10] Hitler, who lived in Vienna in the years before the First World War, later noted his admiration for Lueger as a political strategist, but found him wanting because his anti-Semitism was allegedly insincere. His ideological sympathies lay, he claimed, with the much less successful Georg von Schönerer, leader of the Pan-German movement in Austria.[11] (Hitler's own, later, account of his political development should not be taken at face value, and the extent and nature of his anti-Semitism during his Vienna years has been questioned.) It seems unlikely, however, that as a supporter of the Schönerer movement, and reader of the *Deutsches Volksblatt* he remained impervious to the pervasive and virulent anti-Semitism around him.[12] The goal of the Pan-German movement was the union of all Germans within a single 'Greater Germany', a development that had been thwarted with the creation of the 'small German' Reich by Bismarck, and the effective exclusion from Germany of the Germans in the Habsburg empire. This rankled with German nationalists in Austria, who felt beleaguered and outnumbered in the multi-national 'dual monarchy', and many of them wanted, in Schönerer's words, 'to be rid of Bosnia and all that rabble'.[13] Anti-Slav sentiment was a mainstay of the *völkisch* movement in Austria, and tensions were particularly acute in the ethnically mixed territories of western Bohemia.[14] It was in Bohemia that one of the most clearly recognisable precursors of the Nazi movement emerged shortly after the turn of the century. The German Workers' Party (*Deutsche Arbeiterpartei*, DAP) was founded in 1904. Its establishment was prompted by anxieties about the influx of cheap Czech labour from the countryside, and Czech labour had been used to break strikes involving German workers. It was only later that this racism was extended to the Jews and translated into street violence. Nevertheless the party was a clear forerunner of the Nazi Party itself. When the Habsburg empire collapsed in 1918 separate 'successor' branches of the party were established in Austria and Czechoslovakia, and both had close connections with Hitler's own movement in Munich.[15]

Despite such ideological continuities it would be wrong to see Nazism as an inevitable or even an obvious outcome of pre-1914 developments. The *völkisch* movement had a pernicious effect on public opinion, but remained on the margins of politics. The catalyst for the outburst of violent political extremism that nurtured the Nazi Party was the First World War itself. Political opinion became increasingly polarised during the war, and by 1917 the left was pressing for immediate peace and domestic political reform, while the country's military leaders and their political allies made it clear that they were only interested in a 'victory peace'. At the extremes radical left-wingers split off from the SPD to form the Independent Social Democratic Party (*Unabhängige Sozialdemokratische Partei Deutschlands*, USPD), and the increasingly radical right regrouped around the Fatherland Party (*Deutsche Vaterlandspartei*), which was founded by Admiral Tirpitz and Wolfgang Kapp. The latter movement had over a million members by the end of the war, mainly among the middle classes, and the punitive Treaty of Brest-Litovsk, imposed on revolutionary Russia in March 1918, seemed to bring it nearer to fulfilling its expansionist aspirations.[16] Within Germany itself, however, social order was breaking down, and there was growing industrial and political unrest. There were widespread food riots in Berlin during the summer of 1917, accompanied by violent demonstrations and confrontations with officials who failed to control profiteering, or even enforce the authorities' own decrees as people took to plundering food directly from the countryside. In January 1918 a strike movement broke out, not only in Germany, but in Austria and Hungary as well, and workers' councils were elected.[17] The government and the Fatherland Party responded to the situation with an intensified propaganda campaign in which demands for dictatorship, territorial annexations and populist racism (both anti-Slav and anti-Semitic) played an increasing part. When defeat eventually came in November 1918, many on the right preferred to believe the assertion of Field Marshal Hindenburg that Germany had been 'stabbed in the back' at home by Jews and revolutionaries rather than defeated on the battlefield, and the founding of the Weimar Republic was accompanied by a torrent of anti-Semitic propaganda, co-ordinated by the Pan-German League and paid for by nationalist businessmen.[18]

Germany's war-time leadership not only relinquished power belatedly, and with great reluctance, but sought to ensure that the transition to parliamentary democracy was as difficult as possible. Political power passed for the first time to a government responsible to parliament, under the leadership of Prince Max von Baden, which meant that Ludendorff and the military leadership were able to evade the responsibility for negotiating humiliating peace terms. As the new parliamentary administration began to dismantle the virtual military dictatorship that had developed during the last years of the war, however, senior naval officers ordered a final engagement with the Royal Navy in order, as they saw it, to save the honour of the service. This prompted mutinies in northern German ports, and proved to be the trigger for the November revolution of 1918. Unrest spread from naval bases to the army, and to industrial workers in the major cities. Workers' and Soldiers' Councils were formed, and Max von Baden resigned, handing over power to a 'Council of People's Deputies' under SPD leader Friedrich Ebert.

Although the terminology of the Councils' movement was reminiscent of the Soviets of revolutionary Petrograd, the reality in Germany was very different. Most people, including most of those on the councils themselves, did not see the movement as an alternative to parliamentary democracy. The leaders of the SPD – the 'Majority Social Democrats' shared the widespread anxieties about Bolshevism; they too were eager to contain the threat of political radicalisation and to restore order. In order to do so the government accepted recognition by the army in return for a guarantee that its command structure would not be dissolved, and this was reinforced by a far-reaching agreement (already arrived at in early November) between the leaders of the Social Democratic ('Free') trades unions and leading businessmen. The German revolution was something of a compromise with the old regime, in so far as it reformed the political system, but left undisturbed the economic power, political influence and social status of the old elites. This alliance between the republicans and the old establishment worked smoothly when threats to the political stability of the republic came from the Communist left, and the Spartacus uprising was the first of several Communist insurrections to be suppressed speedily and brutally by the authorities. The army proved a much less reliable ally, however, when the republic was threatened by the right, and stood aside when the government was driven out of Berlin during the Kapp putsch of 1920. The coup was eventually defeated by a general strike, and when its leaders were arrested they received indulgently lenient punishments.

Although the Kapp putsch had failed, sympathy with its aims persisted. The radical right had been transformed by war and revolution. In the Reichstag it was represented by the German National People's Party, which was formed by merging the imperial conservative parties with the Fatherland Party, the Pan-German League, the Christian Socials and two other anti-Semitic parties. Tirpitz and Kapp were both members. The party thrived in the polarised political climate after the war, exploiting opposition to the Versailles Treaty. Its membership reached almost a million in 1923, shortly before its greatest electoral success (in 1924, when it won almost 20 per cent of the vote, and polled particularly well among women). Political horse-trading compelled the moderate wing of the DNVP (*Deutschnationale Volkspartei*, German National People's Party), led by the party's parliamentary delegates, to develop a pragmatic relationship with republican institutions during the 1920s, but most of the rank and file remained profoundly hostile to the republic, and despite the loss of some members to the more radical *Deutsch-Völkische Freiheitspartei* in 1922, a substantial Pan-German anti-Semitic wing remained.[19] The party responded to electoral losses in 1928 by moving further to the right under the leadership of the newspaper tycoon Alfred Hugenberg, and making common cause with the then marginal Nazis, only to be left behind by the latter in the 1930 elections.

Outside parliament the most significant *völkisch* organisation after the war was the *Deutschvölkischer Schutz- und Trutzbund* (DVSTB). Founded on 13 September 1918, it had a membership of 30,000 by the end of the following year, recruited mainly from among the old anti-Semitic groups, and especially from the Pan-German League, and the pre-war *Deutsch-Völkische Partei*.[20] By 1921 it had over 150,000 members, predominantly from the lower middle classes, and above all from among white-collar workers in both public and private sectors. The DVSTB effectively formed an organisational bridge between earlier *völkisch* groups and the emergent Nazi party.[21] Alongside the political formations of the right there were the *Freikorps* and *Wehrverbände*, paramilitary organisations recruited in the winter of 1918–19 from among soldiers who for one reason or another had not returned to civilian life as the German army had disintegrated. They were formed to suppress the radical left, and also fought against the Bolsheviks in the Russian civil war, and against the Poles in Upper Silesia. It was from such organisations that the Nazis recruited their stormtroopers – and many of the leading figures in the Nazis' security head office.[22] The extremes of German politics in the early 1920s were particularly manifest in Bavaria. In February 1919 Kurt Eisner, the outgoing head of the Bavarian government and a member of the USPD, was murdered by an aristocratic officer. His assassination was followed by a popular uprising, during the course of which a 'Councils' Republic' was declared, and power passed to a group of Communists (who were largely independent from the KPD in Berlin). This new government raised a 'Red Army', and prepared to defend Munich against the anticipated counter-revolutionary forces of the republic. Most of the troops that entered Bavaria to suppress the Munich 'soviet' were Prussian *Freikorps* units. They quickly defeated the Bavarian 'Red Army' and took Munich by 3 May. During the 'White Terror' of the following fortnight Communist leaders and suspected red guards were indiscriminately beaten up, tortured and murdered.[23]

Hitler and the Nazi Party

Munich became a haven both for far-right political movements and for paramilitary organisations formed by former *Freikorps* members (*Vaterländische Verbände*). The early Nazi Party was one of many similar groups. It was founded as the German Workers' Party (*Deutsche Arbeiterpartei*, DAP) in January 1919 by Karl Harrer, a toolmaker, Anton Drexler, a journalist, and other members of a small group called the 'Workers'

Political Society' (*Politischer Arbeiterzirkel*). Hitler, then a demobilised soldier working as a political spy for the army, first turned up at a meeting in September of that year, after attending a series of army indoctrination courses in 'anti-Bolshevism' at Munich University during the summer.[24] After intervening heatedly in the discussion, he joined the party the same day. The DAP was a small marginal party, even in its provincial context, and Hitler proved to be such a great asset that he was quickly able to impose his own agenda on it. By 1921 he had made himself its undisputed leader. His great contribution to the party was his skill as a speaker, which he used at public meetings throughout Bavaria to attract hundreds of new members. As his colleagues were only too aware, however, many of those attracted to the party by Hitler's rhetorical *tours de force* owed their first loyalty to him personally, rather than to the party. Moreover, he was often able to define party policy while ostensibly clarifying it for an external audience.

This is not to say that Hitler impressed everybody – indeed, many people disliked him immediately; or that he necessarily expected to become leader of the DAP from the outset. He was scathing about the party's democratic procedures, but his impatience with the party's structures arose as much from his distaste for democracy as from his own personal ambition, and shortly after joining he pressed for internal reforms which would give the executive a stronger role.[25] He collaborated with Drexler on the formulation of the party's 'unalterable' 25-point programme of February 1920, and represented the party – now renamed the National Socialist German Workers' Party (*Nationalsozialistische Deutsche Arbeiterpartei*, NSDAP) – at an international congress of national-socialist parties held in Salzburg in August of that year. He very quickly made an impact on the fortunes of the party – and not least in a literal sense, by charging admission fees for his public appearances and attracting significant one-off donations. The issue of his position in the party came to a head in the summer of 1921, when the old leadership backed the merger of the party's Augsburg branch with the local branch of the German Socialist Party (*Deutsch-Sozialistische Partei*, DSP). Both were tiny groups, and the move was ostensibly a practical one, aimed at consolidating the forces of the radical right in Augsburg, but Hitler was against it because the DSP favoured taking part in local elections, a strategy he opposed. He was also irritated that the decision to merge had been taken in his absence, and at the beginning of July he resigned, making his rejoining the party conditional upon his election as leader with dictatorial powers and a free hand to introduce reforms. It would be easy to read into this incident an attempt by Hitler to maximise his power within the NSDAP as quickly as possible, but rather than manipulating developments to suit his own ulterior motives, he seems to have been reacting to events, and uncertainly at that. He had been offered the chairmanship of the party before, but had consistently turned it down. (It was also not the first time he had resigned from the party.) Although he was not averse to consolidating his base within the party, he seems to have been motivated primarily by instinct, and above all by a determination to prevent the party from taking what he saw as a wrong turn. For Rainer Zitelmann, his insistence on the party chairmanship was a 'means of crisis management'; for Ian Kershaw his tantrums were a sign of inflexibility and weakness, not strength: he was, quite simply, frustrated at not getting his own way, and his own egocentric logic dictated that it was better to start again with a new party than to give in. His behaviour was a relatively ill-prepared response to the first significant crisis of his political career, a defensive move to protect rather than enhance his position.[26]

In the event Hitler's stand-off succeeded, although the outcome of the crisis was by no means inevitable, and he was unanimously accepted as chairman. Once elected leader he proceeded to establish his control over the party by promoting his allies to key posts and establishing central authority over local branches: this was to be a party based on the leadership principle – a 'Führer party' – not an internal democracy. During the course of the next 2 years the NSDAP developed in a number of ways. In the political climate of counter-revolutionary Bavaria the party's membership more than doubled, to nearly 5000. The largest social group in the party was the lower middle class, which accounted for nearly a third of all members, and skilled craftsmen were also well represented.[27] Despite this modest social profile the party also had a significant number of influential contacts among the educated middle classes of post-war Munich, many of whom had been involved with organisations such as the Thule Society or the DVSTB.[28] Among these was Ernst Röhm, a *Reichswehr* officer and deputy to the local *Reichswehr* commandant. Röhm organised local armed militias and became the effective leader of the party's own paramilitary 'storm division' (*Sturmabteilung*, SA), founded in 1921. *Reichswehr* funding, and financial help from a wealthy local journalist, Dietrich Eckart, enabled the party to acquire its own newspaper, the *Völkischer Beobachter*, in 1920.[29] The president of the Munich police, Ernst Pöhner, and his assistant Wilhelm Frick ensured that the Nazis were not called to account for their violent activities.

At the outset of his career as a beer-hall rabble-rouser in Bavaria, Hitler's thinking reflected that of the Pan-Germans, and he railed against Britain, France and the Treaty of Versailles, reiterating the conventional revisionist demands of the *völkisch* right. During the course of the next few years, however, he came increasingly under the influence of a group of anti-Semitic Baltic German émigrés in Munich, including Alfred Rosenberg and Max Erwin von Scheubner-Richter, the leading figure in an organisation of White Russian exiles called *Aufbau* (Reconstruction), which described itself as an organisation for the political and economic reorganisation of the East. It was from this milieu that Hitler's preoccupation with Bolshevik Russia came, and in particular the fusion of anti-Semitism and anti-Bolshevism in the single idea of a Jewish–Bolshevik conspiracy that now took precedence over an earlier obsession with the evils of Jewish finance capital. As the focus of his attention moved from the 'plutocratic' Jewish west to the Bolsehvik Jewish East, the destruction of the Soviet Union to create living space for the restless German nation took shape as a racial and ideological crusade.[30]

For the time being these ideas remained rhetoric; but an opportunity for more practical action seemed to present itself in 1923, a year of crisis which began with the occupation of the Ruhr by French and Belgian troops and ended with hyperinflation. The Reich government's policies for dealing with the crisis were seen by the right in Bavaria as a betrayal, and a number of right-wing groups and individuals, including Hitler, joined together in a 'combat association' (*Kampfbund*) with the intention of mounting a coup against the 'Marxists' in Berlin. At the beginning of November, however, the authorities in Munich, who had done much to antagonise the Reich government by refusing to ban the *Völkischer Beobachter*, began to realise that the national crisis was effectively over, and warned the would-be putschists not to proceed. Gustav Kahr, the commissioner general of Bavaria, Hans von Seisser, commander of the Bavarian police, and Otto von Lossow, the commander of the Bavarian *Reichswehr*, had all been implicated in the planning of the coup until the last minute; but on the night they could not be persuaded to lend their support to the action, either by Hitler's bullying, or by General Ludendorff, the only remaining significant figure from the conservative establishment remaining among the putschists.

Without the support of army, police or leading political figures, the coup had no chance of success, but Hitler could not now back down. He had become leader of the *Kampfbund* only against opposition from other *völkisch* groups, and it was not only his position in the party that was at stake, but his political reputation as well. He would also have found it difficult to retain his authority over the stormtroopers had he tried to restrain them at the last minute. So, after theatrical declarations in the Munich *Bürgerbräukeller* the putsch went ahead. Its inevitable failure marked a turning point in Hitler's career. His former allies appeared as witnesses for the prosecution at his trial, and Ludendorff's part in the affair was discreetly understated. As a result the 'beer hall putsch' was remembered not for what it was, a broad conspiracy of the Bavarian right with the complicity of the government and security forces in Munich, but as a national revolution led by Hitler, perfect for a mythology of struggle and betrayal, and complete with martyrs, heroes and traitors. The NSDAP was banned, but Hitler himself was treated with remarkable sympathy. Sentenced to 5 years imprisonment, he was released only 10 months later in December 1924.

In any case the moment had passed. It was not only that the strategy of a direct assault on the authority of the state had been revealed to be futile, but that the political turmoil which had enabled Hitler to make something of a name for himself during the post-war crisis had given way to apparently more stable conditions. In addition the NSDAP had been unprepared for the blow it had been dealt in 1923, and there had been no plans for underground activity in the event of the party's prohibition. Its supporters had been compelled to find a sympathetic haven with other *völkisch* groups, and in doing so had split along broadly generational as well as political lines. The older members in Bavaria – the 'pioneers' had joined the Greater German National Community (*Grossdeutsche Volksgemeinschaft*, GDVG), while the younger, more radical Nazis of the 'front generation' had joined the National Socialist Freedom Party (*Nationalsozialistische Freiheitspartei*, NSFP).

The NSDAP was refounded in February 1925, and both the GDVG and the NSFP voluntarily dissolved themselves shortly afterwards. This was not the end of the latest conflict within the party, however. Hitler's comeback was staged in Munich, and consolidated largely in Bavaria, on territory he knew. The response was initially enthusiastic in all parts of Germany, but political differences persisted between Bavaria and the north. It was in Bavaria that Hitler was most secure, not least because he was best-known and most often seen and heard there, but also because it was here that the party leadership in Munich had most effectively imposed its central authority over local branches. Hitler's charismatic leadership was systematically underpinned by the bureaucratic authority of the party machine. The northerners, emboldened by the rapid growth of the party in northern Germany, were more sceptical, and believed that the success of their own tactics, which included flirting with pseudo-leftist rhetoric, entitled them to participate in decision-making about the party's overall strategy.

Matters came to a head in 1926, when a number of urgent issues arose. The northerners, who were struggling to recruit industrial workers, resisted the new strategy of 'respectability'. Where Hitler now repudiated putschism, and favoured participation in elections, the northeners embraced political violence as a possible means of winning power; and where Hitler hoped to attract the support of business, the northerners talked of expropriating the princes. The split was not just about political disagreements – after all the northerners' revolutionary rhetoric was more propaganda than policy. More serious was the challenge to Hitler and the authority of the party leadership in Munich, which culminated in the drawing up of a new party programme. Hitler responded by calling a party conference in the Bavarian town of Bamberg, where he convincingly asserted his own authority, and followed up his triumph by appointing two leading members of the northern faction, Gregor Strasser and Joseph Goebbels to important new positions. Strasser became propaganda chief in Munich, and Goebbels became *Gauleiter* of Berlin.[31]

The Bamberg conference established the authority of Hitler and the central leadership in Munich. The years that followed were ones in which a corresponding nationwide organisation was established along hierarchical lines. Germany was divided into regions or *Gaue*, roughly corresponding with the country's electoral districts, and these were run by *Gauleiter* (regional leaders) directly responsible to Hitler.[32] Beneath them were the descending levels of authority, each corresponding to a lower level of government or administration and a smaller division of territory: *Kreisleiter* (district leaders), *Ortsgruppenleiter* (local leaders), and so on. Beneath the level of the local organisation the party was divided into cells (*Zellen*) and 'blocks'. There were territorial adjustments over the years, but the leadership principle, remained. Pseudo-medieval terminology was used alongside the more modern, pseudo-revolutionary vocabulary of comradeship and community for ordinary members of the party, who were referred to as 'party comrades' (*Parteigenossen*), and eventually for all Germans (*Volksgenossen*), which reflected the party's ambiguous attitudes towards modernity.[33]

Although the structural framework of the NSDAP was relatively well established by the late 1920s, the party was unevenly developed in practice, and even senior positions in the hierarchy were often filled by whoever happened to be available on the spot at the time. In addition the nature of the authority bestowed by leadership was ill-defined. At the top were competing institutions of central control, each trying to assert its primacy over the others in the manner that was to typify the institutional rivalry of the Nazi state itself after 1933. The *Gauleiter*, for example, were a crucial link in the chain of command between the bureaucratised party machine on the one hand and local branches on the other. But despite the attempts of other Nazi leaders to establish control over them the *Gauleiter* were able to exploit a special relationship with the Führer himself. They were appointed and dismissed directly by Hitler, and were still able to gain direct access to him after the party came to power. Careers were built on personal relationships between patron and client, and political authority and the limits of administrative competence were attached to the individual rather than his office: 'charismatic' rather than bureaucratic authority was exercised not only by Hitler, but at all levels of the NSDAP, and this meant that despite the complexity of the party's organisational structure, and all its fine gradations of rank and status, the reality was one of confusion and conflict.

By 1927, meanwhile, membership growth was stagnant. Existing members were increasingly apathetic, and the party was constantly short of funds as it struggled to make an impact in the unpromising political and economic circumstances of the Weimar Republic's years of relative stability. For some months the party had directed its appeal towards the industrial working class, despite the overwhelming odds it faced in the working-class districts of major northern cities and industrial conurbations. The party's attempts to make headway in the strongholds of the SPD and KPD were undermined by Hitler's refusal to countenance the establishment of Nazi trades unions (although, typically, there had been no clear directive on the issue). At the same time his attempts to win the sympathies of big business had met with little success.[34] The result was that the middle classes were alienated by the extremism of Nazi radicals in the cities, while local branches atrophied as they reverted to the empty 'clubiness' (*Vereinsmeierei*) that had typified associational life in the provinces before the war. Even in Munich, party members had not paid their dues, and donations from sympathetic businessmen were also declining.

These problems were addressed at the 1927 party congress in Nuremberg. A number of administrative reforms were undertaken, but above all a change of tone was discernible in the party's propaganda, which was now increasingly orientated towards the middle classes. This reorientation was also reflected in the changing social composition of the senior and middle-ranking leaders. New *Gauleiter* now no longer tended to come from lower-middle-class backgrounds, and some of those already in post were now judged either too radical or too incompetent and came under pressure to step down.[35] The party continued to attract members from the lower classes, but they were now increasingly concentrated in the rank and file of the movement, and especially in the SA (where there were grumbles about pen-pushing bureaucrats taking over); and even here they were under-represented, although the social pattern of recruitment varied considerably from place to place.[36]

Who Supported the Nazis?

The social base of Nazism before 1933 has received a great deal of attention from historians, and has generated some controversy.[37] The earliest interpretations characterised the party as a movement of the lower middle classes: a *Mittelstandspartei*. The party seemed to fill an obvious gap, representing a social group squeezed between the skilled working class organised in the Social Democratic labour movement, and the better educated and more affluent sections of the middle and upper classes (*Bürgertum*), from which more established Protestant bourgeois parties drew support.[38] The *Mittelstand* was certainly over-represented among the Nazi Party's members and voters before 1933, and its ideology was dominated by typically petit bourgeois concerns.

The designation *Mittelstandspartei* was problematic for a number of reasons, however. First of all it bracketed together the established occupational groups of the 'old *Mittelstand*', such as small farmers and artisans, with those of the 'new *Mittelstand*' produced by industrialisation and urbanisation, the salaried white-collar workers whose incomes were scarcely higher, and often lower than those of skilled manual workers. All these groups, along with shopkeepers and other urban small business people, belonged to the same social stratum, between wage earners and the propertied middle classes; but clerks and craftsmen, smallholders and shopkeepers lived in social cultures that were worlds apart, and espoused irreconcilable political values. (The tension between provincial conservatism and 'modern' mass politics within the party reflects these differences.) Secondly, the party itself explicitly sought to transcend sectional interests and appeal to the whole electorate, to be not just nationalist, but national as well. The idea of the 'national community' (*Volksgemeinschaft*) meant putting the national interest above 'selfish' materialist motives – like the more equitable distribution of wealth. The very name of the party reflected its ambition to recruit manual workers, and considerable effort was put into campaigning among them during the 1920s, albeit with such little success that it redirected its appeal very clearly towards the middle classes in the late 1920s.[39]

By the time it reached the peak of its electoral success in July 1932, the NSDAP represented a greater range of social and economic groups than any of its competitors. Despite the diversity of the party's appeal, however, the middle classes remained over-represented both as members and as voters before 1933. Salaried employees made up a quarter (25.5 per cent) of party members, but only 15.9 per cent of the population; civil servants (including teachers) constituted 8.3 per cent of all party members, twice the proportion in the population as a whole (4.4 per cent); and the self-employed accounted for over a third of the Nazis (34.4 per cent), and only 17.4 per cent of the employed population of the Reich. Workers on the other hand were under-represented in the NSDAP, where they comprised 28.1 per cent of the membership, as opposed to 45.1 per cent of the employed population in Germany as a whole.[40]

The hierarchy of the Nazi party reflected the conventional hierarchies of German society. The middle classes were even more heavily represented in the leadership than in the party as a whole, while the proportion of members from the lower classes was greater in the SA, and particularly among rank-and-file stormtroopers. Although the rise of the Nazi Party has often been associated with the phenomenon of mass unemployment, those out of work were strikingly resistant to the party's appeal, and decidedly *under*-represented among the party's members and less likely to vote for it. The class composition of the party's membership and electorate has been a much more controversial issue than gender, generational or regional variations. Definitions of class inevitably contain an element of subjectivity, and cannot simply be equated with notionally 'objective' categories, such as the social and economic groups defined by government departments. German census enumerators, for example, count all wage-earners (including agricultural labourers) as 'workers', but to understand what determined the very different cultures of urban and rural politics we need to be aware of the diversity of social identities within such an all-embracing group. Many urban industrial workers lived in relatively homogeneous communities and were integrated into a range of labour organisations from trades unions to consumer co-operatives and brass bands, and such 'political schooling' was central to the development of political behaviour. Such workers were far more likely to be 'immune' to the appeal of Nazism than agricultural labourers, manual workers employed outside manufacturing industry or workers in small rural towns.

There are similar difficulties in identifying the Nazi electorate. Our knowledge of it is necessarily based on general observations and correlations between the share of the vote and the social, economic and confessional composition of the constituency. We cannot know the occupation, income or status of individual voters because we do not know their identity; but some general points can nevertheless be made. In the elections of 1928, the last before the Depression, the Nazis managed to win only 2.8 per cent of the vote. Two years later, in September 1930, that share had risen to 18.3 per cent. The party's popularity peaked in July 1932 (37.3 per cent). In the last free election held during the Weimar Republic (November 1932), the party's share of the vote fell back to 33.1 per cent. (The 43.9 per cent of March 1933 was achieved only by intimidating the other parties, above all the Communists.) One of the most striking features of the Nazi vote during these years was its regional distribution. Despite the fact that its early successes had been in Bavaria the party did much better, both in 1930 and in 1932 in rural Protestant northern and eastern Germany than in the Catholic south and west or in the major cities. The Nazis' biggest electoral successes came in places like Oldenburg, Pomerania, East Prussia, Schleswig-Holstein, and the Prussian province of Hanover. In Thuringia the Nazis emerged as third largest party in elections to the provincial diet (*Landtag*) in 1929, and Wilhelm Frick joined the state government as the first Nazi minister in 1930.

Large cities and industrial conurbations remained relatively resistant to the Nazis. In July 1932 when the NSDAP won 37.3 per cent of the vote across the country, the Nazi vote was 28.7 per cent in Berlin, and it was 33.3 per cent in Hamburg. In Protestant cities such as Frankfurt and Hanover the Nazis did better, with 38.7 and 40.2 per cent of the vote respectively. In predominantly Roman Catholic cities on the other hand they did much worse: 24.5 per cent in Cologne, and 28.9 per cent in Munich and Düsseldorf. In the industrial cities of the Ruhr the Nazis' share of the vote was lower still: 27 per cent in Duisburg, 23.8 per cent in Essen and 19.5 per cent in Dortmund. In all cities the party did better in the more affluent reaches of suburbia, and least well in districts with large communities of industrial workers.[41] The Nazis would not have made their breakthrough, however, without support from workers or Catholics, and it is more useful to think in terms of shifting political identities, based on a combination of social origins, cultural affiliation and prior political allegiance, than a simple relationship between voting behaviour and confession or class.

Although the Nazis attracted a significant number of new voters, their gains came largely at the expense of other parties, so it is worth looking at the electoral performance of other parties during the Depression. The most stable share of that vote was for the Centre Party, which barely fluc-tuated. Similarly, the combined vote of the labour parties (SPD, USPD, KPD) remained relatively constant between 35 and 37 per cent, although an increasing share was taken by the Communist Party as politics became more polarised. This polarisation was far more dramatic on the right: the combined share of the vote for the conservative and liberal parties of the Protestant middle classes (DNVP, DVP, DDP) fell sharply, and in direct proportion to the rise of the Nazis. It only recovered a little when the Nazi vote fell back in November 1932. The Nazis also mopped up the support of the small special interest parties, which had benefited from an emergent middle-class protest vote in 1928. They also did better when the turnout was higher, suggesting that they managed to mobilise non-voters or those with weak political allegiances. But above all the Nazis took advantage of the collapse of the bourgeois parties, and succeeded in uniting the support of the hitherto politically frag- mented Protestant middle classes largely behind their own agenda. The political and economic conditions of the early 1930s, then, seem to have prompted voters to shift their support to more radical parties, but mainly within their own broad political camp; it is possible that some left-wing voters switched directly or indirectly to right-wing parties, as has been suggested, but it is unlikely that this happened on any significant scale without a corresponding shift of voters in the other direction.[42]

German women gained the right to vote in 1918, and a provision of the republic's electoral law, permitting but not requiring local author- ities to register men's and women's votes separately, makes it possible to make more confident statements about gender differences in elect- oral behaviour. The law was not implemented consistently, except in Cologne, but its intermittent use has enabled historians to make some general observations. The turnout of eligible women voters was consist- ently lower than that of men (except in the 1919 elections to the republic's constituent assembly), but in the critical elections of the early 1930s the gap between male and female turnout narrowed. The single most important beneficiary of women's suffrage was the Centre Party, 60 per cent of whose voters were women; in Protestant areas the DNVP and *Deutsche Volkspartei* (DVP) benefited disproportionately. Women voters were a minority on the left. The difference was slight in the case of the liberal *Deutsche Demokratische Partei* (DDP), more marked in the case of the SPD, and very clear in the case of the Communist Party, despite its radical feminist policies. Women's votes, like those of men, were determ- ined by their social background rather than primarily by gender, but with the important proviso that women did not by any means always 'vote the same way as their husbands': they were more likely to support the less radical party within their social and political milieu. This meant that on the whole women were less likely to vote for the Nazis than men. However the gap narrowed quite rapidly during the Depression, and by November 1932, and especially by 1933, there were constituencies in which the recorded female vote for the NSDAP was higher than the male vote. In terms of electoral support, the party was less of an 'out and out man's party' than it had been.[43]

The scope for more active involvement by women remained strictly circumscribed, however, in keeping with the party's very clear position on separate spheres: women were admitted to the party only on strictly subordinate terms and not permitted any leadership role, except in the women's organisations, nor were they allowed to represent the party as candidates in elections at any level. Women attracted to the Nazi movement were generally from conservative Protestant backgrounds and believed, in keeping with one of the most fundamental tenets of Nazi ideology, that a woman's place was in the home; but they were determined to serve the nation in public life too – while carefully denying any feminist agenda or desire to promote women's rights generally. A number of women's groups worked alongside the party from the early 1920s, among them Elsbeth Zander's *Deutscher Frauenorden*, which was recognised as the party's women's organisation in 1926 and incorporated into the party in 1928. It was dissolved in 1931 to make way for a new unitary Nazi women's organisation (the *NS-Frauenschaft*), a move which further curtailed the independence of the women's groups. As the political situation became more polarised the threat to women's rights became a political issue that concerned not only feminists, liberals and the left, but even right-wing women affiliated to the DNVP Protestant organisations, who reasserted the right of women to participate in politics.[44]

Above all the Nazi movement was a young movement, a fact which was very clear to contemporary observers. More than half of those joining the party in the late 1920s, and over a third of all party members in 1933 were under the age of 30; and almost two thirds were under the age of 40. The average age of a party member in 1930 was 31. The stormtroopers terrorising German cities during the early 1930s were clearly young, and student elections at German universities suggested strong support among young middle-class men. As Jürgen Falter has pointed out, the Nazi electorate must have had a somewhat different age profile, or there would have been few young people voting for other parties (and we know that the Communists in particular recruited heavily among young people). In fact it has been shown that the Nazi vote was higher the more older or retired people there were in an electoral district, and that Nazi gains in 1930, July 1932 and 1933 were also more clearly evident here than in constituencies with younger profiles, where the evidence for strong gains is 'anything but overwhelming'.[45]

The Demise of Parliamentary Democracy and the Rise of Hitler

Despite the scale of the Nazi electoral breakthrough, and the diversity of the constituency the party attracted, the German people never elected a Hitler government. Some two thirds of the electorate voted against the party in the Reichstag and presidential elections of 1932, when the Nazis were at the peak of their success, and even after the Nazis had been given free rein to terrorise the opposition, they failed to win an absolute majority. Parliamentary democracy had effectively ceased to function, however, even before the Nazis' electoral breakthrough. For although some leading conservatives had become 'rational republicans' (*Vernunftrepublikaner*) and although there had been some pragmatic, if often reluctant support for the republic from business, the country's elites had never been happy with the political settlement of 1918, and the economic crisis provided them with the opportunity to challenge it. Anti-republican posturing gave way to a serious reconsideration of the appropriateness of liberal democratic institutions for Germany, and some politicians and military leaders, along with businessmen, landowners, senior civil servants and other members of the traditional ruling class hoped to find ways of installing a more authoritarian form of government.

In 1930 the increasing hostility of business to basic welfare provision during the gathering Depression brought down the last government that was properly accountable to the Reichstag. In December 1929 the National Association of German Industry called for lower taxes on capital and cuts in welfare expenditure. When the issue was forced to a vote in March of the following year the 'Great Coalition' led by Hermann Müller (SPD) – a broad government embracing parties of left and right – collapsed over the issue of employers' insurance contributions. The 'fractional alteration' in the rate of contributions was symbolic; the real issue was the social policy that was a focus for all the political antagonisms that culminated in 1930.[46] The next government, formed by Heinrich Brüning, a right-wing member of the Centre Party, was a minority government, and depended largely on presidential decrees from Hindenburg in order to enact legislation, in accordance with Clause 48 of the constitution. Friedrich Ebert had used this measure in the early 1920s to bring stability and order to the republic and ensure its survival, and both Hermann Müller and Carl Severing (the Social Democratic Prussian interior minister) were among those recommending it now as a solution to the parliamentary impasse. Moreover Clause 48 stipulated that presidential decrees could be rescinded at any time by the Reichstag.[47] The increasingly 'presidential' government that followed was not inevitable in 1930, therefore, nor did it imply a slide towards authoritarianism, and Brüning first of all attempted to establish a working majority within parliament, rather than confronting it directly. His minority government immediately faced difficulties, however. It enjoyed Hindenburg's legal backing, but there were no supportive political gestures from the president, who more or less withdrew from politics, intervening only when it suited him. The DNVP, now led by the right-wing newspaper tycoon Alfred Hugenberg, was not convinced that the 'Hindenburg cabinet' marked a political turning point and remained hostile. The SPD quickly regretted the downfall of Müller, but Brüning's freedom of movement was restricted: any co-operation with the Social Democrats risked incurring further hostility from the German Nationalists and vice versa. Seeking to head off opposition, Brüning sought to produce a finance minister and a budget which might win SPD support without alienating the DNVP. He failed, and when he attempted to force through his plans anyway with a presidential decree the two parties joined forced to rescind it, and the chancellor carried out his threat to call fresh elections.[48]

Although it was clear before the election that the chancellor and his allies could not win a majority, the outcome – an enormous increase in support for the Nazis – was nevertheless a shock to everybody, and concentrated the minds of both the chancellor, who had expected the centre-right to emerge strengthened, and SPD leaders, who not only recognised the significance of the Nazi gains, but had themselves also lost ground to the Communists. Brüning now had no alternative but to rely on the 'toleration' of his government by the SPD, while the SPD had an interest in avoiding new elections which might bring fresh gains to the two anti-republican parties. This pragmatic working arrangement might have been extended to closer co-operation between the Reich and Social Democratic Prussia, had it not been for the entrenched hostility of some members of the cabinet and many of the president's circle to the Prussian government. Prussia was determined to defend the republic by applying sanctions against political extremism to the right as well as the left. Hindenburg was irritated by the implications of such a policy for the *Stahlhelm*, the most important of the right-wing veterans' associations; and the Reichswehr ministry questioned the Prussian interior ministry's assertion that membership of the NSDAP was incompatible with a position in the public service. Brüning himself was drawn increasingly into the anti-republican camp.

The chancellor's immediate problem was the economic crisis, which was exacerbated by the sudden recall of American loan capital and alarm among foreign investors at the political extremism in Germany. The effects of these developments on the economy were aggravated by Brüning's own deflationary economic policies, which hit the worst off hardest as the chancellor refused to countenance deficit spending, despite the deteriorating political situation. Military expenditure was maintained and the landed estates of eastern Germany were propped up through the 'eastern aid' (*Osthilfe*) policy, while austerity measures for the rest of the population included cuts in wages, salaries and welfare benefits. It was a policy which also sought to exploit the country's economic difficulties in order to demonstrate Germany's inability to make reparations payments, and thereby gain concessions. Whether alternative economic policies would have worked better is a matter of debate. Some historians, notably Knut Borchardt, have argued that the German economy was structurally weak before the Depression began, not least as a consequence of high industrial wages, and that Brüning had no realistic alternative to the policies he implemented: he was victim of the circumstances he inherited, and above all of the long-term consequences of the unreasonable demands of labour. Other historians have pointed out that wage increases in the 1920s were in line with productivity increases, and that if German industry suffered from low profitability the problem was its own lack of competitiveness as a result of cartelisation. In any case, the problem was less an economic than a political one: it was not that German wages were high by international standards, but that industrial workers were perceived to have gained from a shift in political power since 1918, and this generated resentment among those who felt dispossessed. Brüning's policies were not reluctant measures, but deliberate political choices in a society where powerful interest groups saw 'every tax on themselves as a mortal low to their existence, and . . . every subsidy or benefit to other groups as imposing an intolerable burden upon themselves.'[49] This is not to say that big business was instrumental in the downfall of the Weimar Republic, and by extension in the establishment of the Nazi dictatorship, as has sometimes been suggested. Business interests were disparate and conflicting, and some branches of industry were less hostile to the republic than others: it largely depended on their own economic fortunes. Similarly, although some individual businessmen donated money to the Nazi party, such support was limited, and less important than the smaller but more numerous donations from small business people. After the 1930 election, when it looked more likely that the Nazis might join a coalition government, the NSDAP was simply added to a list of other right-wing parties that received regular financial contributions from businessmen.[50] The economic crisis was accompanied by a rapidly deteriorating political situation. As the country dealt with the consequences of the financial collapse of 1931 and unemployment approached 6 million the level of political violence escalated in conflicts between Nazis and Communists on the streets of German cities. The violence of Nazi stormtroopers during the presidential election campaign of 1932 prompted a ban on the SA and the SS on 13 April. Less than a fortnight later the Nazi Party recorded spectacular gains in regional elections in Prussia, where the Braun government lost its majority and there were now moves to bring the Nazis into a coalition. The Nazis also made massive gains in Bavaria, Württemberg, Anhalt and Hamburg; and in May they won an absolute majority in Oldenburg.[51] The terminal crisis of the Brüning administration developed during the spring of 1932, but the occasion for the chancellor's dismissal came with a proposal for an emergency decree to expropriate some of the most hopelessly indebted landed estates in eastern Germany, a move which alienated agrarian interests, and was denounced by the DNVP as 'Bolshevism'. More importantly the chancellor had lost support among Hindenburg's circle and the president refused either to authorise any more emergency decree or countenance changes to the cabinet, effectively dismissing Brüning to make way for a move to the right.[52]

The president was more sympathetic to Brüning's successor, Franz von Papen, whose chancellorship marked a further stage in the dismantling of Weimar democracy. Papen's most destructive anti-republican measures were taken immediately. Before dissolving the Reichstag he lifted a ban on the SA and SS imposed by the government only a few weeks before (while leaving in place a similar ban on Communist paramilitary organisations), and thereby immediately enabled the Nazi Party to initiate a campaign of street violence and intimidation of their political opponents, culminating in the Altona 'bloody Sunday' of 17 July.[53] Three days later the government of Prussia was dismissed and Papen became 'Reich commissioner', an unconstitutional step with far-reaching implications, which proved to be an important milestone in the establishment of the dictatorship.

The elections which followed brought the Nazis their greatest success, but Hitler was denied the power he wanted: Hindenburg invited him to join the government, but refused to appoint him chancellor. He was also instructed by the president to keep the SA under better control. He retaliated by supporting a KPD vote of no confidence. Papen now had no alternative but to call another round of elections. These were held on 6 November, in the middle of a transport strike in Berlin supported by both Communists and Nazis. Although the NSDAP lost support, it was still the largest party in the Reichstag, and without its support the Papen administration was effectively finished. Again Hindenburg urged Hitler to join a government of 'national concentration', and again he refused to do so unless he was appointed chancellor. With the Reichstag due to reconvene on 6 December, Papen reported to Hindenburg that his government could not command a majority in the Reichstag, and asked him to suspend it for a short time. With most of the cabinet against Papen's reappointment, however, along with advisers warning Hindenburg of the possibility of civil war, and the army giving notice of its inability to cope, the president reluctantly had to let the chancellor go.

Papen was replaced by his minister of defence, Kurt von Schleicher, who had been closely involved in negotiations with the army and the Nazis.[54] Schleicher's attempts to win broad popular backing for his short-lived administration, largely from the trades unions and the Nazis, came to nothing, however. Gregor Strasser, who had indicated a willingness to break ranks with the Nazi leadership and accept ministerial office under Schleicher, was forced by Hitler to resign his post as Reich Organisation Leader of the NSDAP, and promised to resign his parliamentary seat too (although he did not do so until the March elections of the following year). The Social Democrats, who thought that the tide had turned with the Nazis electoral losses in November, were both suspicious of Schleicher and unwilling to back him. In the end the new chancellor was compelled to ask for the suspension of the Reichstag and the postponement of new elections until the immediate crisis had been dealt with. Hindenburg was not prepared to give him the support he wanted. The president was aware that Papen, resentful at being ousted, was involved in negotiations with Hitler. The two had met at the Cologne house of the banker Kurt Schröder on 4 January, and further talks were held at the house of Joachim von Ribbentrop. The conspirators had close contacts with members of Hindenburg's circle, and at the end of January the president was finally persuaded to appoint Hitler as the head of a conservative-dominated coalition.

Hitler's appointment to the chancellorship on 30 January 1933 brought with it the support of the largest party in the Reichstag, but had little to do with parliamentary democracy, and much to do with the intrigues of Papen and the Hindenburg 'camarilla'. Conservatives had seen the possibility of an authoritarian revision of the constitution recede in the wake of the November elections, and as the options narrowed a Hitler cabinet – long resisted – now looked like a more promising way forward than a populist Schleicher administration, or new elections that might bring fresh gains for the Communists. The decision to appoint Hitler was not one that was taken enthusiastically, nor was it greeted with much enthusiasm outside the ranks of the Nazi Party and their supporters: most Germans, as we have seen, remained unconvinced by Hitler. Hitler did not win power, but he did not seize it either. Despite the street violence of the stormtroopers, both before and after 30 January, the Nazi 'seizure of power' (*Machtergreifung*) is a misnomer for what in reality was a negotiated 'takeover of power' (*Machtübernahme*). Hitler's appointment was the decision of a small and unaccountable group around the ageing president, albeit one with connections and resonances among a broader circle of powerful interests. When they turned – finally – to Hitler their concern was not whether they could control him so much as what aims they had in common and what immediate objectives they could work on together.

Chapter 2: The Nazi Dictatorship

Hitler came to power as leader of a coalition cabinet largely made up of conservatives and nationalists, many of them aristocrats unaffiliated to any political party, who had served in the 'cabinet of barons' under Papen and then under Schleicher. Papen himself became vice-chancellor and Reich commissioner for Prussia. They lent the new government a spurious air of respectability, and created a false sense of continuity. Outside the cabinet room the true measure of the political watershed was evident in the torchlight procession of stormtroopers through Berlin: here the German Nationalist *Stahlhelm* was clearly in a minority, and had only been included belatedly at the insistence of Hindenburg.

Hitler himself was one of only three Nazis in the cabinet. The other two were the new Interior Minister Wilhelm Frick, and Hermann Göring, who was appointed minister without portfolio. Frick, the son of a school teacher with a doctorate in law from Heidelberg, had been Hitler's contact in the Munich police during the early years of the Nazi movement, and had been the first Nazi to hold ministerial office (as interior minister in Thuringia in 1930). Göring, the son of a colonial civil servant, had been educated at military college and decorated as a fighter pilot during the First World War. Like Frick he had been a close associate of Hitler's since the early 1920s, but their relationship had been cemented by his role in the negotiations that had brought Hitler to power. He had been President of the Reichstag since the July elections in 1932. In addition to his Reich ministerial position he was also appointed commissioner for the Prussian interior ministry.[1]

The Consolidation of Power

Although the Nazis were outnumbered there was little possibility of Hitler's authority being challenged or checked from within the cabinet, or for that matter by Hindenburg. The only other political party represented was the DNVP. Its leader Alfred Hugenberg, a wealthy industrialist and press baron, had been one of the founders of the Pan-German League before the war. He had also been a key figure in the (strained) co-operation between the DNVP and the Nazis during the Depression, and had used his newspapers to help win support for the Nazis. Anxious to stem the haemorrhage of support for his own party, he opposed new elections and proposed banning the Communist Party in order to engineer a Reichstag majority for the new government; Hitler preferred a dissolution, and the rest of the cabinet agreed, with Papen observing that 'it would be best to decide now that the coming election to the Reichstag would be the last one, and a return to the parliamentary system is to be avoided for ever'.[2] Hindenburg was persuaded to sign decrees calling new elections to the Reichstag (and simultaneously to the Prussian Landtag).

There were immediate steps to ensure the best possible conditions for the government during the election campaign. The Decree of the Reich President for the Protection of the German People, issued on 4 February contained wide-ranging provisions for press censorship and the prohibition of public meetings if the government felt that leading officials had been maligned, or that the interests of the state were being put at risk by the spreading of 'false information'.[3] With Göring in control of the Prussian police the Nazis' opponents were subject to the most violent intimidation on the streets. The police were directed to shoot members of 'organisations hostile to the state' if necessary (17 February); and five days later stormtroopers, SS men and members of the nationalist *Stahlhelm* were enlisted as auxiliaries, a move which effectively enabled the Nazis to murder their political opponents without fear of arrest.

The political tension was dramatically increased by the Reichstag fire of 27 February, apparently an act of arson by a young Dutch Communist, Marinus van der Lubbe, which generated countless conspiracy theories about the Nazis' own involvement. More importantly it provided the government with an excuse to introduce even more draconian measures during the last week of the election campaign. It seems unlikely that the Nazis themselves were responsible for the fire, not least because the immediate action they took against members of the Communist Party gave the impression of being rather hasty and unprepared. But the new regime exploited the opportunity to the full. Virtually all civil rights were suspended by the Decree of the Reich President for the Protection of People and State (28 February 1933), and the state police were empowered to arrest individuals and detain them without trial in 'protective custody'. Despite the high turnout (89 per cent) and extent of repression and intimidation, the Nazis still failed by a substantial margin to win over a majority of the electorate. The party's share of votes cast rose to 43.9 per cent, and it now had 288 of the 647 seats in the Reichstag. Although the DNVP performed poorly it returned the same number of deputies (52). This meant that although the Nazis could not form a government alone, the government parties together could now manage a majority in the Reichstag.[4] The Nazis' opponents did much better than might have been expected: apart from the KPD they managed to hang on to their voters. The number of votes cast for the Centre Party increased, and the SPD suffered only minor losses, while even the Communist Party, virtually an illegal underground organisation by the time of the election, won nearly 5 million votes. A contemporary observed that 'Social Democrats, regardless of the scandalous pressure exercised against them and the complete paralysis of their propaganda, have lost only a hundred thousand votes, the KPD only a million. That is astounding and a wonderful tribute to the imperturbability of the "Marxist Front"'.[5]

These last, flawed elections had not yet acquired the character of the 'plebiscitary democracy' to come. They were scarcely an indication of universal approval for the new regime, and in a number of electoral districts up and down the country the NSDAP failed even to make first place in the poll. The Centre Party won an absolute majority of local electorates in dozens of communities in Silesia, Westphalia, Hesse, the Rhineland, Württemberg, Baden, and in some Catholic enclaves in East Prussia and lower Saxony; and the Bavarian People's Party led the field – often with over half the vote – in parts of Bavaria. The tiny communities of Westphalia and the Rhineland where the Centre Party could rely even now on the support of over two thirds of the electorate were exceptional, however. Niederfischbach in the Altenkirchen district of the Rhineland is probably the most extreme example of Catholic immunity to the Nazis' appeal: here only 4.4 per cent of the 1175 voters supported the party, while 71.6 per cent supported the Centre and 18 per cent the SPD. The KPD retained its lead in the working-class districts in and around Berlin such as Wedding, Friedrichshain and Neukölln, and the Nazis trailed behind either SPD or KPD in a number of districts in central and western Germany, although the labour vote was often split between the two.[6]

The resilience of the opposition meant more than just loss of face for the Nazis: if they wanted to preserve at least the appearance of constitutional propriety as they swept away parliamentary government, they would need a 'double two thirds majority' of the Reichstag in order to amend the constitution: that is, two thirds of all the deputies would have to be present, and two thirds of those present would have to consent. The problem of ensuring the necessary quorum (in case the Social Democrats should absent themselves) was avoided by changing the standing orders of the house so that Göring, as president of the Reichstag, was empowered to determine who was legitimately absent. Those absent without leave could simply be discounted. Although it was scarcely any longer necessary under these circumstances, Hitler had secured the support of the Centre Party by granting a number of concessions to Catholic interests. In the absence of the Communist deputies (and some Social Democrats), who had either been imprisoned or gone underground, the SPD was the only party to vote against the law which brought parliamentary government in Germany finally to an end, a courageous gesture undertaken in the face of threats of violence both inside and outside the chamber.

The events of March 1933 revealed the 'dual' nature of the Nazi state at its very inception. The Weimar constitution technically remained in force, subject to the modifications introduced by the Decree for the Protection of People and State and the Enabling Act, which became the constitutional basis of the dictatorship's political authority. Although the government now no longer needed either the Reichstag or the president in order to enact legislation, much government business was still conducted according to 'normal' procedures. This was important: while many of the government's supporters shared its aversion to parliamentary democracy, not all of them were as eager to abandon constitutional government and the rule of law entirely. On the other hand the new political order the Nazis wanted could be neither established nor maintained without the 'exceptional measures' that characterised the 'national revolution' during the spring of 1933: arbitrary arrest and imprisonment, intimidation, violence and torture, summary justice and execution. There was little or no public discussion of the 'exceptional measures' – at best, perhaps, a euphemistic reference in the press. Important politically independent newspapers that had once written critically about the Nazis were nervous of boycotts and bans, and increasingly reticent in their coverage of the wave of state terror. Many communities saw little or nothing of the violence of the 'national revolution'. Victims were abducted and taken outside the towns and cities to the isolated spots where the beatings and murders took place: 'Dead men were found in the surrounding forests, and no one dared to know anything about them. People disappeared without a sound, and their best friends did not have the courage to ask where they had gone.'[7] The violence was directed not at the fabric of the old political order, however, but very specifically at the regime's defeated political opponents. Despite its pseudo-revolutionary rhetoric the Nazi 'seizure of power' was a myth, and the Nazi Party did not carry out a political revolution in the classic sense. Although the pace of development in Germany was much swifter, the political transformation that took place was closer to that in Italy under Mussolini during the early 1920s than in Bolshevik Russia. In Russia the revolutionaries had come to power in a political vacuum and reinvented the state, albeit not without opposition. In Germany, as in Italy, the system had not collapsed, and the traditional ruling classes had co-operated with fascist movements in pursuit of their own agenda. In addition the NSDAP was a very different organisation to the Bolshevik party. For a number of reasons it had been impossible to impose a rational unitary organisational structure on the party in the years before 1933. When the Nazis came to power it was a fragmented collection of semi-independent organisations incapable of exercising power in remotely the same way as the Bolsheviks had done in Russia. The regime did not seek to alter social and economic relationships fundamentally, still less dispossess the ruling class or interfere with its vital economic interests; nor did it attempt to sweep away or re-found existing social and political institutions (the army, the bureaucracy, churches, universities), partly because it could not have succeeded, and partly because the Nazis did not want that degree of change. Such purges as were undertaken were directed at a minority and the frequently declared intention was explicitly *restoration* rather than revolution.

The theme of restoration – of authority, order, leadership, greatness – while no less a rhetorical device than the party's revolutionary posturing implied a return to a time uncontaminated by the party politics of the 'system' (as the right disparagingly termed 'parliamentary democracy'), common ground that the Nazis shared with their conservative allies. Accordingly, one of the regime's first objectives was to do away with the political pluralism of the Weimar republic, a process which had begun with the banning of the Communist Party, and was concluded by July, by which time Germany had become a one-party state. The point was not to establish rule by the NSDAP, however; during the first weeks and months of the dictatorship it was more important for the regime to contain and thwart the aspirations of some of the more radical members of the party than to transform it into an instrument of government.

The party's purpose in opposition had been propaganda and electioneering, and with its leaders now in power, and elections abolished, its original purpose was fulfilled, and it diminished in significance as its subsidiary organisations began to form their own particular relationships with existing institutions. After 1933 the party's responsibilities at local and regional levels were largely restricted to morale-raising and, increasingly, welfare initiatives: the party's job was to mobilise and sustain popular support for the regime, to elicit the acclamation expressed in plebiscites and rallies, and above all – at least as far as Hitler was concerned – to prepare people for war. Hitler himself was not keen to see authority centralised in a national leadership that might threaten his own position, but the party could not be allowed to degenerate entirely into a propaganda organisation. Its continued existence was necessary as a counterweight to the state and its bureaucracy, and to this end large numbers of regional and local party leaders (*Gauleiter* and *Kreisleiter*) assumed corresponding roles in the political hierarchy of the state, as provincial and district governors, mayors, chairmen of local councils and so on. In the long term, however, the party lacked members with the skills essential for the administration of a modern state, and could not reasonably hope to attract them.[8] There were few Nazis in the senior ministerial bureaucracy, either because there were so many non-Nazis in the cabinet, or because there was a preference for professional expertise over political commitment; and there were relatively few Nazis in civil service posts at regional level, especially outside Prussia. Although by 1935 nearly 80 per cent of German mayors were Nazis, only about half of these were genuine party veterans, who had been members of the NSDAP *before* 30 January 1933; and of the 50,000 mayors of municipal districts, some 40 per cent were non–Nazis, and only a third of the remainder had been party members before 1933.[9]

Opposition parties were not the only obstacle to the monopoly of political power claimed by the Nazis, and they set about bringing a range of institutions into line with new political order. The term *Gleichschaltung* (co-ordination) was used to describe the process of Nazification – and in many cases enthusiastic self-Nazification – of institutions, corporate bodies and private associations during the first months of the new regime. It was applied above all to the transfer of power to agents of the new regime in the federal states (*Länder*) and the purging of the civil service of Social Democrats and Jews. In the case of Prussia, by far the largest of the *Länder*, the process had been anticipated by the authoritarian precedent of the 'Prussian coup' (*Preussenstreich*) of 1932: Papen's dismissal of the elected government and its replacement by Reich commissioners. In addition the Nazis held power anyway in a number of smaller states: Thuringia, Braunschweig, Anhalt and Oldenburg. The process of 'co-ordinating' the rest began in March and conformed to a broadly similar pattern throughout Germany. Stormtroopers were used by local *Gauleiters* to manufacture a crisis of public order by means of demonstrations, street violence, the occupation of municipal offices and so on. At the same time the interior ministry in Berlin applied pressure from above, culminating in the appointment of a Reich commissioner on the grounds that the local authorities could not keep order. The process began first in Hamburg, where SPD senators had resigned over the issue of press censorship shortly before the election, and local policemen had raised swastika flags on public buildings. Alfred Richter, a member of the SA, was appointed Reich police commissioner for Hamburg on 5 March, and events followed a similar course the following day in Bremen, Lübeck and Hesse. The process was completed in the other states during the course of the next two days.

There was no constitutional basis either for the appointment of Reich commissioners or for the formation of Nazi regional governments. In Hamburg, Württemberg and Hesse the appearance of constitutional propriety was maintained: in the absence of Communists and Social Democrats there was now a majority of Nazis and conservatives in the regional assemblies (*Landtage*), each of which proceeded to elect a suitable new administration. No such niceties were observed in the other states, where thinly veiled threats of renewed public disorder from the Nazis forced the existing governments to resign, and further Reich commissioners were appointed to head the various government departments. Nazi *Gauleiters* were also appointed to the post of *Oberpräsident* in the Prussian provinces, except in a few cases in western Germany where German nationalist aristocrats, including the Hohenzollern crown prince, August Wilhelm, took over the position.

The Provisional Law for the Co-ordination of the *Länder* with the Reich (31 March 1933) legalised the control the Nazis had asserted over the states by brute force. It effectively dismissed existing state governments and appointed new ones without elections, but using the Reichstag elections of March 1933 as a basis. It gave state governments the power to legislate, to change or deviate from the constitution, and alter the administration of the state without reference to the *Landtag*; and it abolished the representation of the Communist Party. This was not enough: Hitler wanted to appoint commissars to supervise state administrations and a commission was established under Papen to draft a second law, comprising Frick, Johannes Popitz, and the right-wing constitutional and legal theorist Carl Schmitt. For Schmitt the new law would be an attempt to resolve the latent conflict between particularist interests and strong central government. It was irrelevant whether such a move was legal under the Weimar constitution. Schmitt believed that the Enabling Act inaugurated a new legal order (and had published an article on it within a week of its promulgation). The Second Law for the Co-ordination of the *Länder* with the Reich (7 April 1933) created the new institution of Reich governor (*Reichsstatthalter*). In political terms this was a move intended to counter the aspirations of local Nazis by placing centrally appointed place-men as local representatives of the Führer. This would prevent party radicals from developing regional power bases. Hitler himself became Reich governor of Prussia, restoring the personal union between Prussia and the Reich which had existed under the emperor; this meant that Papen was now superfluous to the government of Prussia, and the way was open for Göring to take over as minister-president. In the other *Länder Gauleiters* were normally appointed Reich governors, many of them relinquishing the office of minister-president to a party colleague in order to take up the post.[10]

A further potential obstacle was the civil service, an institution with privileged status perceived as the embodiment of the sovereign power of the state itself rather than merely public servants implementing the policies of the executive.[11] The Prussian bureaucracy had shaped the constitution from the Reform era in the early nineteenth century, and had ensured a degree of constitutional continuity through a period of considerable political upheaval, while the Reich and Prussian bureaucracies had shaped policy and institutions from the time of Bismarck to the end of the First World War. Civil servants were widely respected, and their prestige and position had survived defeat and revolution largely unscathed. Nevertheless both they and political conservatives alike felt that the role of the civil service had been undermined by the republican political system. The Weimar constitution had made bureaucrats responsible to elected masters, who were in turn accountable to parliament, and many civil servants resented such accountability. Political appointments to civil service posts were resented, especially if the appointees did not come from the appropriate social class; so were the reductions in the size of the bureaucracy in the 1920s, and the salary cuts enforced by Brüning during the Depression. Since 1930, however, the civil service had resumed something of its earlier role. The ministerial bureaucracy began to negotiate as meetings of the Reichstag became more and more infrequent. Ideally many civil servants would have liked to institutionalise an authoritarian but constitutional system along these lines. A loyal elite of expert administrators would govern in the best interests of the nation, thereby putting an end to 'divisive' party politics. Yet in practice, bureaucrats were being increasingly politicised in the service of a specific right-wing agenda.[12]

Despite Hitler's own antipathy to bureaucrats, they had joined the Nazi Party from its earliest days, and in increasing numbers from the late 1920s. By 1933 support for the party among civil servants was disproportionately high, and they had great expectations that the new regime would see them restored to their former position even though many Nazis wanted the state bureaucracy subordinated to the party. The Law for the Restoration of a Professional Civil Service of 7 April 1933 was the centrepiece of the Nazi 'co-ordination' of the bureaucracy. Its provisions applied to all 'officials' (*Beamte*) at national, state and local levels including, for example, teachers in schools and universities, and other categories who shared 'the rights and duties' of state officials; it also applied to workers and 'employees' (*Angestellte*, or white-collar workers) in state employment. It therefore covered a much wider range of state employees than is understood by the English term 'civil service'. The educated, euphemistic language of the officials who drafted the law was less coarse and confrontational than that of Nazi propaganda, but the law effectively provided for the dismissal of Jews and Socialists. All officials 'of non-Aryan descent' were to be retired, along with the politically unreliable.[13] Among other things the law was a reassertion of central control, by the regime, over a purge which threatened to come about anyway as a result of direct action by radical rank-and-file Nazis. It should also be seen in the broader context of the long-term need for a reform of the civil service, and there were provisions permitting the government to override tenure protection and move civil servants to other posts in the interests of efficient administration.[14]

The 'National Revolution'

The imposition of political authority from above was accompanied by unrestrained violence from gangs of stormtroopers and SS men, who raided and looted the premises of trades unions, political opponents, consumer associations, co-operatives and newspapers. Banks and finance offices and Jewish shops and businesses were also targeted. Occasionally the victims were set upon in their own homes. Wilhelm Sollmann, for example, a Reichstag delegate for the SPD was attacked and beaten up in his flat in Cologne before being brought before the local police president at the NSDAP Gau headquarters, along with a Socialist journalist, and sent to a prison hospital. Political opponents were bullied, beaten, arrested and imprisoned, tortured and even – as in the case of Georg Landgraf, editor of the *Chemnitzer Volksstimme* – murdered more or less with impunity. In many cases the dismissal and arrest of Jewish and left-wing officials were brought about by means of direct action until the passing of the Civil Service Law, and Social Democratic members of regional parliaments (*Landtage*) and councils were compelled to give up their seats voluntarily. In Braunschweig the SPD offices were ransacked and looted by the SA and SS, supported by the regular police, employees were beaten up and a salesman was murdered; and two days later two Jewish department stores were laid waste by a group of SS men. Their leader, a lawyer, later condemned the incident, blaming it on Communists, and was subsequently appointed state justice minister.[15]

The so-called 'national revolution' was a mixture of 'illegal' violence and 'legal' procedures. Technically, political opponents of the regime were detained in 'protective custody' (*Schutzhaft*). Politically unreliable citizens had been locked up under the terms of this provision by the imperial authorities during the First World War, and by local Reichswehr commanders during Communist insurrections in the early 1920s, but the Reichstag Fire Decree had made it much easier to imprison people arbitrarily. It freed the police from the necessity of judicial investigation in the case of those arrested 'preventively'. An estimated 25,000 people were arrested in Prussia alone during March and April, and the numbers made it necessary to provide much larger prisons, separate from those of the police and justice ministry. In Bavaria the number of arrests rose so sharply after the appointment of Adolf Wagner as state commissioner that he foresaw the problem of prison overcrowding, and recommended to the State Commissioner for justice, Hans Frank, 'the use of methods formerly employed in dealing with mass arrests of former members of the National Socialist German Workers' Party. . . . [T]hey were shut up in any empty ruin and nobody worried whether or not they suffered the inclemency of the weather.' He recommended the setting up of separate quarters to deal with protective custody arrests, and at a press conference on 20 March, the SS leader Heinich Himmler, who was now also police president of Munich, announced plans to use the site of a derelict factory outside the city. 'On Wednesday the first concentration camp will be erected near Dachau, with a capacity for 5000 people', the party newspaper *Völkischer Beobachter* reported the next day. The report continued,

All the Communists, and as far as is necessary, all the *Reichsbanner* and Social Democratic functionaries who endanger the security of the state, will be brought here, because it is not possible in the long term to accommodate these functionaries in court prisons, and places too great a burden on the state is too overburdened. It has become evident that it is not appropriate to leave these people at liberty, as they continue to agitate and create disorder. We must take this measure in the interests of the security of the state and without regard to pedantic objections.[16]

Further camps were set up on the Dachau model throughout the Reich during the 1930s, among them Sachsenhausen, near Berlin, in 1936 and Buchenwald, outside Weimar, in 1937.

In addition to these 'legal' camps, other unofficial (or 'wild') concentration camps were set up, outside the jurisdiction even of the Nazis' dubious notions of legality, and those abducted to such makeshift sites were treated even more brutally. The memoirs of Rudolf Diels, head of the Gestapo, recalled that 'there were reports of camps near Oranienburg, Königswusterhausen and Bornim'. The 'wild' camp established in an old brewery at Oranienburg in March was retained and financed by the interior ministry, and was one of the few to remain in use after the excesses of the national revolution. The SA also had 'interrogation posts' (*Vernehmungstellen*) in Berlin itself, along with private prisons in many districts. Diels reported visiting the Columbia prison, operated by the SS, with police teams, and finding victims with festering wounds on the point of starvation in rooms strewn with straw. The prisoners had been beaten repeatedly for hours by a dozen men with iron bars, rubber truncheons and whips and there was none whose body was not covered with bruises.[17]

The process of *Gleichschaltung* was well-advanced in all spheres of public life by the middle of the summer, but for many in the party the regime had not gone far enough. For Hitler's conservative allies on the other hand the bullying tactics of the SA were becoming a cause for concern. On 6 July, anxious to avoid alienating powerful allies in the army and big business, Hitler announced the end of the 'national revolution'. A week later, on 14 July, Germany was officially proclaimed a one-party state. Complaints continued throughout the autumn and winter, however, of increasing Nazi interference in all levels of administration, in industrial relations and in the judicial process. Matters came to a head in the early summer of 1934, by which time the SA was considerably bigger than the army and, despite a warning from Hitler himself, had been engaging in military activities. Hitler felt under increasing pressure to curb Röhm's ambitions and the activity of the stormtroopers, especially in view of the weakness of the economy and Germany's international position. Conservative criticism of the stormtroopers was increasingly outspoken, and the SS (still technically part of the SA), finding its own ambitions thwarted, encouraged the antagonism and fostered rumours of an SA conspiracy to stage a coup. Finally, when Papen denounced the SA in a speech at Marburg university on 17 June 1934, Hitler knew that his ambition to succeed the ailing Hindenburg by combining the offices of president and chancellor would now depend on how he acted now to deal with the radicals in his own movement.

The purge of the SA leadership – the 'night of the long knives' – was painstakingly prepared. A meeting of SA leaders was called at Bad Wiessee in Bavaria at the end of June, just as members were about to take a month's leave. After putting the army and SS on alert, Hitler cancelled the remainder of his schedule for 29 June and flew to Munich. Early the following morning the SS, accompanied by Hitler himself, burst into the hotel where the stormtroopers' leaders were staying and arrested them. They were sent to Stadelheim prison, where Röhm and a number of others were murdered. A similar purge was carried out by Göring in Berlin, and further murders were carried out both there and in Silesia. In addition large numbers of SA leaders (30 per cent in some parts of Germany) were dismissed from office. Nor did Hitler miss the opportunity to take revenge on old enemies or to hit back at conservative critics. Both Gregor Strasser and Kurt von Schleicher were shot, as were Gustav von Kahr, Edgar Jung, the author of Papen's speech, and Herbert von Bose, Papen's press secretary and a leading conservative. Papen himself was forced to resign as vice-chancellor and was sent to a diplomatic posting in Vienna.

Although the killings were clearly illegal on any reading of the law, approval of Hitler's actions was almost universal. The army expressed its support for the purge through Defence Minister Werner von Blomberg, and on 3 July the cabinet approved a retroactive law which consisted of one sentence justifying the episode in the interests of state security. In a speech of 13 July Hitler characterised his actions as those of Germany's supreme judge, taking decisive measures in the national interest, an argument echoed by Carl Schmitt, who argued that Hitler *protected* the law from the gravest abuse by acting in times of danger and, as 'Führer', making law directly: 'The true leader is always a judge as well.'[18] Beyond the narrow circle of political leaders and commentators, Hitler's standing was enhanced rather than diminished by the news of the purge, not least because it reinforced the image of a leader not only above the petty villainies of ordinary Nazis, but willing to punish them too.[19] It also strengthened the image of Nazism as a force for order in Germany, particularly since the homosexuality of some SA leaders, including Röhm, was well known, and had detracted from the party's image. Reports on popular opinion reaching the exiled SPD leadership in Prague confirmed the impression that Nazis and non-Nazis alike generally approved of Hitler's action, although – they added – reports of food costing 30,000 marks and 'abnormal orgies' had not gone down well among the party's middle-class supporters in Berlin, and some people had 'made comparisons between the dead and the living', wondering what the latter were probably still getting up to. The dominant impression in popular opinion was positive, however: 'Hitler's speech makes him appear as the strong energetic man', a report from Dresden began, 'who strikes with an iron hand'. Anxieties about what the government might even now be hiding from the people, or 'where the German people was heading', were secondary.[20]

The Röhm purge marked something of a turning point in the establishment of the Nazi dictatorship, in so far as it helped determine the shape and political development of the regime over the next 3 years. On 20 July the SS became an independent organisation as a reward for its part in the blood bath;[21] and Hitler's own position was consolidated when the offices of chancellor and president were combined following Hindenburg's death on 2 August. A new personal oath of loyalty to Hitler as *Führer* was introduced for civil servants and the armed forces later that month, and a Führer chancellery was created on 17 November. The political change brought about by the Nazis during their first 18 months in power was rapid and far-reaching, much more so than that achieved by Mussolini's Fascist regime in similar circumstances a decade earlier. Although there had been no revolution, and although the country's elites remained in place, retaining both their wealth and their social status, Germany felt like a very different place.

'Polycratic' Government and the Cumulative Radicalisation of Policy

The regime's violent confrontation with the SA closed off the possibility of a second, more radical revolution, but by no means neutralised all the potential for political conflict. Despite the monumental façade of discipline and order presented at rallies, and the focus and drive suggested by the regime's propaganda, the government of the Third Reich was fragmented, disorganised and riven by infighting. Cabinet government was more or less abandoned within a matter of months: it met several times a week in the spring of 1933 but there was barely one meeting a month following the retirement of the ailing president of East Prussia at the end of that year, and from the end of 1935 cabinet meetings were called only intermittently, and when it was expedient to get a number of new laws passed together. It met for the last time on 5 February 1938.[22] Cabinet government was replaced by a system where business was conducted by bilateral meetings or by written correspondence and co-ordinated by Hans-Heinrich Lammers, the head of the Reich Chancellery. The fiction of collective government was kept alive when the Enabling Act was renewed in 1937 and 1939. Hitler's attempts to have it changed to designate him as sole lawgiver were challenged by civil servants in the interior ministry, and it was renewed unchanged, pending the promulgation of a National Socialist constitution. In reality over half of all legislation took the form of Führer decrees or Führer orders.[23]

Although the power of ministers was ostensibly increased by the abolition of the *Länder*, their authority was undermined by the appointment of 'plenipotentiaries' to lead specifically designated organisations charged with undertaking urgent tasks: Fritz Todt, for example, as General Inspector for German Roads from 1933, worked outside the jurisdiction of any ministry. Other organisations were technically subordinate to a government department (as in the case of the Reich Labour Service), or to the party (as in the case of the Hitler Youth), but in practice operated as quasi-autonomous institutions.[24] Similarly, ministers and ministerial bureaucrats found themselves at odds with specially designated agencies led by 'plenipotentiaries' or 'Reich commissioners' appointed by Hitler, and staffed by a mixture of civil servants, ambitious party members and professional experts or advisers. Quasi-governmental organisations proliferated as the professional civil service lost its grip on the day-to-day business of routine administration. This was not simply a matter of the party usurping the functions of the state and the civil service: there were too few qualified or competent Nazis available to make that possible. What appeared superficially to be simple conflicts between party and state were often more complicated, and had originated elsewhere among the confused, 'polycratic' governmental structures of Nazi Germany. Departments, offices and agencies multiplied and institutionalised conflict became endemic.[25]

Hitler's first intervention was relatively conventional (the creation of a new ministry) but nevertheless established a pattern for the new approach to politics and government. The sphere of interest of the Ministry of Popular Enlightenment and Propaganda (*Reichsministerium für Volksaufklärung und Propaganda*, RMVP) overlapped with that of several existing ministries, not least education. The Education Minister Bernhard Rust found himself fighting simultaneous demarcation battles with Goebbels, Baldur von Schirach of the Hitler Youth, and Alfred

Rosenberg, who presided over the party's cultural organisation; and Rosenberg in turn felt that the new Propaganda Ministry trespassed on his own territory. Finally, there was potential for further conflict over the control of leisure and popular culture, this time with Robert Ley's German Labour Front, whose Strength through Joy (*Kraft durch Freude*, KdF) organisation sought to control such activities.[26] Overlapping jurisdiction and latent conflict was similarly built into the regime's economic policy, where Göring's Four-Year-Plan Office faced Schacht's economics ministry and the Reichsbank. Göring in turn was challenged by Himmler in a struggle for control of the police and security forces; and the development of foreign policy was complicated by the influence of Ribbentrop and Hitler's own personal interventions. Powerful leading figures built personal empires which were semi-independent of any other control than Hitler's approval, and whose claim to legitimacy was founded on their ability to maintain themselves and expand. Goebbels, Göring and Himmler were all close to Hitler and could – crucially – get to see him personally without much difficulty. In the case of these powerful senior figures in the party, personal empires were built up through the acquisition of a series of portfolios, apparently at random. Göring, an outstanding example, had responsibilities for Prussia and for aviation, and attempted to control the police before building up a significant power-base in the economy after the establishment of the Four-Year-Plan Office in 1936.[27] Increasingly, political power was invested in the office-holder rather than the offices they held.

The proliferation of offices and organisations, all outbidding each other for the favour of the Führer, produced what Hans Mommsen has called a 'cumulative radicalisation' of politics, in the Third Reich. Individuals and organisations battled to outstrip their rivals and establish or enhance their own position within the system, pushing the regime into ever more radical measures, above all in the drive to achieve territorial expansion and racial purity, making compromise impossible and over-reach, chaos and self-destruction ever more likely. The collapse of the German political system was exacerbated after the outbreak of war by the experience of expansion in the East, where new territories existed almost wholly outside any practical legal jurisdiction. The 'state of exceptions' (*Ausnahmestaat*) found its fullest expression in territories annexed or occupied for 'living space' (*Lebensraum*) in eastern Europe, where SS and party personnel were unrestrained by any constitutional control. Definitive arrangements for the 'new order' were deferred until after the final victory, but the emergence of structures of arbitrary power in the East suggested a model not just for the new territories, but for the

Reich itself, and exercised a considerable influence on the development of politics in Germany.[28]

For Mommsen the cumulative radicalisation of policy options illustrates the way in which the apparatus of the German state degenerated into a collection of uncoordinated organisations which subordinated any rational consideration of objective national interests to the irrational goals of Nazi ideology. This 'functional' analysis of the Nazi regime underpins a broader 'structuralist' approach to the understanding of the Nazi dictatorship, which places Mommsen, alongside Martin Broszat, in one of the two opposing schools of thought that dominated explanations of the Nazi dictatorship during the 1970s and 1980s. Their emphasis on the anarchy behind the 'totalitarian' façade of the Third Reich failed to convince their 'intentionalist' opponents, who had placed the determined (if flexible) implementation of a Hitler programme at the centre of the history of Nazi Germany, rejecting the idea of a 'weak dictator' at the head of the regime.[29] As research on all aspects of the Nazi dictatorship has proliferated, we have become increasingly aware of the countless constraints on Hitler and the Nazis, generated by competition for influence and resources as much as by unforeseen events: it is impossible to isolate political events from their context, their bearing on other projects and their consequences outside the direct field of application. The decision-making and implementation of policy that drives political events was a complicated business, and not best explained as the product of an individual or even a collective will.[30]

The Führer State?

Our understanding of Hitler himself has changed. We have long known that he avoided the responsibility of making difficult decisions. Indeed one of the striking features of Hitler's attitude to government was his sheer lack of interest in many of the more mundane matters that demanded his attention, and this was reflected in his frequent absences from Berlin, and in his late nights and leisurely morning routine even when he was in the capital. It was an approach to government and to leadership that contrasted very starkly with Stalin's obsessive will to control all aspects of policy.[31]

Hitler recognised that too close an engagement with day-to-day government business, particularly in domestic policy, was neither advisable nor necessary. The role of the 'Führer' went beyond the power of his office, and embodied a leadership which claimed to be *above* politics, to project

a heroic persona transcending the rules of bureaucratic political institutions, in order to elicit acclaim for the regime regardless of the short-
comings of its actual performance. Ian Kershaw has explained this role
as a function of Hitler's 'charismatic' authority, in the technical sense
the term was used by Max Weber.[32] Hitler could not engage with the
'normal' bureaucratic routines of modern government without undermining his charismatic leadership; as the embodiment of a national
mission he had to remain exempt from the criticism that might follow
an unpopular decision. Hitler's role was a natural outcome of his position in the NSDAP itself (and of the broader cult of 'strong leadership'
that had long been dominant on the political right in Germany); and
in the absence of the 'traditional' authority the emperor had provided
before 1918, and the democratic legitimacy an elected government had
provided during the 1920s, it also fulfilled an essential function providing
a means by which ordinary Germans – once subjects, then citizens, now
followers – could identify with the nation and state. Hitler did not need
to pursue a divide-and-rule policy in dealing with his subordinates in
order to secure his position; rather, it followed from his approach to
politics and his charismatic function within the Nazi political system of
'plebiscitary democracy': mass politics based on popular acclaim rather
than popular participation.

The establishment of 'Führer authority' was never systematised,
however, to reflect the changes in government and politics under the
Nazis. Attempts to reform the NSDAP before 1933 in order to prepare
it for power and provide it with a governmental programme failed when
Hitler thwarted Gregor Strasser's attempt to institute a bureaucratic hierarchy within the party. He used Strasser's resignation in 1932 to break
up the emergent power apparatus at the centre. Rudolf Hess (deputy
Führer for party affairs) was responsible for party policy in a general way,
despite the ambition of Martin Bormann, Hess' chief of staff, to make
the office of the deputy Führer the supreme authority within the party.
Powerful heads of specialist party offices in Berlin (*Reichsleiter*) asserted
their own independence of any central authority, as did the regional
party leaders (*Gauleiter*) in the provinces, although Bormann and his staff
worked to secure co-operation with the regional and local hierarchies,
and to replace individual *Gauleiters* with somebody acceptable to the
deputy Führer's office when the opportunity arose.[33]

Attempts to reform the state were also thwarted. Wilhelm Frick
proposed government by an authoritarian bureaucracy under the
auspices of his own interior ministry, a plan which foresaw the abolition of all elected institutions, from the Reichstag to local councils, and

the federal system would be swept away; all regional and local government institutions would be subordinate to the ministry, which would determine the broad outlines of policy and ensure that it was properly implemented.[34] These intentions were embodied in the Law for the Reconstruction of the Reich of 30 January 1934 but did little to change political realities because, like ambitions for reform (and centralisation) of the party, it came into conflict with the entrenched positions of the *Gauleiters*, this time in their capacity as Reich governors.[35] (Local rights had withstood the encroachments of central authority in Germany for centuries, and the tension still persisted.) Moreover, attempts to reform the state, like those to reform the party, generally entailed a bid for supremacy in relations between the two, and for one to gain such a precedence over the other might threaten the position of Hitler himself, whose role – as we have seen – transcended state and party institutions. Constitutional reform was thwarted above all by the emergence of autonomous power bases loosely connected to both party and state, but effectively independent of either, and with no other authority than the approval of the Führer. The Law on the Head of State of the German Reich of 1 August 1934 marked an important staging post in the development of the dictatorship. It effectively combined the Hindenburg's death on 2 August, thereby introducing the party's leadership into constitutional law. This effectively removed all constitutional and legal constraints on Hitler's power by replacing the constitutional role of the state – in the view of ministerial officials and constitutional lawyers – with that of the Führer's 'single will'.[36] The regime then sought to legitimise this fundamental change to the constitution by plebiscite: the electorate was invited to approve the new law in a referendum of 19 August, which returned an official yes vote of 88.9 per cent. The implications of the changes were neatly summarised in an analysis published by the exiled SPD leadership in Prague, and sub-titled 'Caesar Hitler': 'As Party leader, Reich chancellor, Reich president, and supreme war commander he combines in himself a fullness of power that far exceeds that of Mussolini. Responsible to nobody and undismissible, his position seems to be comparable only with the crowned heads of the absolute monarchies of past times.'[37]

Hitler was now free to conduct government as he pleased. He was rarely at his desk before lunch and left Berlin during the summer. He felt no need to concern himself with discussion of matters that did not bear directly on his immediate concerns, and the preparation of routine legislation was taken over by civil servants. A range of Reich authorities enacted legal provisions in a variety of ways, without consulting each other, effectively making laws which invalidated existing law, often unwittingly. Attempts by Frick and the interior ministry to stem the confusion by at least insisting that new legislation be published in recognised organs became bogged down in inter-departmental wrangling in the autumn of 1936.[38] In the meantime the regime faced no real political threats. The political left had been dealt with very quickly in 1933, and any remaining latent threat from underground resistance groups evaporated as the Gestapo, detected, infiltrated, uncovered and rounded up resistance cells, and turned its attention to turbulent priests and the persecution of minorities. Nor was the regime confronted with disaffection so widespread as to be unsettling during much of the 1930s. Many among the middle classes, particularly the lower middle classes, were disappointed, but saw little alternative. Similarly, if there had been some wishful thinking on the part of reporters for the Sopade's *Deutschland-Berichte* during the early years of the regime that stirrings of discontent persisted, there were few illusions by the autumn of 1937, when a summary of 'reports from the shop floor' reiterated a familiar formula: 'All reports agree that the workforce is passive [. . .] but that the National Socialists have not succeeded in winning them over.'[39]

In fact the 'night of the long knives' seemed to be followed by a period in which Germany achieved a degree of political stability, however illusory. Certainly the later 1930s, and even the first 2 years of war, were perceived as good years by many Germans who lived through the Third Reich.[40] The return to full employment did much to alleviate the poverty suffered during the Depression by many working-class families, and did much to limit opposition. Hitler's foreign policy triumphs – the incorporation of the Saarland into the Reich in 1935, and the remilitarisation of the Rhineland the following year – were seen as milestones in the restoration of Germany's international position; and his foreign policy did not yet, quite, seem so alarming as to induce real anxiety about the possibility of another war (although it was always a relief when tension was resolved).[41] These were also the years in which Nazi Germany built up its reputation among admirers abroad for strong government at home and decisive action on the international stage, much to the frustration of Hitler's beleaguered opponents in Germany.[42]

The creation of a stable authoritarian Germany was not the point of the Nazi dictatorship, however, and the radicalisation of policy gathered pace in the late 1930s. Behind the façade of a stable, ordered, peaceful Germany on show for foreigners at the Berlin Olympics in 1936, pressure was being stepped up on the churches and the Jews, who were being systematically marginalised and impoverished; and new victims were being sought out by the Gestapo – 'asocials', homosexuals, and members of minority sects such as the Jehovah's witnesses. Pressures were also building up in the economy as reserves of gold and foreign currency dwindled, and labour shortages threatened to set off wage inflation.[43] Germany was already embroiled in a foreign conflict, having committed its support to General Franco's rebellion against the Spanish government in 1936, and Hitler himself was increasingly preoccupied with the time-scale of the coming war.[44]

The winter of 1937–38 marked a sharp radicalisation of the Nazi regime.[45] In November 1937 Hitler set out his plans for aggressive expansion within a few years. Hjalmar Schacht, the economics minister, who was in favour of restraining rearmament in the interests of a more balanced and sustainable economy, resigned on 26 May, although he stayed on until January 1939 as president of the Reichsbank, and remained in the government as minister without portfolio until 1933. (Although he had been appointed Plenipotentiary for the War Economy in 1935, Schacht had effectively been excluded from responsibility for economic policy with the construction of the Four-Year-Plan office the following year, and he now resigned from this post too.) He was replaced, both as minister and as president of the Reichsbank, by the more pliable Walther Funk, but the real control of the economy was now with Göring, who had recruited senior civil servants from the labour, agriculture, economics, and transport ministries into his own organisation.

Conservative critics of the regime's policy were removed from senior positions in the armed forces. General Beck, chief of the Army Command and head of the General Staff, was forced to resign, as was General Fritsch, chief of the Army High Command, after being accused of homosexuality. The Defence Minister General Blomberg, who had married a woman later exposed as a former prostitute and compromised Hitler (a guest at the wedding), also resigned. The defence ministry was dissolved and the supreme command of the armed forces (*Oberkommando der Wehrmacht*, OKW) was established in its place under General Keitel. This was an office directly answerable to Hitler, who now took over the command of the armed forces that had hitherto been in the remit of the defence minister. General von Brauchitsch was appointed supreme commander of the army. Finally, the Foreign Minister Konstantin von Neurath was replaced by Joachim von Ribbentrop, who had been promoted through a number of foreign posts during the 1930s (including London, where he was known for his embarrassing and awkward enthusiasm for the Nazi salute).[46]

The direction of policy in 1938 very quickly reflected this radical restructuring at the top. Hitler soon increased the pressure on the Austrian Chancellor Kurt von Schuschnigg, both at a meeting in Berchtesgaden in February and on the streets of Vienna, where adolescent

Nazis now marched and rioted with impunity. The invasion and occupation of Austria followed shortly afterwards, and with it came a sharp
radicalisation of the regime's anti-Jewish policy, first in Austria and then
in the Reich itself as the 'Vienna model' of anti-Semitism was exported,
culminating in the pogrom of November 1938. By then the Munich crisis
and the occupation of the Sudetenland had raised foreign policy stakes
considerably, and the annexation of Bohemia and Moravia the following
spring set Germany on an irreversible course to war. Popular opinion
became increasingly anxious as the pace of foreign policy accelerated,
and there was now scarcely time to be relieved after one war scare was
defused before another flared up. Within days of the Germans marching
into Prague, Nazi formations (SA, SS and police) in Danzig were put
on alert and press agitation against Poland intensified to the point of
hysteria.[47] The outbreak of the war was followed by an 'escalation of
legal terror' that included a crackdown on habitual criminals, asocials
and other outsiders in the national community. Punishments became
more severe as new, vaguely defined categories of 'internal enemy' were
identified in open-ended legislation which extended the scope of the
penal law and encouraged severity in order to protect the Reich from
another 'stab in the back'.[48]

The outbreak of war also marked a turning point in the government of the
Reich. On 30 August Hitler authorised the establishment of a Ministerial
Council for the Defence of the Reich under the chairmanship of Göring;
the other members were Hess, Frick and Funk (respectively plenipotentiaries for the administration of the Reich and the economy), Lammers
and Keitel. It was not meant to signal a return to a form of cabinet government, so much as a committee that would deal swiftly with matters arising
from the war, and it had the power to issue decrees, without necessarily
consulting Hitler. In addition, decrees could by issued jointly by Frick,
Funk and Keitel. The result was an effective deregulation of the process of
drafting legislation. There was a further confusion and a blurring of lines of
jurisdiction between the different legislative procedures, and the situation
deteriorated as communications and relationships between competent
departments broke down during the war. Laws were drafted and published
without consultation, without consent, and often without the knowledge
of all the interested or affected parties – because there was no higher
office to adjudicate. The Ministerial Council for the Defence of the Reich
never became a responsible, coherent, collective government, and was
never intended to, although it remained notionally responsible for author-
ising legislation. Measures were agreed at ad hoc meetings of two or more
members, and although 30 people attended a meeting in November 1939,

there was never a full meeting after that; and Hitler himself intervened
to ensure that its authority was not extended to occupied Europe.[49]
Hitler was not prepared to see a source of political authority emerge
which might remotely challenge his own position, but did not adequately
fulfil the function of adjudicator over departmental differences either,
which led to friction as individuals simply took matters into their own
hands. Much depended too on who had Hitler's favour: if Göring was in the
ascendant at the beginning of the war, Goebbels staged a comeback during
the conflict, and relatively new figures in the leadership assumed considerable importance: chief among them being Albert Speer and Martin
Bormann. In May 1941, following Hess's flight to Scotland, Bormann was
promoted to take over his duties as Führer's deputy for party affairs, but in
fact the staff of the Führer's deputy now became the 'Party chancellery' and
Bormann its head. Bormann, a former farm manager from a Nazi family,
had worked for the party since the mid-1920s, and using the Party chancellery now set about building up a power base. Bormann controlled access
to Hitler, who made him Secretary to the Führer in 1943, a post which Hess
had also occupied. Hitler became increasingly reliant on Bormann, especially after the assassination attempt of 1944, and in so far as Bormann and
the Party chancellery managed to encroach on the authority of Lammers of
the Reich chancellery, the party finally seemed to have the opportunity to
assert itself over the state.[50] In practice a rather different development was
taking place: the consolidation of position by a handful of leading figures
such as Himmler, who was appointed Reich commissioner for the Strengthening of Germandom at the beginning of the war, and became interior
minister in 1943, and instinctively sought to restore the position of the state
vis-à-vis Bormann and the party. Similarly Goebbels became Reich plenipotentiary for total war following the defeat at Stalingrad, and sought in turn to
secure the support of the party in his attempts to recruit more manpower.[51]
   The proliferation of offices that had typified the regime remained
its hallmark to the end. So too did the internal rivalries and conflicts,
which continued in the ruins of Berlin during the spring of 1945. When
Göring sought to succeed Hitler, it was Bormann who denounced him
for treason, and he was summarily dismissed from all his offices by a
leader who commanded little beyond the bunker in which he was now
trapped. Nonetheless, the spoils of defeat continued to be contested,
and Himmler convinced himself not only that he could succeed, but
that he could also continue the anti-Bolshevik crusade against the Soviet
Union after making a separate peace with the Western Allies. In the
event Admiral Dönitz decided to take over the government after Hitler's
suicide, albeit only for the purpose of surrendering unconditionally.

Chapter 3: Nazism and the Economy

The early Nazi party of post-revolutionary Munich made much of its opposition to 'capitalism', and several points in the party programme of 1920 might seem at first glance to bear out its claim to be a national 'socialist' party. It demanded the abolition of income unearned by work, the confiscation of war profits, the prohibition of speculation in land, and the punishment of profiteers and usurers. It also demanded state intervention to control big businesses, especially those that were held to damage the interests of the small firm. The programme further demanded land reform, the nationalisation of corporations, the placing of state contracts with small traders and the communalising of department stores. There was to be state spending on health and education, investment in old age pensions and the prohibition of child labour. This ostensibly radical social and economic agenda differed from that of the Republic – which had in any case already established the most progressive welfare state in Europe – in that it was a critique of capitalism from the right, and one that was not unusual in the early twentieth century.

Nazi Economic Ideology

While Nazi propaganda appropriated the fighting talk of European labour movements the alternative they proposed was neither socialist nor democratic, but authoritarian and corporatist, and drew on non-socialist critiques of economic liberalism that had circulated since the beginning of the nineteenth century. Friedrich List, for example, a forerunner of the 'national' school of economics, had argued that free trade and free markets worked in the interests of the dominant economy. At the time he was writing this was Great Britain, a country which – he pointed out – had built up its position by earlier protecting its own industries. Similarly, the German 'historical' school of economists had argued that the economy should not be run according to the dictates of the supposedly universal laws of the free market, but in the interests of the real national economy, in its social, historical and institutional context. There was a strong element of anti-modernism in right-wing critiques of liberalism: a nostalgia for a harmonious lost world of small communities with strong local roots and identities, with a social system based on estates that bound together all members of an occupation in a single corporate entity, irrespective of wealth or status, but characterised by fixed hierarchies where everybody derived security from knowing his or her place. Such corporatist ideas gained wider currency during the late nineteenth century, when this fictional world of sleepy half-timbered home towns seemed more appealing than the teeming cities of industrial capitalism; and the appeal was reinforced in Catholic Europe by the ideological influence of the papal encyclicals *Rerum novarum* (1891) and *Quadragesimo anno* (1931) in which the corporatist vision of a conflict-free post-liberal society was strongly reflected. The years between the two World Wars saw something of a resurgence of corporatist ideas, particularly on the radical right. Mussolini's corporations, the Austrian 'corporate state' (*Ständestaat*) and Salazar's *Estado Novo* in Portugal all drew on this tradition of thought.[1] Similarly, the very notion of the national community (*Volksgemeinschaft*), which is at the core of the Nazi conception of society, is clearly a corporatist idea.

Despite the anti-capitalist rhetoric there was no fundamental disagreement between Nazism and business, even in the early days and even on the so-called 'left' of the party. This is not to say that there were no differences at all, especially when it became clear that the Nazi regime was intent on subordinating the economy to its ideological objectives.[2] It sought to harness Germany's resources as fully as possible to its programme of rearmament, war and territorial expansion: the economic policies of the Nazi state only make sense when they are seen as part of a greater, combined economic and foreign policy.[3] Conversely, territorial expansion, and above all the acquisition of 'living space' (*Lebensraum*) in the East, was at the heart of the regime's solution to the country's economic problems. By the 1920s there was a growing and influential body of opinion which held that only a 'greater economic region' (*Grossraum*) could survive in the modern world. For decades German politicians, intellectuals and businessmen had found the country's position in the existing world order problematic, and advanced strategies to increase Germany's clout in the emergent global economy.

On the one hand there was a body of opinion that envisaged a coming world of heavily armed protectionist empires run by 'world powers' such as Britain, France, Russia and the United States, and argue that Germany too must become a world power – or go under. Wilhelmine *Weltpolitik* envisaged a colonial empire like Britain's with overseas territories concentrated in Africa. On the other hand there was also a party, drawing particularly from those with interests in agriculture and heavy industry, who thought in terms of a continental power base comparable with that of Russia. If businessmen remained divided before 1914 about the best strategy for economic expansion, the advocates of *Mitteleuropa* were the dominant voice when the war broke out.[4] Bethmann Hollweg's September programme of 1914 set out a blueprint for a European '*Grossraum*' based on a union of Germany and the Habsburg Empire, strategic territorial annexations in France, and the domination of the Balkans and other parts of a putative new European economic order.[5] The programme was not simply a consequence of the outbreak of the war, a bolt from the blue without precedent in public discussion, but reflected the opinions of a strong and vocal political and economic lobby on behalf of territorial expansion in Europe. In a memorandum to the governor of Alsace-Lorraine the industrialist Hermann Röchling had suggested adjustments to the border with France, and adding that the ethnically mixed population should be driven out by Germans. Similarly, Walther Rathenau had written to Bethmann Hollweg on 7 September on the matter of Germany's strategic aims, suggesting that the ultimate war aim should be 'central Europe (*Mitteleuropa*) united under German leadership, politically and economically secured against England and America on the one hand and Russia on the other'. Such positions were not developed overnight, but drew on a long-standing economic rationale for German territorial expansion.[6] Little was said about eastern Europe, but it was here that real German expansion took place during the war.[7] Defeat, revolution and the loss of territory under the terms of the Treaty of Versailles changed perspectives in Weimar Germany; but for many the same issues, linking economic security with territorial expansion, remained on the agenda throughout the 1920s. They were advanced again with greater urgency during the 1930s, when 'Reform' economists looked forward to a post-liberal economic future based on economic self-sufficiency (autarky) in the context of large regional economic blocs.

The Re-ordering of Industrial Relations

In the meantime, however, the new regime had to deal with the pressing economic problem of the present. German agriculture had been in severe crisis since the late 1920s, the banking system had collapsed and the country was in the throes of an industrial Depression which had seen unemployment rise to over 6 million. The first priority for the Nazis was the re-ordering of industrial relations, an objective they shared with their conservative coalition allies. Many of the problems of the Weimar Republic were attributed to the advances made by the working class after 1918: the country's economic problems were felt to be a consequence of the drain on the economy resulting from high wages and welfare spending. There was also a political dimension to the reckoning with organised labour, whose network of parties, unions and co-operatives would now be dismantled.

The Nazis could not afford to alienate the industrial workforce entirely, however, and they were always careful to express respect for the dignity of labour and the 'true' German worker, who resisted the temptations of international Marxism to join in the building of the new national community. The rhetoric was backed up with conciliatory gestures and symbolism: May Day became a public holiday, and one on which Hitler claimed to recall his own experience of manual labour. The language of proletarian solidarity was replaced with that of service to the nation, and the supposed national virtues of the Germans, such as orderliness and cleanliness, were attributed to workers in the specific context of their workplace.[8] The next day the offices of trades unions all over Germany were ransacked by stormtroopers and SS men, and union leaders were imprisoned. The (social democratic) 'free' trades unions were placed under the authority of the 'Action Committee for the Protection of German Labour'; the other, non-socialist unions were similarly 'co-ordinated' the following day.

Despite their claims to be a workers' party, however, the Nazis' own attempts to organise among shop-floor workers had been unsuccessful, and there was no existing Nazi organisation into which the old unions could be readily absorbed. Factory cells had been set up from the early 1920s, and in 1928 the National Socialist Factory Cell Organisation (*Nationalsozialistsiche Betriebszellenorganisation*, NSBO) was established in Berlin. Yet, although it made some headway among white-collar workers in the commercial sector and uniformed workers employed by the state it was less successful among industrial workers in factories. The NSBO was strongest in Berlin, Saxony and the Ruhr conurbation, but even in the Ruhr there were only 2600 members in 1931. National membership rose rapidly following the Nazis' electoral breakthrough, from 39,000 members in 1931 to 170,000 shortly after the July 1932 election, and 294,000 by January 1933. Yet even this was a tiny fraction of Germany's industrial workforce, despite the readiness of the NSBO, unlike other right-wing unions, to take part in industrial action. In elections to factory councils in 1931 the number of Nazi and Stahlhelm candidates together accounted for fewer than 0.5 per cent of all candidates elected. Even after the Nazi takeover of power the NSBO won only 11.7 per cent of factory council votes, while free trades union candidates won 73.4 per cent. The results were even more extreme in individual factories, such as the Berlin electricity works, where Social Democrats won 91 per cent of the vote. Where workers defected from the free trades unionists, as in the Berlin gas works, they switched to the Communists.[9]

At the same time the NSBO was considered too radical by Nazi leaders, and felt to be an inappropriate vehicle for the organisation of industrial labour in the Third Reich. It was effectively sidelined by the founding of the German Labour Front (*Deutsche Arbeitsfront*, DAF) by Robert Ley on 10 May. The DAF was an organisation which would reflect the corporatist concept of 'national community' at shop-floor level, bringing together workers and employers in a 'factory community' (*Betriebsgemeinschaft*). It was technically a subsidiary organisation of the NSDAP, and with 25 million members and over a million functionaries by 1942 it became the largest mass organisation in the Reich. It inherited the organisation of the old unions, including their assets and income from membership dues, but it had no legal authority within the factory to negotiate between workers and employers. The employer was cast as 'works leader' (*Betriebsführer*), and the workforce, in pseudo-medieval language, as his 'retinue' (*Gefolgschaft*). Moreover, in order to ensure that the DAF did not become a real union, capable of genuinely representing workers' interests, a law of 19 May 1933 empowered 12 regionally based officials – the Reich Trustees of Labour – to regulate wage levels. The Law on the Ordering of National Labour of 20 January 1934 codified – to some extent retroactively – the new regime in industrial relations.[10] Unable to represent the workers' basic material interests, the DAF directed its energies into subsidiary organisations such as Beauty of Labour (*Schönheit der Arbeit*), which existed to improve conditions in the workplace, and the leisure organisation Strength through Joy (*Kraft durch Freude*, KdF), which sought to provide cheap entertainment and popularise holidays away from home. Councils of Trust (*Vertrauensräte*) were created to 'deepen mutual trust within the factory community', but had none of the rights of Weimar factory councils (*Betriebsräte*) to be consulted on such matters as mass redundancies.[11] The workers' response was reflected in the results of elections to the new councils in March 1934. In many places fewer than 50 per cent of the workforce voted in favour of the lists of Nazi candidates, and a great many votes were declared invalid. In some places Nazi candidates could not be found, and the old Social Democratic shop stewards who stood instead got much higher votes. According to Social Democrat sources the issue of the elections had led to political differences within the regime, and Hitler himself had been disturbed by the results; leaders of the Labour Front had been forced to admit that some two thirds had voted against the Nazis, and Ley had tried to shift the blame on to the employers.[12]

The 'co-ordination' of the trades unions shifted the balance of power in industrial relations very sharply in favour of the employers. No such radical steps were taken to reorganise business or its representative institutions. Leading members of the Reich Association of German Industrie (*Reichsverband der deutschen Industrie*, RDI) had assisted in the formation of the Hitler cabinet, and the association wrote to Hitler declaring its loyalty to the new regime. Göring invited leading industrialists to a meeting on 27 March 1933 to cement the friendly relationship, and promised to refrain from interfering in the organisation of business. Although the headquarters of the RDI were occupied by stormtroopers on 1 April 1933, the radical measures that had been planned to deal with 'corrupt' business men were quietly abandoned. Following pressure from more hardline Nazis for leading members of the association to resign, the Chairman Gustav Krupp wrote to Hitler, assuring him that the RDI accepted the leadership principle, while the association's executive committee simultaneously insisted on freedom from state interference. Hitler's response was to merge the RDI with the union of German employers' associations (*Vereingiung deutscher Arbeitgeberverbände*) to form a single organisation, the *Reichsstand der deutschen Industrie*. Jewish members were expelled, and members of the old RDI executive committee resigned, to be replaced by Nazis, or at least by men more sympathetic with the aims of the regime. The leadership principle was accepted, and business was thereby more or less voluntarily reorganised along corporative lines as the 'estate of German industry'. In practice however, any further progress towards the corporative model for industry demanded by some radicals, including the establishment of some kind of guild structure, was successfully resisted by big business during the summer of 1933.[13]

This is not to say that industrialists had the upper hand in their relationship with the Nazi regime. The so-called 'puppet theory', which suggested that the Nazis were controlled by big business was rarely taken seriously after 1945 outside the official historiography of the Soviet bloc.[14] Hitler needed the co-operation of business leaders in order to address the economic problems of the Depression and launch his rearmament drive. Although industrialists affirmed their support for Hitler's foreign policy in 1933, the subordination of the economy to the regime's expansionist objectives inevitably gave rise to tensions. Some sectors, such as mining and heavy industry, stood to gain from rapid rearmament; others, particularly those in the consumer goods sector, stood to lose, as increasingly scarce resources – raw materials and labour – were allocated to munitions by the state. Nevertheless the relationship between big business and the new regime generally remained good.

Thwarted Expectations: The Mittelstand and the New Regime

On the other hand, small business people could not help but be disappointed, such were their expectations of the regime. The urban *Mittelstand* had provided the core supporters of the NSDAP before 1933, but the Nazis had made few specific promises, and they did little when they came to power to satisfy petit bourgeois expectations. For a short time during the spring and summer of 1933 the ideological spokesmen for the *Mittelstand* thought they were on the brink of seeing their ideas implemented. The language of nostalgic corporatism, embodied in the very term *Mittelstand* (middle estate) itself, was at the centre of these expectations, and although the terminology of estates had long outlived the social and economic arrangements they had once described, it remained a powerful rhetorical device, and a mainstay of conservative and nationalist political discourse during the crises of the inter-war years. In practice it did not necessarily reflect reactionary or anti-modernist agendas on the part of the lower middle classes or their champions, still less a genuine wish to return to pre-modern conditions. It provided a symbolic language that enabled the lower middle classes to articulate present-day antipathies to the forces by which they felt they were being squeezed out of existence – big business on the one hand, and the labour movement on the other – and it helped them to express essentially modern aspirations.[15] Many middle-class voters had migrated to the NSDAP via single-issue parties in the late 1920s, and behind the circumlocutions of corporatist ideology there were often very straightforward demands or grievances. So if there was no immediate transformation of Germany into a *Ständestaat* in 1933, it was perhaps because that was not the point: it was more important for the regime to identify the real issues and to address the specific preoccupations of the various occupational groups and thereby halt and reverse the decline of the *Mittelstand* as a whole.[16] At first the political situation seemed promising. The sustained attack on the labour movement was immensely popular, and the Nazi Combat League for the Commercial Middle Class (*Kampfbund für den gewerblichen Mittelstand*) organised boycotts against department stores and consumer co-operatives up and down the country. Meanwhile organisations representing small-business interests, including chambers of commerce, were nazified in much the same way as other organisations, and Nazis replaced the politically unreliable in leading positions. 'Co-ordination' was accompanied by some limited measures of benefit to the small business sector. In May 1933 the Law for the Protection of the Retail Trade prohibited the creation of expansion or chain stores, the addition of new lines of merchandise in existing shops, and eliminated the practice of installing self-contained craftsmen's shops or restaurants in department stores. In September 1933 the building trade profited from the introduction of tax benefits and subsidies for house repairs and construction worth 500 million Reichsmarks. In 1934 the establishment of new businesses was limited by the introduction of a licensing system imposing certain requirements on the proprietor. Compulsory guild membership was also introduced in 1934, and in 1935 a certificate of qualification was introduced, to the irritation of big business and the delight of artisans' associations, who saw it as a turning point in their fortunes – the Magna Carta of National Socialist legislation. In practice, however, the effect of the measure was diluted by a number of qualifications and exceptions.[17]

Small shopkeepers in particular had expected some action from the Nazis to limit the competition they faced from department stores (demonised by Nazi propaganda as essentially Jewish establishments) and co-operatives. Both the German financial and business community and the civil service rejected the idea of punitive legislation against department stores, however, and they survived sporadic boycotts and discriminatory taxation; the *Länder* were empowered, for example, by a law of 15 July 1933, to impose their own taxes on department stores. Local authorities were also able to impose other sanctions. In Chemnitz, for example, the city authorities withdrew the drink licence from two department stores, forcing them to close their refreshment rooms.[18] Co-operatives ceased to receive state subsidies, and the weaker ones were liquidated, but many of them continued to trade, much to the irritation of members of the Nazi trade and commerce organisation (*Nationalsozialistische Handels- und Gewerbetreibende Organisation*, NS-Hago). The co-operatives themselves tried to come to terms with small retailers by promising (in a pact of 1934) not to campaign for new members, but ultimately their survival, like that of the department stores, was a triumph of pragmatism over ideology: they could not be closed down without creating more unemployment and disrupting food distribution.

The general thrust of Nazi economic policy was bound to work against the economic interests of the lower middle classes, and it very quickly became clear that there was widespread disillusionment among the regime's core constituency of support.

The most vociferous criticism of the regime seemed to come from the Mittelstand, from people who 'could not shout loud enough when Hitler became chancellor, and voted solidly for him for years' in the words of an underground reporter for the Social Democrats. 'Now they say furiously that they had not imagined it would be like this.' Unemployment was supposed to be falling, but business did not seem to get any better, and people's purchasing power had certainly not increased. Business people were caught between the continuing slump in trade and endless pressure to donate to party causes. Farmers, craftsmen and shopkeepers all complained incessantly, consoling themselves that things could only get better. Others, typical small business people, had already had enough of the Nazis, among them a hairdresser and his wife from south-west Germany, seven times Nazi voters ('but never again!'); a hotelier in Dresden, who objected to providing free meals for stormtroopers, and had cancelled his subscription to the *Völkischer Beobachter*. Meetings of the NS-Hago were badly attended and bad-tempered: speakers were shouted down, and up and down the country people were walking out of conferences and guild meetings during Nazi speeches (except where the doors were kept closed and guarded).

The regime's own internal reports on morale (by local authorities and the police) recorded similar findings. There were very specific complaints from small businesses about the lack of contracts, shortages of materials, taxes and contributions to the new organisations. Shopkeepers complained about price regulation (and regulation generally), about Jewish firms and the lack of purchasing power among their customers.[19] There were widespread complaints that credit was tight, and that the regime had still not done away with department stores. The discontent continued into the autumn of 1934, and Sopade reporters noted – with some Schadenfreude – that farmers and petit bourgeois seemed to be vying to outdo each other in cursing the government, and the content of these reports was confirmed by the regime's own. Shopkeepers in particular continued to be squeezed: taxes remained high, and help from the government was unforthcoming, shortages drove prices up, and held back the recovery of trade, and the shopkeepers themselves became scapegoats for popular discontent. The NS-Hago was finding it increasingly difficult to get their members to pay their subscriptions. On top of other difficulties small businesses were being starved of the foreign currency they needed to buy goods from abroad. Cargoes waiting in container ports in the Netherlands could not be imported, or in some cases had to be sent back because the firm could not find the hard currency to pay for them. This inevitably led to lay-offs by small manufacturers in the consumer sectors, in branches such as textiles and leather goods, and as a result more craftsmen were becoming dependent on social security. The construction industry suffered similar difficulties: raw materials were scarce, taxes were high, and guild subscriptions were going up – doubling in some cases. Finally, although this was one sector where targeted public intervention held out some promise of relief, there were soon complaints that work commissioned effectively by the authorities was not being paid for, as for example in the case of state-subsidised housing repairs in Saxony, where small businesses finding themselves out of pocket.[20]

Minor frustrations about shortages, taxes and contributions to guilds had fuelled a mounting sense of general disappointment in the new regime. Complaints continued to pour in from all trades and all parts of the country, from painters and decorators in Saxony, shopkeepers in the Rhineland, hoteliers in Hanover and publicans in the south-west. The chicanery of the new authorities at local level compounded the resentment. Butchers in Hamburg, for example, were incensed to find that RM 46,000 in their life assurance fund had been signed over to the NS-Hago, and that simultaneously the payout in case of death was being halved, from 1000 marks to 500, while monthly payments doubled from 1 mark to 2. Finally, the regime's new corporatist ideology was not to all tastes. In the opinion of some small business people it reflected 'a narrow-minded guild mentality' that was felt to be restrictive and expensive, replacing 'lively self-administration with expensive compulsory organisations'.[21]

It quickly became clear that the economic priorities of the regime were not those of the 'little people' who had supported the party most devotedly, and many of them now even began to deny that they had ever really been Nazis at all. Nor did the morale of the lower middle classes much improve when the rearmament boom really took off in the later 1930s; after all, rearmament not merely favoured the big industrial enterprise, it also pushed up wage costs, starved retailers of consumer goods and failed to deliver the disposable income and consumer boom that small businesses needed. So the litany of grumbles continued throughout the 1930s. On the eve of war Sopade's *Deutschland-Berichte* published a special report on the 'decline of the commercial middle class' based, as usual, on reports from within Germany, and followed by a detailed account of the problems of the retail sector in Berlin. The self-employed middle classes, it argued, had seen Hitler as a saviour in time of crisis, but had been bitterly disappointed: 'the great industrial concerns were not dissolved, the department stores were not closed'; in fact both had received support from the authorities. The shortage of retail goods in the capital was catastrophic, and such items as were to be had were of poor quality. Shopkeepers were allocated supplies of meat at fixed prices inflated to keep the farmers happy. They were then compelled to sell at fixed prices, this time lower than they liked, to keep consumers happy. Craftsmen were still constantly short of essential materials: plumbers could not get lead, for example, and decorators could not get oil-based paints. Finally the shortage of industrial labour had prompted the regime to close down ailing small businesses, especially those paying little or no tax, to free up workers for the munitions industries, and while it squeezed out 'uneconomic' business it also squeezed a whole section of the *Mittelstand*.[22] In general, however, the first wave of dissatisfaction among small business people seems to have receded somewhat during the later 1930s, only for new anxieties to emerge with the outbreak of the war as the sector took the brunt of shortages. Morale deteriorated rapidly after 1943 as shortages became more widespread and businesses were closed down, a policy which also encountered some reluctance among local authorities sceptical of the policy's effectiveness.[23]

'Blood and Soil': The Impact of Nazi Policies in the Countryside

If expectations of the Nazis were high among urban small business people, the same was also true of their rural counterparts, and the importance of the countryside itself to the Nazi view of the world cannot be emphasised too strongly. The party's ideology and propaganda, like that of other contemporary fascist parties, was distinctly anti-urban: cities were perceived as hives of criminality, political subversion, degeneracy and vice. The regime wanted to halt and reverse the headlong flight from the land by reinvigorating rural society, and it was from here after all that the party drew its most solid support during the prolonged agricultural crisis of the late 1920s and early 1930s. In return Hitler promised farmers that he would make agriculture profitable again, even if it meant higher food prices for the consumer: the problems of German agriculture would be solved within 4 years, and it was hoped that Germany would dramatically reduce its dependence on food imports. The tension arising from these conflicting aims became clear when measures undertaken to protect farmers by Hugenberg, the new agriculture minister, had the effect of increasing food prices. The agriculture price index rose, albeit marginally, for the first time in years, and the regime was popular in the countryside. Support for agriculture at the expense of other sectors of the economy was short-lived – as was Hugenberg's career as agriculture minister. He clashed with Walther Darré, who was overseeing the 'co-ordination' of agricultural organisations and interest groups, and replaced Hugenberg as minister on 29 June.

In September all agricultural organisations were united in the Reich Food Estate, under Darré's leadership as Reich Peasant Leader.[24] It was a body which had some 17 million members in the 1930s and controlled all aspects of the production and distribution of food through 26 regional farmers' organisations and their local branches. Reich offices were established to oversee the import of foodstuffs, quotas were set for domestic farmers and prices were regulated by marketing boards. Through these controls and increased productivity the regime hoped to achieve greater agricultural self-sufficiency. In fact farmers from Pomerania to Bavaria resented what they saw as interference in their business by the new 'bigwigs', particularly the regulation of food marketing and distribution.[25]

Beyond the reorganisation of agricultural organisations the most pressing problem for the regime was indebtedness and the threat of farms being broken up as a result. The DNVP had already put together a scheme for debt relief in 1931, and Hugenberg proposed to register all farmers unable to meet their obligations. Laws preventing the break-up of farms in Prussia were introduced in May 1933, and the Reich Entailed Farm Law of 29 September extended such arrangements to the rest of the Reich.[26] A great deal of emphasis was placed on the benefits of the measure to the racial health of the nation, not least by Darré himself, and those not of German blood excluded from its provisions. ('German blood' came to be a category defined very broadly in practice to include all Europeans). This clause, directed primarily against the Jews, had little impact as few of them were farmers in any case, and they were still permitted to own their own land. The law had a limited impact: fewer than a quarter of all farms were eligible under its provisions (although they accounted for more than a third of all farmland), and the proportion varied from region to region. There were more eligible farms in north-eastern Germany, for example, and in Bavaria, than in other parts of the country.

Responses to the new legislation were mixed. Its provisions were not well understood, and it generated anxiety in the countryside. Would childless widows, for example, now be forced off their farms? Above all, the measure was perceived as unwanted state interference in the business of farmers, who were now felt to be little more than administrators of their own property.[27] Entailed farmers lost the right to sell or mortgage property, which meant that those who did not inherit could not use the property to raise money. (That they were destined, in Darré's grand scheme, to settle new land in the east was little consolation.) A Sopade reporter from northern Bavaria, noting the unpopularity of the laws, summarised the observations of local farmers: 'What good is an entailed farm that will be free of debt in about 30 years, when we can't get any money now because nobody will give us any.' 'Dissatisfaction everywhere' was reported from Brandenburg, among farmers and their families: eldest sons were coming back from the city and driving out younger siblings. The only people who seemed to benefit from the law were insurance salesmen who preyed on the farmers' anxieties. By 1938 it was acknowledged that the scheme promoted inactivity and opportunism on the part of the farmers, and worst of all that it reduced the birth rate.[28]

There was also resentment in the countryside on a number of other issues, above all the 'coercive economy' (*Zwangswirtschaft*) regulation of food production and distribution.[29] Farmers resented having to deliver their produce to state collection points for fixed prices, in order, as they saw it, to featherbed a bloated Food Estate bureaucracy. These feelings were echoed by the food processing industry: firms claimed to be paying much more to the Food Estate in dues than formerly to independent associations.[30] Where one woman had collected eggs there were now six state employees, as one complaint from Bavaria had it. Attempts to thwart or circumvent the regulation were widespread. A farmer from the Palatinate, who had tried to sell some of his milk on the black market, preferred in the end to pour it away rather than surrender it to the authorities. From Bremen it was reported that the authorities had set up road blocks to put a stop to the local black market in butter; in Breslau the main market was raided by 50 officials and goods were confiscated.[31] Yet despite these measures to rationalise and improve food distribution the regime failed in its intention to reduce Germany's dependence on foreign imports, and particularly fats, the lack of which contributed to the general economic crisis of 1935–36. At the same time the cost of food rose, while the consumer was scarcely in a better position than during the Depression. Finally, the regime failed to prevent the continuing 'flight from the land', and one of the most serious problems facing the agricultural economy by the mid-1930s was the shortage and cost of labour.

Economic Recovery and Economic Crisis

If the regime's agricultural policy enjoyed only limited success and met with a mixed reception, its policies in the industrial sector seemed to be dealing better with the economic crisis. Germany had long-term economic problems, and had been hit harder by the Depression than most developed countries. The relative economic stability of the mid-1920s had proved to be illusory, interest rates had remained high and growth was sluggish. As the economy had deteriorated in 1929, the situation was exacerbated by the sudden large-scale withdrawal of capital from Germany. Industrial production and foreign trade had collapsed, agricultural prices had fallen and unemployment had risen sharply.[32] The Brüning government had addressed the crisis by conventional means: by seeking to persuade Germany's trading partners to reduce levels of protectionism in the hope of restoring foreign markets for German goods; by trying to reduce labour costs in order to make German goods more competitive; and by intervening in the financial sector in order to control the flow of capital. But before his demise he departed, albeit marginally, from his deflationary economic policy, and agreed to allocate funds to work creation programmes in 1931. These were taken over (and expanded) by Papen, but the funding allocated to them was so trivial that the effect on unemployment was marginal.[33]

Many of the policies associated with the 'Nazi economic recovery', then – regulation of trade, finance and foreign exchange, agricultural protection and work programmes – were products of the Weimar Republic, and not unusual practice in other European countries. The Nazis had the good fortune to come to power at a time when the world economy began to recover anyway, but took measures to promote and accelerate the recovery in Germany. Above all they established control from above, and reinforced it by regulation and coercion. While subordinating the economy to political objectives, however, the Nazis relied on the expertise of the economic 'establishment' – bankers, businessmen and civil servants – to achieve their economic objectives.[34] The combination

of ideological soundness and pragmatic measures was epitomised in
the former president of the Reichsbank, Hjalmar Schacht, who had
been a co-founder of the DDP, but had turned to the extreme right
during the 1920s, and had raised funds from the business community
for the Nazis during the Depression. Above all he was more sympathetic than the current president of the Reichsbank, Hans Luther, to the
state spending on work creation programmes, was recalled to replace
him in March 1933 and was appointed Reich economics minister in 1934.

The work creation programmes, for which Schacht immediately began
to make funds available through deficit spending, were at the centre
of Nazi economic measures during the first 2 years of the regime, but
the propaganda image of the 'battle for work' was at variance with the
meagre sums devoted to job creation schemes – schemes that the Nazis
had in any case inherited from their predecessors. The voluntary labour
service with its high-profile organisation for low-paid, unskilled labour
was cut back from 1934, and the number of those working in it declined
from 1932 to 1935.[35] The fall in unemployment was not the result of work
creation programmes, as astute contemporary observers were aware; it
was due above all to spending on rearmament, which constituted the
most important shift in Germany's economic priorities during the first
months of the dictatorship. There were other factors, of course: the
regime put pressure on employers not to lay off workers (resulting in
more short-time work for those who remained employed), and there were
assorted ditch-digging and weeding projects. Germans were returning
to work, but for lower wages, in poorer conditions and under greater
pressure from employers, who exploited the absence of the unions.[36]

As business picked up and people returned to work, consumption was
stimulated and investment increased. New problems were encountered
very quickly, however, which raised serious questions about the future
direction of the economy. Should the regime's dwindling reserves of
foreign currency be used to import raw materials for the rearmament
drive? Or should some of it be used to import food in order to maintain popular support for the regime? In brief, should the regime invest
in guns or butter? The response – apart from suspending the repay-
ment of foreign debts – was Schacht's 'New Plan', by which the government effectively allocated foreign exchange according to its own priorities, and regulated imports. The government also tried to redirect the
country's foreign trade away from overseas countries that were tied into
preferential agreements, towards closer trading partners, primarily in
the Balkans – Germany's 'back yard' – where a number of exploitative
bilateral agreements were reached. East European prices were relatively

high by world standards, but Berlin encouraged Balkan states to produce food and raw materials for export to Germany, whose requirements were such that the regime could, at least for a time, insist on paying in marks rather than hard currency, and moreover marks which could only be spent on certain types of German goods: not the heavy machinery the Balkan states wanted, but cheap consumer goods. Effectively a system of barter was established, which worked to Germany's advantage in the mid-1930s, but quickly left the regime's Balkan trading partners disillusioned, and by 1938 the lucrative trade had more or less ground to a halt (but the relationship was revived after 1939).[37]

From early 1935 there were increasing numbers of complaints about rapidly rising prices for potatoes, eggs and butter, and there was some bitterness among industrial workers about poor wages. By the summer both police reports and the Sopade's *Deutschland-Berichte* were dominated by complaints about shortages. Prices were rising rapidly: some fresh vegetables were between 30 per cent and 50 per cent dearer than the previous year; and berries were twice as expensive, because – people were complaining – they were all being used to make jam for the army. Hoarding and smuggling (from Czechoslovakia to Saxony, for example) were widespread.[38] By the autumn there were long queues for food. Shops introduced their own informal rationing system, and the police were increasingly present to keep order as tempers frayed and fights broke out at markets. They also prevented would-be photographers taking pictures of the queues. (Goebbels rather unconvincingly accused troublemakers of deliberately avoiding well-stocked shops and waiting outside those without butter in order to exacerbate the problem.) At the same time the shortage of raw materials was seriously affecting arms production, and industrial workers were being laid off. Finally, the increasing hostility of farmers towards the regime's new regulations was making things worse, as they took to various forms of passive resistance.[39] There was some understanding for the government's dilemma, and many more than might be supposed conceded that 'ore (for munitions) was more important than butter'.[40] Even so the regime's popularity, as assessed by Gestapo reports in January 1936, and then again in March, was continuing to decline.[41]

The Four-Year Plan and the Defence Economy in Peace-time

The crisis came to a head again in 1936, and its outcome was the Four-Year Plan: a decisive shift in economic policy from relatively conservative to 'reform' economics. Despite some unorthodox measures Schacht's policies had still been determined by the thinking of the Depression era.[42] In his view the more radical impulses of the Nazis needed to be contained, and when he recommended Göring to head a commission on the raw materials question it was in the belief that practical experience of addressing economic problems would be good for him. But he had misjudged the situation. Hitler was now determined to bring the economy under more direct party control – something which Schacht had managed to avoid – in order to ensure that preparations for war were prioritised at whatever cost, and this meant a greater commitment to 'autarky'. Göring was appointed commissioner of raw materials on 4 April, and it immediately became clear that the scope of his intervention would be far greater than Schacht had envisaged. This is what Hitler intended. He could have appointed his economic adviser Wilhelm Keppler, or Walther Funk (a pliable party man who would eventually succeed Schacht at the economics ministry), but the point was to put in place a forceful character, who would loosen the conservatives' hold over economic policy.

Göring consolidated his position during the summer while the conservatives in the army and the economics ministry disagreed among themselves. He aligned himself more clearly with the autarky lobby around Keppler, and set about recruiting staff. He asserted his position according to a pattern that was not unusual in the internal power struggles of Nazi Germany: not by taking over an existing institution, but by constructing a rival alternative. As the crisis became more acute Göring solicited advice from economic experts, among them Carl Goerdeler, a leading conservative and formerly price commissioner under Brüning. Goerdeler counselled moderation, and effectively defended Schacht's position, recommending a cut in military spending and the import of raw materials. This might mean a rise in unemployment of up to 2 million, however, which the regime could not countenance. Moreover, events in international affairs – particularly the outbreak of the Spanish civil war – strengthened Hitler's belief that military spending must be maintained, and that Germany must become more self-sufficient, and in September Göring was appointed eich Plenipotentiary for the Four Year Plan.

Hitler's memorandum on the Four-Year Plan emphasised Germany's role as a bulwark against Bolshevism, and foresaw an inevitable military conflict with the Soviet Union. It concluded that both the economy and the armed forces should be ready for war within 4 years. Ultimately, Germany's aim was to acquire 'living space'; this would settle the problem of obtaining food and raw materials once and for all. In the short term, however, Germany must become as self-sufficient as possible in order to reduce her dependence on imports. This meant the development of synthetic substitutes with the co-operation of the giant chemicals cartel IG Farben, which had supported the party financially, and already worked closely with the military. The company, represented by Carl Krauch, Göring's new 'plenipotentiary' for chemicals production, was to become a key player in Germany's economic preparations for war. Almost half of all investment under the plan went into synthetic products.[43]

The Four Year Plan marked a change of course for the regime. It served much of its real purpose in so far as it subordinated economic policy to the requirements of rearmament, and it did so without demanding any great sacrifices from the German people. Göring established an extensive organisation which encroached on the territory of ministers by co-opting senior civil servants from the ministries of labour and agriculture, and undermined the civil service by bringing in 'experts' such as Krauch from the private sector. The organisation intervened extensively in the economy in a drive to divert resources into rearmament at the expense of export industries, and there were increasing complaints from businessmen about interference, bureaucracy and red tape, as Göring's 'strip-mining' of the economy began to make its impact.[44] The Four-Year Plan Office recognised that Germany could not depend entirely on the resources within her present borders. The self-sufficiency envisaged by the plan was clearly unrealistic, and its targets were not met. The majority of Germany's iron ore continued to come form abroad, primarily from Sweden. Nor were the production targets met for synthetic oil. Only the production of synthetic rubber (Buna) was relatively successful. Clumsy attempts to use substitute materials were liable to backfire. Shoemakers, for example, complained bitterly when the regime tried to enforce the use of ersatz leather for shoe repairs for welfare recipients, and most of the small businesses affected did not have the machines needed to work the substitute materials.[45] Nevertheless, autarky provided the regime with resources to continue its rearmament for 2 years, until the annexation of Austria, which placed not only Vienna's gold and currency reserves at the regime's disposal, but considerable quantities of raw materials as well. But the Anschluss also aggravated problems: Austria, and later the Sudetenland, both had important requirements which Germany could not fulfil, while their own exports were now diverted to the '*Altreich*' too.[46]

The annexation of Austria also brought with it reserves of unemployed manual workers, and although they could not be deployed immediately to plug Germany's increasing labour shortages, they did offer some relief for an increasingly urgent problem.[47] According to the labour ministry

there were 1.17 million unemployed in Germany at the end of July
1936, a figure comparable with the late 1920s, and the level of unemployment was falling rapidly. Of the remaining unemployed some were
only temporarily out of work, others were of only 'limited employab-
ility', and some long-term unemployed people, such as older white-collar
workers, had difficulty finding work despite the improved economic situation. On the other hand there were shortages of labour in agriculture,
construction and the iron and steel industry, and employers had to
compete for scarce skilled workers. Workers were restless, and changed
jobs frequently in pursuit of higher wages, raising the threat of inflation.
Workers were also beginning to flex their new industrial muscle, and
euphemistically termed 'strike attempts' and 'work stoppages' were no
longer exceptional.[48]

The regime responded by extending state control over the labour
market, assuming control of labour exchanges, and issuing workers with
a 'work book', a personal record of their qualifications and previous
employment.[49] By 1938 unemployment stood at less than half a million,
and by 1939 it was only 74,000. At the end of 1938 the labour ministry
reckoned that there were a million unfilled vacancies.[50] Some relief was
expected from the annexation of Austria, where mass unemployment
had persisted well into the 1930s, but the long-term unemployed in
Austria needed training, and that in turn required diverting other staff
from their work. Many Austrians resisted being allocated to employers in
Germany – the *Altreich* – and it would take time to modernise and expand
Austria's own industrial base so that the regime could take advantage of
local labour – above all in the new industrial developments around the
Reichswerke Hermann Göring in Linz, a massive undertaking designed to
transform Hitler's home town and underpin its future cultural significance with an economic base.[51]

The labour shortages had immediate and obvious consequences: there
were delays and bottlenecks in the worst-affected sectors, and these had
repercussions throughout the economy. Wage inflation was a further
threat, whose costs would ultimately have to be borne by the government itself. Firms poached workers from each other in order to be
sure of fulfilling lucrative government contracts on time, enticing them
with higher wages that pushed up hourly rates for industrial workers by
10 per cent between 1935 and the outbreak of war, and weekly wages by
over 17 per cent in the same period.[52] Maximum wages were set, with
the threat of fines for employers who exceeded them, but as workers felt
more secure in their jobs, and became aware that employers could not
afford to lose them, industrial discipline suffered: productivity declined,

absenteeism and sickness rates increased, and workers frequently broke their employment contracts in order to take up better offers elsewhere. In addition agricultural workers left the land in increasing numbers to take up better paid jobs in industry, and did so despite a barrage of propaganda and prohibitions from the regime, thereby creating a parallel crisis in the agricultural sector.

Labour shortages, then, contributed to a gathering economic crisis in the late 1930s. Competition between firms for raw materials and foreign exchange, a feature of the earlier crisis (of 1936), persisted and intensified, and the three branches of the armed forces even competed with each other within arms enterprises. Finally, additional demands for resources came from other quarters sanctioned by the state or party – for the redevelopment of Berlin as the grandiose capital of the coming greater German Reich for example.[53] The inflationary pressure this created was compounded by the relative lack of consumer goods, as resources were directed into the capital goods sector. The nature and significance of the crisis has been a matter of dispute among historians. In the 1970s Tim Mason argued that the regime's domestic problems narrowed its foreign policy options during the two years before the war, and thereby influenced the timing of the outbreak of war itself. He attributed the crisis, in part, to the regime's failure to integrate the working class into the 'national community': Nazi leaders were conscious that deprivation during the First World War had led to popular unrest and revolution, and were as anxious to avoid imposing sacrifices on the people as they were to make Germany self-sufficient in order to be independent of food imports in wartime.[54] Critics of this interpretation argued that Mason had read too much into his documentary evidence, or had taken the exaggerated anxieties of bureaucrats too much at face value, given that there is no real evidence to suggest that Hitler and the Nazi leadership were aware of a domestic crisis of such severity that they felt compelled to go to war. Mason himself later accepted that most other historians working in the field had more or less rejected his hypotheses, and accepted that his arguments needed to be refined in some respects, while insisting on the validity of his basic point: the regime was constrained in its choices by its own reluctance to antagonise industrial workers.[55]

The Nazi Economy at War

Indiscipline and industrial protest found their most dramatic focus after the outbreak of war, when a series of measures were introduced to meet the expected demands of the war economy. The provisions of the war economy decree of 4 September 1939 suspended industrial safety regulations, abolished paid holidays, along with bonuses for overtime and shift work, and sought to reduce wages. In addition there was to be more civil conscription and an end to restrictions on the working week.[56] By the end of October it was clear that these measures were unpopular throughout the Reich, and had created a widespread collective sense of disaffection, which was translated into 'passive resistance' of various kinds, including 'refusals to work'. These were not necessarily strikes as such, and often involved a handful of workers refusing to do specific jobs, but also included objections to working overtime or weekend shifts. Sickness rates also rose sharply, and 7 to 10 per cent of the workforce were far above the 2 per cent considered normal by the Reich Insurance Office, or even the 4 per cent considered justifiable on the grounds of longer shifts, the increased pace of work and other pressures. Persistent absenteeism was not the only problem, however, and it was quickly clear that something had to be done. Bonuses for overtime and Sunday shifts were re-introduced on 10 November, and as the government began to make more concessions the mood among the industrial workforce improved. The withdrawal of the measures was also welcomed by the employers, who had derived no direct benefit from them, but had borne the brunt of absenteeism and other labour discipline problems. Where they had gained directly – as with the suspension of paid holidays – the employers opposed the restoration of the status quo, fearing that the backlog of holidays would be expensive, but it was this concession in particular, along with the decision to pay Christmas bonuses, that decisively improved morale.[57]

The regime never took on the workforce head on again in such a fashion. It reasserted greater control over the workers during the war, and the labour discipline problems of the later 1930s proved to have been a relatively short-lived phenomenon. Shortages of labour persisted, however, and the situation was exacerbated by the conscription of working-class men into the armed forces. There was no easy solution to this problem: men had to be recruited to the armed forces, but were also needed on the 'home front' for jobs that were vital to arms production. No amount of taking up slack from the consumer goods sector or 'non-essential' firms was enough. Nor did attempts to impose rigid controls on the allocation of skilled labour provide the necessary numbers. Since the regime was now reluctant to try again to force higher productivity from a dwindling workforce, the only alternative was to find new sources of labour, and there were two possibilities: women or foreigners.

The regime was uneasy about recruiting large numbers of women into the workforce. Such a move would go against the grain of Nazi ideology, which idealised the domestic and maternal roles of women; and it was also likely to be bad for morale. Nevertheless, pragmatism ensured that women were encouraged back to work, even in traditionally male jobs, as labour shortages became more acute in the late 1930s. The number of women in paid employment or seeking work remained the same in 1933 as in 1925 (11.5 million), but had increased by over a million (to 12.7 million) by the outbreak of war – and there were countless others involved in 'hidden work', taking in washing or sewing, or providing other domestic services within the local community to supplement the family income. Nearly all (90 per cent) of single women were in work and, although most married women stayed at home, an additional 2 million joined the workforce between 1933 and 1939. By 1939 over a third of the workforce was made up of women already and it proved difficult to recruit more during the war, despite the introduction of legislation in 1943 to exert greater pressure on women to work. The regulations not only contained loopholes, but discriminated in favour of those women who had never needed to work, by providing an allowance to compensate for the loss of a conscripted husband's income. Allowances for women already in work when the war began were reduced in accordance with their income and this generated some resentment among working-class women, who objected to what was effectively an exemption for middle-class women, many of them still employing domestic servants.[58]

The alternative was equally unpalatable in many respects. The recruitment of large numbers of foreigners and their deployment in industry in the expanding cities of the Reich would be to compound the problem of accelerating urbanisation with that of increasing racial heterogeneity among the working population. It also generated irrational anxieties about 'miscegenation' – illegitimate children of 'mixed blood' as a consequence of illicit sexual liaisons between foreign workers and German women. Nevertheless the temporary deployment of large numbers of foreign workers was perceived in most quarters as preferable to the conscription of German women for war work.[59]

The number of foreign workers 'temporarily' employed in Germany had already risen from 220,000 in 1936 – about a third of them Czechs – to some 375,000 in 1938, most of them working in agriculture; but it was the defeat of Poland which provided the opportunity of impressing large numbers of foreign workers into the service of German industry and agriculture, and which brought the issue to a head.[60] There were reservations about the influx of large numbers of Poles, but these were set aside as their employment was still considered a temporary measure. Nazi leaders were quick to appreciate that whatever threat foreign workers posed to the Reich's racial purity was far outweighed by the economic advantages; and once it was agreed that the Polish workers could be set to work without prior racial selection, a significant concession had been made to the demands of the economic pragmatists over those of ideological purists. This did not mean that foreign workers were accepted as equal to Germans, or treated with respect: they were subjected to a harsh and discriminatory regime. In 1940 a series of decrees were issued – the so-called *Polenerlasse* – which provided for harsher punishment in cases of indiscipline and breach of contract, and for the death sentence for men in cases of sexual intercourse with German women.[61]

By 1944 there were almost 8 million foreign civilians and prisoners of war working in greater Germany, from 26 different countries. Over half of them came from eastern Europe: almost 3 million (2,806,203) were *Ostarbeiter* from the Soviet Union, a further half million were from Poland and over half a million from south-eastern Europe and the Baltic. Over a million were French, and almost half were prisoners of war. Their average age was between 20 and 24, and a third were women; of those from Poland and the Soviet Union, however, over half were women, and most of these were under the age of 20. Foreign workers were deployed in all sectors of the economy, from domestic service, agriculture and small workshops to large factories and public services. A small number of older, male, skilled German workers might have to oversee departments in large munitions works staffed almost entirely by young women from the Soviet Union, and thousands of other Russian girls were maids in well-to-do German households.[62]

The German economy was not fully mobilised for war between 1939 and 1941, and many historians have quite reasonably assumed that this is what Hitler intended. His strategy of 'lightning war' (*Blitzkrieg*), it was argued, required armament in breadth rather than armament in depth, obviating the need to concentrate all Germany's economic resources on the war at the expense of civilian consumption, and thereby reducing the burden on the German people. *Blitzkrieg* was a way of sparing the civilian population from the misery of war.[63] Only after 1941, presumably as a consequence of the difficulties encountered in the campaign against the Soviet Union, did Germany attempt a more thorough economic mobilisation, diverting resources from the civilian sector to the needs of the war.

More recent research has suggested that to see the Blitzkrieg as a deliberate strategy is mistaken: Hitler expected a long war, but one that would be waged from a position of strength once a 'greater Germany' had been consolidated. Richard Overy in particular has argued that there is little evidence to suggest that Hitler was swayed by the short-term considerations arising from the crises and bottlenecks of the late 1930s. His pronouncements on economic questions in the context of international relations – such as they were – indicated that he was thinking in terms of a large-scale and decisive conflict in the long-term rather than taking the necessary measures for a short campaign. If he seemed to want to continue providing resources for the non-military sectors of the economy as well, Overy argues, that was because he did not understand that the two objectives were incompatible: motorways, the Volkswagen and the prestige building projects that would reshape Berlin were as necessary in the Führer's mind as the war itself.[64]

When war came in 1939 Germany was not yet prepared for the full-scale conflict Hitler was anticipating. Regardless of the adequacy of preparations the talk had been of 'total war' based on centralised decision-making, and work had begun on plans for economic mobilisation within weeks of the establishment of the regime in 1933. Early initiatives were superseded by the appointment of a Reich plenipotentiary for the war economy. This was effectively an additional role for the economics minister – first Schacht, and then Funk. During peacetime the armed forces would be responsible for arms industries themselves, while the Reich plenipotentiary would oversee other businesses that were important for the war economy. The uneasy division of responsibilities, typical of power structures in the Third Reich, immediately gave rise to difficulties. The empire-building staff of the Reich plenipotentiary effectively placed under its protection firms which could contribute little to the preparations for war, and should have been rationalised out of existence, while at the same time it could not co-ordinate its sector sufficiently to guarantee the necessary continuity of supplies to the munitions industry proper. Decision-making was further fragmented with the establishment of the Four-Year-Plan office. In this context, and with the further upheavals that came in 1938 – the Reich Defence Council set up that year seldom met – it was difficult to demarcate clear boundaries between these potentially overlapping jurisdictions, and the economy was driven by political pressure to respond to immediate needs rather than long-term planning. The regime had failed to develop any agency capable of overseeing Germany's economic mobilisation, and appropriate institutional arrangements developed only piecemeal, and once war had broken out.[65]

The Polish campaign itself quickly revealed the economy's lack of readiness for war. The first hasty response – the War Economy Decree of 4 September – foundered against a fractious response from industrial workers and its main provisions were quickly withdrawn. By then Poland had been defeated, and the immediate emergency had passed; but the Polish campaign revealed the economy's lack of readiness for war. Long-standing and essentially unresolved problems could only get worse as men were called up, existing materiel was depleted and needed to be replaced, and supplies became more insecure. In the meantime there were simply not enough arms and ammunition to fight another campaign. Above all there still seemed not only no clear plan for accelerating or expanding the production of munitions, but no clear authority for devising and implementing such a plan, although this was not a consideration that Hitler seemed willing to allow to influence his military decisions. In November 1939 he announced that Göring would take measures to prepare for a war lasting 5 years, and shortly afterwards (7 December) effectively gave him almost complete control of the civilian economy, abolishing the office of Reich plenipotentiary for the war economy, and thereby marginalising Funk. It was only in the following February that Hitler resolved to create a new ministry of armaments and munitions; he officially appointed Fritz Todt minister on 17 March, with the immediate task of persuading industry to gear more fully towards a total war economy.[66]

Todt was head of the Nazi party technology office, had impressed Hitler with his work on the construction of Germany's new motorways and had then been commissioned to oversee the construction of the West Wall fortifications. He had then been appointed by Göring to oversee the regulation of the construction sector under the auspices of the Four-Year-Plan office, before being asked to take on 'special tasks' in February 1940, shortly before his ministerial appointment.[67] In tackling the war economy Todt brought his experience on the West Wall to bear, seeing off encroachment from the military authorities, offering profit incentives to business, and permitting the self-regulation of production and the distribution of orders by local committees of industrialists. His attempts to rationalise the economy and streamline decision-making encountered resistance, but by the spring of 1940 the German economy had recovered somewhat from its relative unpreparedness for general war the previous year.

The speed with which victories were achieved seemed to belie the necessity of further preparations for a total war of unforeseeable duration, and to offer the opportunity to restore levels of civilian consumption and thereby improve morale. As it became clear that Britain could not be defeated quickly, and was not prepared to make peace either, a switch of resources to consumer goods was unthinkable, especially in the light of Hitler's determination to press ahead with war against the Soviet Union.

Despite the general impression among the public (and not least among businessmen) that there could now be some relaxation, and planning for a peace based on easy victory, *further* demands, not fewer, were to be made by the war economy, and by November 1940 General Thomas, the head of armed forces economic staff, complained that they bore no real relation to the economy's capacity to meet them. By the beginning of 1941, he was convinced that the economy had been squeezed – by the closing down of plant that was not essential to the war effort, and the 'combing out' of labour from essential industries – as much as was possible. Rationalisation was needed: an end to the quasi-artisanal production methods demanded by the armed forces, which required highly skilled labour while simultaneously holding back productivity, and more mass production. Despite a string of directives from Hitler, arms production was rationalised only slowly during 1941. It was only when it unambiguously became a political goal central to Hitler's strategy (not least as a result of the faltering progress of the Soviet campaign), with an order for the 'simplification and increased efficiency of armaments production' on 3 December 1941, that rationalisation was effectively implemented. Between 1942 and 1944 German armaments production was revolutionised on the basis of the changes introduced in 1941 and implemented by Todt's successor as armaments minister, Albert Speer, following the former's sudden death in plane crash in February 1942.[68] Speer, even more than Todt, was confident of Hitler's backing in implementing the policy of rationalisation and, crucially, was able to establish a supreme authority for the direction of the economy: the so-called Central Planning Board, which combined tasks hitherto the responsibility of different offices. Problems continued, and opposition persisted, but impressive productivity gains were achieved.

This transformation of the German war economy came belatedly, and made an impact only as German cities were being bombed to rubble, and the encroaching Allied armies were removing Germany's sources of plunder in occupied Europe. Even then it had been achieved only when there was no other alternative. With the faltering of the Soviet campaign the expansionist dynamic that had hitherto provided a way out of crises in the war economy was no longer available, and the underlying cause of the problem was unambiguously revealed to be weak leadership. Göring, who had failed to deliver an economy capable of sustaining the epochal conflict in which Germany was now embroiled (or even understand how the economy worked), was now discredited; and so were the leaders of the armed forces, who had squabbled among themselves and squandered Germany's early advantage. The fundamental problem, however, was the lack of clear overall authority: at least as far as the efficient organisation of the war economy was concerned, there was a crucial lack of leadership in the 'leader-state'.[69]

Chapter 4: The Myth of the 'National Community': German Society under Nazism

The Nazis did not merely want to win political power; they wanted to transform German society forever. Hitler's appointment to the chancellorship in January 1933 was not simply a change of government; it was a change of regime, and signified a fundamental change in the political system. Winning power was not an end in itself, Hitler told the Nuremberg party rally in September 1933, the political revolution – which he had declared complete in July – must be followed by an ideological revolution. Yet the Nazis did not have a detailed ideological programme of social reform for achieving this; what they did have was a comprehensive critique of modern society and its perceived shortcomings. They wanted to create a '*Volksgemeinschaft*', a national community of all the people, regardless of wealth or rank, that would transcend the divisions and conflicts of modern society. It was an idea with mythical qualities, promising the restoration of a shared sense of national purpose, and at the same time concealing the 'conglomerate of disparities and contradictions' that made up the Nazi programme in 1933.[1] Many – most – of the Nazis' preoccupations were shared with their conservative and nationalist allies, and embraced the usual targets of right-wing populism: emancipated women and working mothers; lack of discipline in the young and the decline in social deference; and all kinds of culture that offended middlebrow taste, whether pulp fiction and popular film (especially if it was American) or the experimental avant-garde. Nazi propaganda fuelled concerns about criminality and disorder, putting the blame on outsiders in the community (*Gemenischaftsfremde*). This meant not only racial outsiders – generally Jews, but also Gypsies and other racial minorities – but the so-called 'asocial' types as well, such as the homeless, the 'workshy', members of dysfunctional 'problem' families, homosexuals, prostitutes, habitual criminals and alcoholics.

Blood, Soil and Community

The anxieties about modern society that underpinned these prejudices were by no means peculiar to Germany, and nor were the solutions proposed by the Nazis. Across much of Europe rapid industrialisation had thrown up large anonymous cities, which had absorbed millions of migrants from the countryside within the space of two or three decades. The dissolution of traditional ties was unsettling, and many people responded to the social consequences of urbanisation by demonising the city and idealising the countryside. For conservative revolutionaries such as Oswald Spengler the city was associated with cultural decline, rootlessness and alienation. Gottfried Feder echoed the theme of the restless 'nomadic' city, finding it unhealthy and expensive, and its inhabitants immoral and hedonistic.[2] The term 'asphalt' had become an anti-Semitic euphemism. It was used to demonise liberal Jewish publishing firms (such as Ullstein) by suggestively associating the decadence of urban modernity with Jewish influence in such combinations as '*Asphaltliteraten*' for urban intellectuals, and *Asphaltkultur* to dismiss the 'degenerate' culture of the Weimar Republic.

The bleakness of urban life was contrasted with the vitality of the countryside. The title of Walther Darré's *The Peasantry as the Life Source of the Nordic Race* (1929) reflected the close association between countryside and racial hygiene in the Nazi view of the world. Darré argued that the origins of the Germanic race were to be found in a nomadic people of warriors and peasants, and that in Germany's coming new order the peasantry should once again become the first estate in the land. He developed his argument in another book the following year, *The New Aristocracy of Blood and Soil*. Here he argued that the decline and fall of industrial mass society so evident during the Depression resulted from the machinations of Jewish capitalists and Bolsheviks. The cure for Germany's ills was to be found in racial renewal through careful biological selection and a renewed emphasis on agriculture rather than industry. The term 'blood and soil' (*Blut und Boden*, irreverently abbreviated to *Blubo* by the public) came to be used to describe genre of film and fiction that idealised rural life.

Central to these distinctions between rural and urban life, and to the corporatist ideology from which Nazi views about society were drawn, was the idea of 'community'. In 1887 the sociologist Ferdinand Tönnies had made a theoretical distinction between the organic rural community (*Gemeinschaft*), and the 'artificial' society (*Gesellschaft*) of the metropolis or the nation.[3] This idea was taken up and simplified by a new generation of intellectuals and publicists after the turn of the century. For both the neo-Romantics of the fin-de-siècle and the conservative revolutionaries of the Weimar republic the notion of community had connotations of wholeness that stood in sharp contrast to the fragmented nature of modern urban society with its sectional interests, class divisions and diversity. Much of the appeal of the Nazis' national community was in its promise of unity to a society that was riven with conflict. Its emphasis on the supposedly German values of hard work, cleanliness and order reinforced the attraction of the NSDAP for many people in the public service from policemen, teachers and doctors to civil servants and judges, all of whom felt that in one way or another their professional authority had been eroded by democracy.

The authoritarian impulses of the 'national community' were clear. Such a harmonious society was unlikely to come about freely, and it seems improbable that even its most idealistic proponents can have expected that it could. It proved impossible to introduce such a corporatist social and political system anywhere in inter-war Europe without resort to dictatorial methods, and the result was less a functioning system of estates or corporations than an empty shell of formal institutions and constitutional rhetoric. Glaring inequalities of wealth, power and status had to be deliberately overlooked or ignored, and individuals were expected to subordinate their own needs and aspirations to the demands of a greater whole. Similarly, the new Nazi regime of 1933 did not want a real social or political revolution – far from it. It required people not only to accept the hierarchy and authoritarian leadership of the 'national community', but to believe in it too: to 'reinterpret' rather than change social reality. The extent to which this new social consciousness was achieved varied considerably.[4]

Class Consciousness and National Community

For the idea of the *Volksgemeinschaft* to convince, even on the level of perceptions, there had to be some sense that industrial workers accepted it and were being integrated into the nation. During the first decades

of the twentieth century a large part of the German working class
seemed to their middle-class compatriots to constitute not just a different
class, but a whole separate society, a state within the state. Like labour
parties elsewhere in Europe the Social Democrats had sought to provide
for the needs of their constituents from cradle to grave, with trades
unions, consumer co-operatives and clubs and societies to reflect all
tastes and interests. When the political labour movement was suppressed
by Bismarck these subsidiary organisations provided solidarity, and functioned as a cohesive substitute for political activity in tight-knit working-
class neighbourhoods, reinforcing and reproducing a very specific kind
of class-conscious sense of community. This working class was by no
means synonymous with all German manual workers, or even all urban
industrial workers, but it was the definition of working class (or prolet-
ariat) that had the most immediate political meaning for contemporaries.
Many, perhaps most, German workers neither lived in such homogeneous communities nor belonged to the socialist ranks of the politically
conscious, but it was the latter – 'fellows without a fatherland', as the
emperor Wilhelm II had called them – that seemed to stand apart from
the German nation, and pose the greatest challenge in the construction
of a genuinely national community.

The Nazi onslaught on organised labour in 1933 was intended to
break the hold of socialism on the German working class once and for
all, by suppressing not only the political parties and trades unions, but
closing down or 'co-ordinating' subsidiary organisations as well, in the
hope that the political allegiances of industrial workers could be broken
by removing the associational networks and political culture that underpinned them. Other parties were closed down too, and other cultural
organisations were integrated – generally more willingly – into the Nazis'
own; but the onslaught of sheer physical violence against working-class
communities was unparalleled during the national revolution. Stormtroopers, many of them from working-class backgrounds themselves,
were now able to settle old scores from past street-fights with impunity,
protected by their uniforms and the indulgence of a complicit judiciary. Many men returned home after weeks of beatings in concentration
camps – all the worse if it had been one of the unauthorised or 'wild'
camps, which existed outside even the exceptionally lawless jurisdiction
of the new Nazi state.

Afterwards, the police – including the Gestapo – maintained a stronger
presence than ever in working-class districts, policing industrial relations
or snooping around in bars for subversives; many of those arrested under
the so-called 'malice law' (*Heimtückegesetz*) for grumbling, criticising

the regime or merely speaking disrespectfully of the Führer and his henchmen had committed these crimes under the influence of alcohol. Such dissent was suppressed, and attempts to organise political resistance were crushed. Underground resistance groups, which were organised almost exclusively by the political left during the early years of the dictatorship, were quickly detected and often infiltrated by the secret police, and their ringleaders were arrested and imprisoned. SPD leaders, conscious of the movement's weakness in the wake of long-term mass unemployment were nevertheless shocked at the speed and determination with which it was suppressed; and although they shrewdly advised rank-and-file Social Democrats against futile acts of heroism, some of them were taken aback at the speedy retreat of their members into individual and family concerns.[5]

It would be misleading, however, to suggest that working-class responses to Nazism involved only the conspiratorial underground activity of a small minority (generally in Communist organisations) and passive resignation or withdrawal on the part of the majority. People came to terms with the regime in one way or another, whether driven by fear, hopes for the economic improvements promised by Hitler, or wishful thinking that some of the more radical elements in the Nazi movement might be as eager for class conflict and revolution from below as their propaganda boasted.[6] The Social Democrats' strategy was to try and ensure the survival of a collective political consciousness among the rank-and-file of their core supporters by encouraging the maintenance of social contacts while avoiding direct confrontation. Nevertheless there were often collective displays of opposition in public, which the Nazis sometimes felt it was shrewder to ignore. Two such incidents were reported from Hamburg, for example, in the summer of 1934. In one instance workers had taken advantage of Ascension Day to commemorate the first anniversary of the death of Adolf Biedermann, an SPD Reichstag delegate who had committed suicide in 1933. Five thousand people visited his grave and covered it with flowers, including a wreath that seemed to have come from a resistance group. In a similar incident the widow of a former party member rejected a wreath from the NSBO, and instead the old local SPD branch (which continued to exist in all but name) organised the funeral service. Three hundred party members attended the crematorium and the local party leader was reported to have ended his speech with a cry of 'Freedom!', urging comrades to continue the struggle, while the congregation responded by standing up and repeating the cry with clenched fists and 'no action was taken by the police'.[7] Such minor victories were written up enthusiastically by otherwise sceptical Sopade reporters, but the incidents themselves were not wholly improbable; there was a long tradition of such expressions of solidarity, and the authorities now, as in the past, were wise not to intervene. They recognised that such displays were meant to be provocative, but that the occasion did not otherwise threaten their authority.

The Nazis were also keenly aware of the power of rituals and symbols, and openly appropriated or adapted those of both Socialists and Catholics in their attempts to create a new mythical language of collective national endeavour. In particular they used the language of the 'dignity of labour' with imagery and rhetoric designed to appeal specifically to the aspirational members of the respectable working class, cleverly exploiting popular prejudices against the 'workshy' and 'feckless'. Bourgeois values of diligence and orderliness were promoted in order to encourage employees to work harder and better, not only for the sake of a job well done, and in the greater national interest, but also in order to break down the consciousness of class difference, and integrate the working class into the 'national community'. Employers always exhort workers to work harder, but the Nazis had populist touches, such as Robert Ley's meet-the-workers factory tours, which initially at least gave their strategy greater credibility than the old-style paternalistic approach.[8]

Workers and the Workplace

It was economic recovery, however, not propaganda, that was most effective in containing latent working-class opposition. The return to work was slow and uneven: heavy industry recovered far more quickly than textiles, skilled workers went back to work faster than the unskilled, and there were considerable regional variations. But despite this, and although conditions at work were worse and wages poorer, the fall in unemployment meant that the overall position of working-class families was bound to improve. For many people the 1920s had been a time of insecurity and relative poverty, and the onset of the Depression had not so much brought a sharp deterioration in living standards so much as made things worse. So although workers complained about low wages, most were happy that they had work at all, as a Sopade reporter from southern Bavaria noted, adding that although they were not at all well-disposed to those in power they were uncertain, lacked faith and kept their opinions to themselves. Other reporters, assessing workers' attitudes 18 months later, complained about their fickleness: they complained about low wages, high prices and the begging of the Winter Aid Fund (*Winterhilfswerk*), but were happy enough if the boss bought them a drink and handed round cigarettes or cigars.[9]

The Nazi concept of the 'factory community' (*Betriebsgemeinschaft*) was intended to mean more than occasional managerial munificence, however. The workplace was to be modernised, and this meant not only a resumption of the technical rationalisation that had begun in the 1920s, but an increased emphasis on workers' health and welfare as well. Consequently the regime's propaganda in the later 1930s played up the significance of company social policies (*betriebliche Sozialpolitik*) – the measures undertaken by private firms that went beyond minimum legal or contractual requirements. Here too, as in so many areas, the Nazis were building on earlier developments. During the Weimar Republic such policies had been promoted by an Institute for Technical Training and by the institute of 'workplace sociology' set up at the University of Berlin in 1928 (and closed down by the Nazis in 1934). There had been something of a boom in pension plans, company health care and housing. Particularly in the more modern firms, run by professional managers rather than proprietor-entrepreneurs, employees were seen as 'human resources' to be invested in, and new departments were established to administer such schemes, which were also supplemented by sports facilities, improved working conditions and more straightforwardly by productivity bonuses. Among the leaders in the field were IG Farben, Siemens and Bosch.

In the case of IG Farben most of the money spent on social policy went on to welfare schemes (for old age and sickness) and bonuses; only a fraction was spent on 'cultural' projects, whether canteens, sports facilities or entertainments. As more women had joined the workforce, employers were compelled to recognise their particular needs, such as kindergartens and private rooms for nursing mothers. But in practice under the Nazis, and under the extra pressures of war-time production, high-minded concerns about the greater vulnerability of working women went by the board as employers skimped on training and protective clothing. No less than the conveyer belt, company social policy was part of the continuous modernisation of industry, and it was a double-edged development, usurping the responsibilities of a more impartial welfare state, and tying the employee more closely to the paternalistic employer who asserted his role as educator of the modern worker in matters of health and hygiene as a corporate duty.[10] On another level it accorded well with Nazi racial policy and its preoccupation with the eugenic 'upgrading' of the population.

Above all, the Nazis wanted company social policy to be a manifestation of the factory community ideal, a reflection of the factory leader's
concern for his retinue's welfare. It also provided a base for Nazi organisations within the factory. The most important of these were Labour
Front's leisure organisation Strength through Joy (*Kraft durch Freude*,
KdF) and especially its subsidiary, Beauty of Labour (*Schönheit der Arbeit*),
which was concerned initially with improving standards of cleanliness
and hygiene in the workplace, getting rid of some of the dust and grime
from the factory floor, tidying up yards, and cleaning washrooms and
lavatories – all necessary improvements anyway, and ones which were
cheap, highly visible, and therefore good propaganda.[11]

With the slogan 'clean people in a clean factory' Beauty of
Labour inspectors visited companies and reported unacceptable working
conditions, exerting pressure on employers to improve them if necessary. The organisation's propaganda waxed effusive about ways in which
the workplace could be improved: 'Put flowers in the recreation rooms,
build open-air swimming pools, sports fields and gardens for the retinue.'
The organisation grew very quickly, and made a propaganda impact
that was both very effective and very cheap, with campaigns for better
lighting (enthusiastically supported by AEG, Siemens and Osram), clean
air and hot food. The aims of Beauty of Labour were keenly supported
by industrial psychologists and designers alike. Its objectives, like those
of the company welfare schemes, built on the policies of the 1920s,
and drew on earlier developments such as the garden city movement,
and the 'scientific management' associated with Taylorism and Henry
Ford. In Germany, Krupp had been a pioneer of company housing
projects, welfare schemes, cultural programmes and company newspapers to promote corporate identity among the workforce as well as
the management. The journal *Schönheit der Arbeit* was edited by the
former editor of *Die Form*, journal of the *Deutscher Werkbund*, a pioneering
early twentieth-century design movement, and new industrial buildings
were designed by modernist architects such as Peter Behrens – to the
horror of old Nazi ideologues like Alfred Rosenberg. Workers were to
be educated out of the separatist, and politically oppositional mentality
that had characterised the classic age of Social Democracy and educated
into individual aspiration. The aim of 'de-proletarianising' the workforce in the 1930s anticipated the 'embourgeoisement' of workers in
the 1950s.[12]

An assessment of Beauty of Labour based on its grandiose plans and
promotional literature is suggestive of a forward-looking policy, even if
its purpose was to distract from the real political and economic losses

incurred by the workforce under the new regime. In practice, however, there were more flowers than clean lavatories, and Beauty of Labour was mocked as 'façade socialism' or 'plant-pot Romanticism' by workers who often had to undertake the beautification of labour themselves, unpaid and in their own time. Routine maintenance work which employers had once paid for now became a Beauty of Labour project of one kind or another. A group of workers in Silesia, for example, was told to redecorate the factory after work according to a new colour scheme determined by a university professor. Most of the prospective volunteers managed to cry off in this case, and the company had to employ a firm of painters and decorators, but it was not an isolated instance. In other cases workers were required to sign rosters indicating their willingness to put in extra unpaid hours, while other improvements, such as radio sets for the workplace, were paid for with voluntary contributions from employees. Firms themselves were under pressure to prettify their premises for inspections and competitions, and set their employees to work on cosmetic improvements: cleaning up the yard, laying flower beds and – in one case in Bavaria – constructing a children's playground. In February 1938 workers at a factory in Saxony stayed behind in the evening after 11-hour shifts for several weeks to whitewash halls and build bicycle stands. In short, according to one critical observer, there were lots of jobs being done around the place that had once been paid for, but were now done for free by workers just so the boss could cut a dash in competitions with other firms.[13]

The ostensible achievements of Beauty of Labour were paraded before the foreign visitors and dignitaries visiting firms in Berlin, such as Siemens, or the department store Wertheim, where visitors were entertained in the 'staff room'. Here, it was reported, they were told in 'unforced' conversations with the staff how much better things were now that Jews had been purged from the firm, especially for women, who need no longer be afraid of rejecting unwanted sexual advances. (In fact, employees complained, things had got much worse since the management had changed.)[14] In 1937 the *Völkischer Beobachter* reported that the number of factories improved by Beauty of Labour had risen from 2000 in 1934 to 6000 in 1936, and the organisation itself claimed to have visited 70,000 firms, prompting them to spend between them a thousand million marks on canteens, common rooms, gardens and sports fields. Sopade reporters, sceptical as they were about what had been achieved and how, conceded that it had made an impact. A party worker in Saxony quoted a worker who had been 'travelling around Germany for 25 years' and had to confess that 'no bourgeois government has ever done so much for the workers. . . . A worker who is uninterested in politics, and is neither a democrat nor anyting else, is quite happy with conditions at present.'[15]

There was a great deal of truth in this observation. The regime, the Labour Front and Beauty of Labour ensured that more resources were put into company policies during the 1930s than in the previous decade – or at the very least that such policies were identified and represented more coherently as a concerted programme. Great effort, too, was put into psychological and propaganda offensives. Although the Nazi insistence on the leadership principle in the workplace reinforced hierarchical authority, and the tentative democratisation introduced during the Weimar Republic was swept away, the regime sought to compensate for such losses with involvement through rallies and meetings; inclusivity, in the form of social evenings where managers were also present; and propaganda that emphasised the erosion of status differences – in other words a new 'interpreted social reality'. In addition the regime was prepared to make strategic concessions where necessary and possible. Finally the working class was a heterogeneous social group whose political allegiances, or indeed lack of them, reflected its stratifications, along with status, gender and generational differences, regional and confessional loyalties, and their trade or the branch of industry in which they worked. Many industrial workers joined the party or one of its affiliations, and many more were not especially interested in politics – greater numbers perhaps than either the Nazis or the workers' leaders had anticipated.

Consumers and Consumption

Although workers' lives were dominated by their jobs, the regime was acutely aware that the most crucial battles for political loyalty might be won or lost elsewhere, especially among the women who had to make ends meet in working-class households. As real hardship and deprivation had taken its toll at the end of the First World War, women had been in the forefront of the first political disturbances, and the regime was careful to avoid having to exact similar sacrifices. Despite the frequent shortages of specific items, per capita food consumption increased between 1935 and 1938, largely as a result of increased consumption of meat and animal fats, and sugar consumption was higher per person at the end of the 1930s than a decade earlier. Yet while the regime fed popular aspirations to consume, and its propaganda conveyed the impression that things were getting better, women were exhorted to be thrifty and avoid unnecessary luxury or waste. The government intervened increasingly to direct consumption and make Germany more self-sufficient, which meant less imported fruit and more home-grown vegetables. Government regulation of the consumer goods industries also affected other kinds of domestic consumption. Germany barely covered a fraction of industrial demand for wool, cotton, linen and hemp, for example, and although some progress was made towards self-sufficiency, clothes became dearer as the price of wool and cotton rose and the textile industry was squeezed. More artificial fabrics were used as substitutes and the quality of clothes declined, but housewives were frequently disappointed (to say the least) with the results of the first wash, and avoided garments made from *Ersatz* materials until clothes made purely of natural fabrics became virtually impossible to get hold of.[16] The regime recognised that the availability of decent clothes and shoes was important to morale, and it monitored complaints about shortages and responses to regulations in this area, more than for any other kind of mass consumption (other than food), and intervened where it was possible or necessary. Government regulations, in this field as in many others, were not always welcome, however. In 1941, for example, the authorities acted to regulate – and effectively to lower – the prices of ladies' hats, only to find that shoppers generally found the price reductions confusing and illogical, while working-class women and office workers saw it as a measure for the benefit of the rich, because only the prices of the most expensive hats had been reduced. Why not reduce the price of essentials rather than the price of luxury hats?[17]

In principle the regime also recognised the importance of decent housing and basic household goods and furniture, but did little to remedy shortages in this area. While the Weimar Republic had implemented an enormous building programme, it had scarcely covered the demand for public housing created by the decline in new construction during and after the First World War. The contraction of new building during the Depression made the problem worse, and although more new flats were built during the mid-1930s the rate of construction began to fall back after 1936. Company housing, promoted in accordance with the principles of company social policies and much publicised, made only a marginal impact. Although the number of dwellings provided by Siemens in Berlin almost doubled during the 1930s, for example, there were still only 3000 in 1939, and the proportion of Siemens employees living in them actually fell. The most prestigious of all such projects was to be the housing estate for workers at the Kdf-Wagen factory in Fallersleben; at the other extreme were secure estates for problem families and 'asocials' such as Hashude near Bremen.[18]

Beyond the essentials Nazi ideology was opposed to consumerism for its own sake, which was associated with the 'plutocratic' West and above all with Americanism. This hostility was compounded by the need to suppress consumer demand in order to ensure the success of rearmament, and the regime's anti-consumerist propaganda became more strident after 1936 in the wake of the economic crisis that prompted the establishment of the Four Year Plan. Where scarce resources were allocated to consumer goods industries such as textiles the products were often intended for the armed forces. Nevertheless the regime had to accept that there was an expectation, particularly among the middle classes, for all kinds of consumer items that were readily available in the West. Car production, which had peaked at just over 100,000 in 1928 took off again after the Depression and contributed to the economic recovery of the 1930s, peaking again at 276,592 in 1938. The 'people's car' (*Volkswagen*), for which many Germans saved (thereby helping to contain inflationary trends in the economy) is a familiar icon of Strength through Joy propaganda, and was originally called the *KdF-Wagen*. Production was set to begin in 1940 with annual production of 150,000, then increasing tenfold to one and a half million within a couple of years, but none ever made it onto the road.[19] This disappointment notwithstanding, there was a very buoyant demand during the 1930s, particularly among the middle classes, for new consumer products, from cameras and the 'people's receiver' (*Volksempfänger*), to new kitchen equipment. Most of the new consumer durables were for the kitchen or household, where they were intended to alleviate women's work. There was talk of a 'people's fridge', and various domestic appliances were appearing on the market for the first time, from electric irons, which were useful and popular, to vacuum cleaners and hair dryers, which only middle-class women could afford. The larger and more expensive items, such as washing machines and refrigerators, were available only to a tiny minority.[20]

Accommodation and Alienation Among the Middle Classes

The experience of the German middle classes under Nazism has occupied the attention of historians far less than that of industrial workers. Unsurprisingly, given the extent of their support for the Nazi Party during the Depression, the middle classes posed far less of a problem for the regime than the working class. If the language the early Nazi

Party had involved a good deal of 'anti-bourgeois' posturing, that of the party in power was more reassuring. Where working-class organisations, whether political or cultural, were suppressed or 'co-ordinated', those of the middle classes dissolved themselves, were subsumed into the Nazi organisational network in a relatively painless manner, or 'co-ordinated' themselves voluntarily amid a flurry of welcome speeches and resolutions supporting the regime and celebrating the new Germany. This was not primarily because the middle classes were drawn by Nazi ideology. The regime was perceived as a combination of Nazi dynamism and conservative experience, and initially at least it promised a restoration of order, respect for the state and its authorities, discipline in the workplace, and deference towards social status and professional and managerial expertise. The suppression of the trades unions more than restored to management the 'right to manage', and the law for the restoration of a *professional* civil service signalled a return to happier times before the civil service had been 'politicised' in the wake of the November revolution. (In practice the bureaucracy remained the bourgeois institution it had become during the nineteenth century.) There was a little anxiety in some quarters that, in order to deal with the upstarts of the left, some rather disreputable characters had been enlisted (who were no less upstarts themselves). This anxiety was misplaced, however. Although there had been some unpleasant incidents during the 'national revolution', when party radicals had tried to force their way into jobs or public positions, there was little trouble from the uncouth rank and file of the Nazi party. Indeed, many Nazi functionaries, and most of the party's senior personnel were drawn from middle classes themselves: there were to be more doctorates than battle scars among the movers and shakers of the new regime. There were careers and opportunities for social mobility both in the party itself and among the proliferation of quasi-governmental organisations it spawned, first in Germany and later in occupied Europe. Germany's educated and propertied middle classes continued to run the country's public institutions and private enterprises. Beyond the party itself many were less politically hostile to the new regime than they had been to Weimar democracy, and worked more closely with its political leaders than any other section of society. Without the compliance – and in many cases the *initiative* – of a range of senior public servants, lawyers and senior officers in the police and armed forces, the criminal activity of the regime would have been seriously impeded, and it might have ceased to function altogether. 'Oppositional forces in the administration of the *Altreich* appeared only sporadically', the SD noted in a general annual report for 1938 – the year of the Anschluss and the pogrom.[21] Similarly, there was little protest from farmers who relied on the forced labour of Polish peasants, or from companies whose productivity and profits were boosted by slave workers from eastern Europe.

This generally positive consensus was far from universal: Jews were excluded, and significant numbers of public intellectuals, concerned liberals and left-wing dissenters excluded themselves. Catholics were far less inclined to welcome the new regime than Protestants. The German middle class was far from homogeneous, either socially or culturally, and the pressures and concerns felt by the *Mittelstand* – a disparate stratum made up of various largely non-manual lower-middle-class groups – and those of the *Bürgertum* (the bourgeoisie proper) varied as much in the context of the Nazi dictatorship as they had during the 1920s. Nevertheless, studies touching on the experience of the middle class – or classes – under Nazism have either provided a general overview of all its component parts or concentrated very specifically on certain professions, institutions, companies or individuals. The *Mittelstand* has attracted most attention, not least because it was disproportionately represented among the membership, and electorate of the NSDAP, and historians have concentrated very much on their economic demands and the extent to which they were met by the regime. Whatever the extent of their grumbling, it seems clear that significant sections of this group remained broadly supportive of the regime for much of its 12 year duration. As with many people, approval among the lower middle classes of the regime's broader political aims, especially its foreign policy, compensated to a great extent for individual economic grievances, and their continuing support remained an important mainstay of the broad consensus in favour of the regime.[22]

Despite their importance to the functioning of the Nazi state and the war economy, the upper middle classes have received surprisingly little attention from historians. Support for the new regime from this constituency must be seen in the context of the defeat and demoralisation of the German establishment in 1918, and the fragmentation and collapse of Protestant bourgeois political culture during the Depression. Hostility to the Weimar Republic had been widespread and fundamental, and conservative intellectuals had frequently called for authoritarian political solutions as a way out of Germany's deepening crisis. Recent research on middle-class associational life at local level has shown how not only political parties, but sports clubs and music societies struggled with falling membership and cuts in council subsidies.[23] As traditional parties ceded ground to the NSDAP, local worthies lost their seats on the local council or at the Chamber of Trade, and the social confidence and political infrastructure of middle-class conservatism were eroded at local level, and eventually displaced by a Nazi political culture, more aggressive but nevertheless drawing on a similar social milieu for its functionaries and officials.

In this context the new regime could rely on the support of the overwhelming majority of middle-class Germans, whether enthusiastic or grudging. Although they had not been notably reluctant to join the party before Hitler's appointment, for example, civil servants and school teachers flocked to join in the spring of 1933, and were dramatically over-represented in the party's membership rolls. Franz Neumann reckoned that almost a quarter of all Nazi party functionaries in 1936 and 1937 came from the teaching profession, above all from primary schools.[24] Germany's conservative parties, which had suffered a haemorrhage of electoral support during the Depression, were wound up without much protest in the summer of 1933. Middle-class associations and professional organisations were Nazified like any other, in so far as they did not take the initiative and 'co-ordinate' themselves. Much of the middle-class press continued to be published, including the *Frankfurter Zeitung* and *Münchener Neueste Nachrichten*, and in many parts of Germany the number and circulation of bourgeois newspapers continued for some time to exceed that of party publications. The press was censored and self-censored, but it was also often in agreement with government policy. The experience of Jewish property owners, professionals and public servants was very different from that of their non-Jewish counterparts, but with the possible exception of the Freemasons no groups or organisations identified wholly with the middle classes, or their politics were systematically persecuted by the regime.

Unsurprisingly, given the social structure of the party and the nature of its policies, little or no organised resistance or principled protest from the middle classes was evident during the 1930s. Liberals or conservatives who were unable to reconcile their position with that of the regime fell silent or fled abroad. Those who remained, and remained hostile or sceptical, were quickly marginalised, or forced into a passive 'inner emigration', avoiding trouble and hoping not to be noticed. Some, mainly intellectuals and priests, spoke out publicly, but there are few recorded outbursts of sustained political vitriol comparable with those reported from the factory floor, from bars in working-class districts or from markets. Middle-class districts were less thoroughly policed, social or professional gatherings were less public in any case, and larger groups could meet comfortably in private houses. Opposition was muted: concerns were expressed about the encroachment of the Nazi state on professional autonomy, the irresponsibility of government policy, or the brutalisation of professional life. Similarly small gestures of defiance were possible: doctors passed on work to Jewish colleagues feeling the brunt of discrimination. From the universities it was reported that students were 'becoming monarchist', that 'anti-semitism [was] receding' and that some students were deliberately seeking out the company of their Jewish peers.[25] For the most part people got on with their busy lives, as Margarete Fischer, then a Kindergarten teacher, recalled in an interview in the 1980s: 'On the whole everyone felt well.... In the thirties, things went uphill. The order, and there was work. They didn't have these horrible lines of unemployed anymore.... We also had good years. We had *wonderful* years.'[26] Opposition came only later, as Nazi policies became more radical and their conservative allies more dispensable.

Professionals and Public Servants in the Nazi State

Many middle-class professionals, no doubt the majority, carried on as before. It is difficult to ascertain how many actively shared the political outlook or objectives of the regime. Most professions were divided in their attitude to the Nazis, and in all of them there were people who defied the regime or found ways of thwarting its intentions, as well as those who collaborated. The extremes of resistance and fanatical support are misleading if we want to understand the role of the middle classes in the Nazi state. The legal profession is a good example. Our perceptions of the profession in the Third Reich are dominated by the image of the archetypical Nazi Judge Roland Freisler and his hysterical rants in the People's Court, but this is to distract our attention from the routine conformity and quiet collaboration among members of the legal profession, most of whom were not themselves Nazis, but natural conservatives. Lawyers constituted a socially homogeneous occupational group, whose senior members (and their wives) were either the children of judges and lawyers themselves, or came from very similar backgrounds, with parents in the professions, the civil service or the managerial classes. Lawyers joined the NSDAP in large numbers after 1933, and even more were affiliated through the Nazi Lawyers' Association (*Bund nationalsozialistischer deutscher Juristen*). The most enthusiastic attended the new training camp for National Socialist lawyers set up in Brandenburg in 1933. Judges and public prosecutors were more circumspect: but even so almost a third of Germany's senior judges had been party members during the Weimar

Republic (far more than were associated with either the DNVP or DVP), and most of the rest joined the party in 1933 or 1934. By 1941, 31 out of a total of 34 presidents of the high courts were party members. The Association of German Judges (*Deutscher Richterverein*) effectively became the League of National Socialist Judges (*Nationalsozialistischer Richterverein*) in 1933. And 8 of Germany's 35 public prosecutors had been party members before 1933, and a further 14 joined the party in that year, followed – eventually – by all of their colleagues. Here, as in other professions, there was no doubt some pressure to conform, but approval of the regime and self-interest were also factors. Like other professionals, managers or 'experts', many members of the legal profession welcomed the freedom from criticism and accountability. Moreover, by anticipating, and acting in line with the direction of Nazi policy – 'working towards the Führer' – they could expect rapid professional advancement.[27]

The objectives of the Nazi regime were bound to come into conflict with the rule of law. Nazi ideology was fundamentally opposed to the liberal notion of the *Rechtstaat*, in which the constitution made the executive legally accountable. The Nazis did not feel bound by this legality, and from the outset many of the actions of the new regime were outside the law, giving rise to a duality in the state between legal normality (*Normenstaat*) and exceptionalism (*Ausnahmestaat*). The house press of the legal profession reflected the hope of many lawyers in welcoming the new state but at the same time reaffirming the value of legal restrictions placed on the state by the German system of administrative courts (*Verwaltungsgerichtsbarkeit*).[28] In practice most members of the judiciary and the ministerial bureaucracy found that there was little conflict with the regime in routine matters until the last months of the war, when the relationship broke down as the demands of the political leadership increased.

Literate professionals, whose meetings were minuted and who published frequently, have left a far more extensive account of their attitudes and experiences than many other social groups, and have consequently attracted greater attention from historians. Recent research on doctors, scientists and academics has made increasing use of scholarly publications. German scholarship in the Third Reich was impoverished by the dismissal and emigration of Jewish and politically compromised intellectuals. The loss of leading figures with high public profiles, such as Einstein, no doubt had a devastating impact in specific research areas, but thousands more remained in Germany to make an important contribution to the goals of the regime as 'experts' and 'technocrats', and some equally important figures, such as Martin Heidegger and

Richard Strauss, were prepared to make their endorsement of the dictatorship public. Similarly, the regime itself was pragmatic in its attitude to science and scholarship. Eccentric theories were certainly promoted in some quarters, not least by Himmler, who used his SS power base to encourage the proliferation of institutions which were intended to challenge conventional science, but were as often as not related to the more marginal reaches of 'race theory', neo-paganism and the occult rather than scientific research. As Margit Szöllössi-Janze has argued, such clearly offbeat theories as the 'world ice cosmogony' – which purported to explain all human history (including Noah's flood) in terms of a universe constructed of ice – distract us from the routine co-operation with the new authorities of the vast majority of scientists and scholars working in German universities, hospitals, research institutions and private organisations. For the overwhelming majority neither 1933 nor 1945 constituted a point of discontinuity in their work.[29]

Intellectual assumptions fundamental to the view of the world crudely simplified by Nazi ideology were to some extent shared – and often promoted – by scholars from a variety of disciplines ranging from medicine and the natural sciences to law and economics, as well as history, culture and political science. For example, historians, geographers and other specialists were influenced by an historically disdainful view of Poland, which was traditionally seen as a chaotic country, incapable of self-government and fit only to be ruled by others. A more nebulous, but widely disseminated conviction asserted that Germans had been instructing the Slavs in order and industry since the time of the Teutonic Knights. Interdisciplinary research in the region was promoted during the early twentieth century by the creation of university chairs and specialist research institutes in Königsberg and Breslau (Wrocław), along with the establishment of periodicals such as *Osteuropa*, whose subtitle proclaimed it to be a journal for the study of all questions related to the European east. People such as Albert Brackmann, professor of medieval history at Königsberg, co-editor of Germany's leading historical journal the *Historische Zeitschrift*, and one of the leading figures in the world of east European studies, were not Nazis themselves – Brackmann had been a member of the DVP and DNVP during the 1920s – but the results of their research furnished the regime with practical knowledge and ideological justifications for its policies of occupation in eastern Europe.[30] Similarly, German geographers used both maps and theoretical approaches to the conceptualisation of space to advance Germany's expansionist claims. The manipulative concept of *Volks- und Kulturboden* (national and cultural land) was particularly important, in that it obscured the difference between those territories that were populated by Germans and those where Germany claimed to have wielded wider cultural influence, whether through the direct agency of a flourishing German community or indirectly through the imprint of the social and economic activity of Germans on a landscape they had subsequently abandoned: in brief – and in the popular interpretation – signs of advanced or successful economic activity were easily ascribed to German influence.

It was not that cartographers and academic geographers collaborated under pressure with the promotion of the regime's concept of *Lebensraum*; they proceeded from a common assumption of the civilising influence of Germans in the East, and at the same time, like many other Germans, they shared Nazi resentment at the loss of German territory after the First World War. As respectable scholars they secured research funding where explicitly political *völkisch* groups would have found it difficult, and their research findings had the greater plausibility as the results of 'objective' scholarship. When territories were occupied by Germany in the early 1940s the professional expertise of geographers and regional planners was indispensable. As with many other professions, the relationship between the regime and the experts on which it relied was symbiotic.[31]

As with individuals, so with institutions: German universities and research foundations were not simply forced to bend to the will of a monolithic totalitarian state intent on promoting the eccentric theories of marginal cranks. Many individuals and organisations offered their expertise willingly, and some experienced the 'self-co-ordination' (*Selbstgleichschaltung*) not uncommon among middle-class institutions, adapting themselves to suit the new circumstances in their own way rather than waiting to be pushed: as in other professional fields, there was as much continuity as change for academics, and some perceived improvements.[32] In many fields the government's specific interests meant increased funding for favoured projects and less discriminating appointments. Prehistory and archaeology, for example, which coincided with Himmler's researches into the 'Germanic' past, enjoyed something of a boom.[33]

There was very little resistance from universities to the new dispensation introduced by the Nazis in 1933, which replaced traditional forms of relatively democratic self-governance with the more managerial 'leadership principle'. Nor was there much protest at the dismissal of Jewish colleagues, or those deemed politically unacceptable. The number of dismissals varied from one institution to another, depending on the proportion of Jewish scholars. It is estimated that about 30 per cent of staff were dismissed from Berlin and Frankfurt, 20 per cent or fewer from Cologne, Hamburg and Göttingen, and 2 per cent from Tübingen.[34]

Similarly, some subjects were more dramatically affected than others: chemistry and bio-chemistry, for example, depended on the work of Jewish scientists, and were more affected than most.[35]

Young People in the Third Reich: A Nazi Generation?

University students in the 1930s continued to come largely from middle-class backgrounds. It was expensive to study at university, and most students from lower-middle-class or working-class backgrounds were effectively excluded, and the economic circumstances of the 1920s had often made student life difficult even for the impoverished sons of upper-middle-class families.[36] The most change in the intake of students came during the war, when women students – a small minority during the 1930s – began to outnumber men. By the autumn of 1943 there were more female than male students at a number of leading universities, including Vienna, Munich, Heidelberg, Freiburg, Leipzig, Tübingen and Marburg. Women also massively outnumbered men among students registering for the first time at a number of other leading universities, including Prague and Erlangen. Men still outnumbered women nationally in certain disciplines, above all law and medicine, but also theology (a discipline whose numbers were dwindling for other reasons); but there were more than twice as many women as men studying natural sciences, some six times as many studying cultural subjects and four thousand (almost a quarter) more women than men studying economics. The authorities accepted that there were good reasons for admitting more women to universities, not least the shortage of recruits into graduate careers – a problem that was expected to continue after the war as a consequence of the number of men killed. University teachers themselves were often less enthusiastic, and complained that women wanted to be spoon-fed, and that their interests differed from those of male students so much, particularly in the arts and humanities, that new lectures had to be written.[37]

There were strong and long-standing traditions of nationalism, anti-Semitism and radical right-wing politics among students, and they were disproportionately represented in the membership of the Nazi Party. In elections to student representative committees (AStA) in 1929 and 1930 the Nazis attracted support far in excess of their electoral support in the country at large (18.3 per cent in the 1930 Reichstag election): over half the votes at Greifswald (53 per cent) and Erlangen (51 per cent) in the academic year of 1929–30, for example, and over 30 per cent of the vote at half a dozen other institutions. The following academic year the Nazis won 76 per cent of student votes at Erlangen, almost 71 per cent at Breslau, and two thirds of the votes at Jena and the technical university in Berlin. In other universities support among students was much lower. In Munich for example the Nazis won a third of the AStA vote in 1930–31 (still twice the support for the party among the Bavarian electorate as a whole).[38] Although there were also liberal students at German universities, progressive politics was marginalised during the first half of the twentieth century, when a university education was more or less out of the question for the working class. German universities were predominantly middle-class institutions whose graduates were recruited into management, the professions and the country's elites. Many senior Nazis and most of the leading figures associated with the regime had a university education behind them, and in many cases a doctorate; conversely many graduates had strong affiliations with the political culture of the *völkisch* milieu they had experienced as students – and all the more so after 1933 as political commitment to the NSDAP became increasingly important in career terms.

Youth was at the core of the Nazis' vision of national regeneration, and education was central to the regime's attempts to transform society. But for the Nazis education was not an aim in itself, the 'formation' (*Bildung*) of an individual in accordance with the ideals of German educational thinking, but the training of a generation in the service of the community. In order to achieve this they intervened in the education system in a number of ways. Teachers were civil servants, and – like university lecturers – were therefore subject to the provisions of the Law for the Restoration of a Professional Civil Service. This effectively meant the dismissal of all Jewish teachers, and those affiliated with left-wing political parties. Although Jewish pupils (and students) continued to attend schools and universities, the Law on the Overfilling of German Schools and Universities of 25 April 1933 restricted them to a quota of 1.5 per cent of registrations, purportedly in order to reflect the proportion of the population that was Jewish. (In fact only 0.8 per cent of the German population was Jewish in 1933.)

Schoolteachers' organisations, like those of the other professions, were Nazified more or less immediately. The National Socialist Teachers' Association (*NS Lehrerbund*, NSLB) had been founded in 1929, and membership was open to all non-Jewish teachers and related professionals in any German educational institution (including universities). Its head office was in Bayreuth, and its first leader was Hans Schemm, the education minister of Nazi Bavaria. In addition the regime modified the school curriculum to reflect Nazi priorities. This meant more physical education and sport, and a greater emphasis on race and heredity, accompanied by calls from Nazi educationalists for anti-Semitism to permeate all aspects of the school curriculum. Similarly, biology was considered a fundamental discipline that had been unduly neglected during the Weimar Republic, and one which was necessary for the understanding of racial hygiene and pro-natalist policies. Geography was similarly politicised and text books increasingly reflected a preoccupation with race and the idea of *Lebensraum*.[39] History was an obvious candidate for political intervention, and the revised curriculum placed a much greater emphasis on German history, and especially on the great historic achievements of Germans in the past. Finally, the curriculum was modified to reflect Nazi conceptions of gender roles: boys and girls were to be taught differently and to learn different things, with a greater emphasis on domesticity for girls.

Reform of the curriculum in the spirit of Nazism was often a means of career advancement, both for teachers in schools and for lecturers in teacher training colleges and government officials concerned with formulating policy. New school books were provided with the aim of inculcating Nazi values at all levels from primary school pupils to university students. The family values that dominated books for young children became a vehicle for the transmission of political propaganda: children were encouraged to love the Führer in the same way they loved their parents, and scenes of domestic activity incorporated political details, such as swastika flags and, particularly after the outbreak of war, uplifting stories of willing self-sacrifice. Children were depicted collecting material for recycling or for the Winter Aid Fund (*Winterhilfswerk*), or they were shown enjoying the self-denying broth that was meant to be eaten on 'one-pot Sundays' (*Eintopfsonntag*). Racism and an ideological emphasis on innate inequality were reflected in all parts of the curriculum, ranging from the fable of the cuckoo laying her eggs in the nest of another bird in the vain hope that her offspring would learn to sing, to mathematical exercises about the state expenditure on the handicapped.[40]

In addition to the reform of the state school curriculum new Nazi schools were founded to train the political elites of the future. In 1933 the education ministry established National Political Educational Institutes (*Nationalpolitische Erziehungsanstalten* or Napolas), which recruited pupils who were 'completely healthy, racially unobjectionable, of clean character, and above average intellect'. Former Prussian cadet schools – on which the institutes were modelled – were converted into Napolas from the spring of 1933. There were some 93 Napolas (for boys), which had recruited some five thousand pupils by the outbreak of war. All pupils automatically became members of the Hitler Youth, and they were gener-ally destined for military careers. In 1937 Robert Ley and Baldur von Schirach set up a new kind of boarding school for the recruitment of future leaders, the 'Adolf Hitler Schools', which were financed by the party and intended to inculcate 'revolutionary' values opposed to those of the 'bourgeois' *Gymansium* (grammar school). And 50 of these schools were planned, with a total enrolment of 15,000, but in the event only 10 were completed. The best pupils from these schools went on to a rigorous political, ideological and physical training in the *Ordensburgen*, self-consciously elite institutions named after the medieval Order of Teutonic Knights. Three of these were built, one each in Pomerania, the Eifel and the Allgäu, and a fourth was planned for Marienburg in West Prussia. Despite their pretensions, however, the *Ordensburgen* attracted relatively few applications, and these were mainly careerists, many of them unemployed party members, rather than the future elites at which they were aimed. The reform of girls' education along these lines was not considered a priority, and there was no attempt to seek out future leaders from among the country's young women. Only two girls' Napolas were established, and there were no Adolf Hitler Schools for girls.[41]

Control of the education system as an instrument of propaganda and ideological training was not enough for a regime that was making a total claim on the loyalty of the individual. During the first half of the twentieth century children and adolescents had more leisure than earlier generations outside the structured activities of formal education, paid employment and domestic work, and a whole range of institutions, including political parties, the churches and the state, were eager to take control of that free time by recruiting them into youth organisations. The most successful youth movements during the Weimar Republic had been those of the Catholic church and the Social Democratic movement, along with the loose collection of politically independent, largely middle-class and ostensibly youth 'unpolitical' organisations referred to collectively as *bündische Jugend*. The churches negotiated to retain their youth move-ments in 1933, and the Catholic church made this a condition of their support for the enabling bill, and the youth wings of political movements were suppressed along with the opposition parties. The *Deutsche Freischar*, the main organisation of the *bündische Jugend*, was dissolved in 1933, and under the auspices of Ludwig Müller, leader of the German Christians, the Evangelical youth movements were absorbed into the Hitler Youth in December 1933. Most of the remaining youth organisations were banned by the Law on the Hitler Youth of 1 December 1936. Catholic organisa-tions survived for another year or so.

Instead, children were organised in the Hitler Youth movement (*Hitler-jugend*, HJ), which had its origins in an organisation called the *Jungsturm*, an offshoot of the SA. It was still insignificant in terms of membership by 1933. It then expanded rapidly, and had almost four million members by 1935 – over half of all young Germans. Membership became compulsory in 1939, by which time it had risen to over seven million (out of a total population of almost nine million 10- to 18-year olds). In 1933 its leader, Baldur von Schirach, was named 'Reich Youth Leader', and the organisation became affiliated directly to the party. Schirach was replaced by Artur Axmann in 1940.

Within the youth movement there were four separate divisions. The term Hitler Youth applied to the organisation as a whole, and to the section for boys between 14 and 18 years of age. From 1930 girls aged between 14 and 18 were organised in the league of German Girls (*Bund deutscher Mädel*, BdM). Girls were slower to join the Hitler Youth initially, and accounted for only about a quarter of members in 1933, but by the end of the 1930s there were roughly the same number of girls as boys. Young boys between the ages of 10 and 14 belonged to the *Deutsches Jungvolk*, and young girls of the same age belonged to the *Jungmädelbund* (young girls' league). In addition there was a separate organisation for young women between the ages of 17 and 21, *Glaube und Schönheit*, which was intended to prepare them for marriage, with courses in housecraft, hygiene and practical nursing, as well as a wide range of sports and gymnastics, and an emphasis on eugenics and racial hygiene.[42]

While the Hitler Youth projected an essentially meritocratic image of success and achievement based on personal aspiration and collective endeavour, its ideology was based on the assumption of innate physical and intellectual inequality. People could be trained and educated, but only up to a natural limit. In the words of Hellmut Stellrecht, a leading figure in the youth movement, 'This limit is clear. The most obvious example is provided by sport. With the best training, the best teachers, the best living conditions and the strongest personal will, a man will reach a specific limit of achievement, for example in the high jump.' This – according to Stellrecht – constituted a first, natural limit, and could be improved on with exceptional effort and commitment, but the effort required would now be out of all proportion to the effort hitherto expended. The same principle applied to intellectual ability; in mathematics for example, where natural limits of understanding would eventually be reached. Even in terms of personality or strength of character it was impossible to exceed one's natural limits – although things were less clear in this area. Commitment in the service of an ideal, for example, could not be expressed in terms of monetary value.[43]

For many of its members the Hitler Youth was about sport, camping and other supervised leisure activities rather than politics. Such ideology as they encountered came in the form of patriotic songs and oaths of loyalty to the Führer, and in the daily motto and the 'community hour' – mainstays of the routine at summer camps. There was much that was appealing to young people, from the range of activities, the quality of the facilities (in buildings as often as not appropriated from the Nazis' political opponents), and the simplicities of conformity, hero worship and competitiveness. Where genuine enthusiasm was lacking it was reinforced by peer pressure, the teasing of outsiders and by beatings. Circular letters were written to those children who did not join, and to their parents, demanding to know why. By the end of 1934 there were already signs of disgruntlement from some of the young people enlisted in the movement, who resented collecting for the Nazis, selling badges, and the endless parades and marches, but membership continued to rise, and for many the positive outweighed the tedious. 'I believe I am right in saying that among my 150 boys there isn't one who knows what fascism is', an 18-year-old works foreman told Sopade reporters in 1937. 'The boys are enthusiastic, but it's not the idea of National Socialism . . . It's the enthusiasm for sport, technology, romanticism, for the parades. Young Germans no longer want to be tram conductors or train drivers; they want to be aviators. National Socialism has done an excellent job of taking the interest in all things technological and organisational which already exists in young boys, and using it for its own purposes.' Asked if there were differences of attitude among Hitler Youth members, he thought that his own charges were unwilling, disobedient shirkers – but not because they were anti-fascist, but because they were 'inferior', reluctant to obey any kind of order. 'After watching these boys closely', he added 'I have the feeling they would not behave differently even in a Socialist state'.[44]

Did the Hitler Youth produce a generation of Nazis? The evidence suggests that both its potential and its real impact were limited by poor leaders, untrained themselves in the finer points of Nazi ideology, and that for most of the boys and girls involved the sports and other outdoor pursuits were the main attraction: certainly, that is how adult Germans after the war preferred to remember their earlier involvement in the movement. It was only for a few years that the majority of young Germans were recruited into the Hitler Youth, and even then it was at a time when the appeal of the movement was beginning to fade anyway. Boys grew tired of the increasingly military nature of its activities, but above all the young generation of the 1940s identified it with their parents. What had been rebellious opposition to an older generation and the political status quo during the Weimar Republic now seemed respectable and authoritarian. Rebellious middle-class youths took to wearing their hair longer, speaking with an English accent and listening to jazz or swing music – small symbolic acts of defiance against the received taste of the Third Reich. Their working-class peers were more likely to become involved, however fleetingly, with the urban gangs that increasingly dominated the sub-culture of the northern industrial conurbation and other large cities, causing problems not just for the Nazis, but for the Allied occupation authorities that succeeded them in 1945. Although groups such as the 'Edelweiss pirates' have been associated with political opposition, their hostility to authority was not restricted to the Nazis.[45] Above all the era of the institutional youth movement was passing away, and although the churches and democratic political parties resurrected their youth organisations after the war, these too declined steadily until they were finally eclipsed by the commercial youth cultures associated with pop music and fashion.

Compromises and Conflicts of Interest: The Churches and Nazism

With the elimination of political opposition, the suppression of dissent, and the Nazification of social and professional organisations the churches, which remained relatively independent throughout the Third Reich, remained the only potential source of ideological opposition to the regime, and their responses to the new order reveal a great deal about Nazi society as a whole. The relationship between Christianity and Nazism (or the *völkisch* movement before it) was bound to be problematic. The early Nazi party had the character of a sect, with spiritual claims and mystical leanings of its own (and a recent school of interpretation has looked at fascism generally as a 'political religion'[46]). Hitler was pragmatic about relations with the established churches, was shrewd enough to recognise that constant confrontation with the churches would be both exhausting and fruitless. He insisted that the party concentrate on political goals, and was disdainful of the pseudo-religious fringe of the *völkisch* movement. In any case many clergymen welcomed Nazism, and easily found common ground on issues such as politics, race, women's rights and homosexuality; and while many historians have emphasised the Nazis' anti-clericalism and contempt for Christian values, more recent research has found that not only collusion between the churches and the regime, but a convergence between the sincerely held, if sometimes unorthodox Christian beliefs of many leading Nazis and their political engagement.[47]

As the party became more popular and successful it attracted many recruits and supporters who were also practising Christians, but confessional differences began to emerge more clearly. The Nazis consistently achieved their best electoral results in Protestant areas, and the worst in Catholic districts, where the unshakeable appeal of the Centre Party was a formidable obstacle. Similarly, there were different responses among church leaders to the party's breakthrough in 1930. Catholics were adamant that the differences between the church and the NSDAP were irreconcilable, and the diocese of Mainz went so far as to declare that no party member could be a Catholic (albeit without agreement from other Catholic bishops). The relationship between the state and the Evangelical church had always been close, and many senior churchmen were opposed to the Weimar republic and sympathetic to the Nazis. The 'Faith Movement of German Christians', which grew out of a local group in Thuringia founded in 1930, was popular among the younger Protestant clergy. Its members styled themselves 'stormtroopers for Jesus Christ', and sought to combine evangelical theology with racial nationalism, hoping thereby to broaden the appeal of the church in the age of the 'masses'. Although the German Christians attracted support among northern Protestants in church elections in 1932, it was significantly less than the level of support for the Nazis in parliamentary elections at the same time. There was a surge of interest after Hitler's appointment, however, and the German Christians won two thirds of votes in synod elections following the establishment of the Reich church during the summer. As a consequence Friedrich von Bodelschwingh (1877–1946), who had been elected Reich Bishop in May, was replaced by the German Christian leader Ludwig Müller, a personal acquaintance of Hitler, and the Nazi revolution in the church seemed complete, as other supporters of the regime were rapidly promoted to important positions. The opposition to these developments was led by the 'Pastors' Emergency League', organised by Martin Niemöller and by the 'confessing church', which eventually became a second Evangelical church (21 October 1934) – albeit not one recognised by the secular authorities, and subject to internal divisions between the Lutheran and Reformed wings. Its theology was expressed in a declaration at the synod of Barmen in 1934, and drew heavily on the work of the Swiss theologian Karl Barth.

Moves towards the creation of a national Evangelical church had been hastened by the reception among senior Protestant clergymen of the regime's concordat with the Catholic church, concluded on 20 July 1933. This followed negotiations between the church, which was represented by the papal nuncio in Berlin (and future Pope Pius XII), Eugenio Pacelli, by Ludwig Kaas of the Centre Party, and Franz von Papen for the government. The German concordat signified the end of political Catholicism in Germany, in so far as the Centre Party (along with the Bavarian People's Party) was sacrificed in exchange for a guarantee of the independence of the church in Germany to organise its own affairs, including the administration of church schools. It did not remove all tension from the relationship between church and state. The regime sought to apply various restrictions on Catholic associations and publications, and found ways to persecute individual Catholic priests, prompting a public rebuke in the papal encyclical *Mit brennender Sorge* of 1937.[48] Catholics were not opposed to all aspects of Nazi policy, but the relationship between the regime and the Catholic communities in Germany was frequently characterised by conflict and covert opposition. If the concordat ensured that there was no dramatic confrontation in the manner of the 'conflict of cultures' (*Kulturkampf*) of the nineteenth century, there were nevertheless countless minor struggles, particularly in defence of Catholic associational life. Catholic clubs and societies could not simply be suppressed like those of the labour movement, but would not be quietly 'co-ordinated' either. Conflicts over the control of education were sharper, as was demonstrated by the adamant – and successful – opposition of Catholic teachers and parents to the removal of crucifixes from schools in Oldenburg.[49] The result of this particular conflict was a substantial no vote among the electors of Oldenburg in the plebiscite held shortly afterwards to acclaim the 're-unification' of Austria with the German Reich.

The regime's relationship with the smaller Christian sects was similarly problematic. Fringe groups such as the Seventh Day Adventists, Mormons and Christian Scientists attracted a few thousand, mainly middle-class adherents in Germany. Although they were not political opponents of the regime, and shared many of the Nazis interests and values, they were a cause for concern in other ways. They not only had their roots and headquarters in the United States, but also paid too much attention to the Old Testament and the Jewish elements in Christianity. Such groups had only small numbers of adherents in Germany, however, posed no direct political challenge to the regime and many members of such communities shared the Nazis' own racial prejudices, and some Mormon communities banned Jews. The Jehovah's Witnesses were a rather different case. The sect had come to Germany in the early twentieth century, had nearly 4000 members by the end of the First World War, and some 25,000 by 1933, most of them from working-class or white-collar backgrounds in large towns and cities. (Three quarters of the male Witnesses in Augsburg during the 1930s were workers, and half of these were unskilled.) Although they did not oppose the Nazis politically this was because they rejected political engagement of any kind, and they were so intransigent on points of principle, above all in defence of their refusal to take up arms, that they immediately came into conflict with the regime. Their head office in Magdeburg was raided in April 1933 and 25 lorry loads of literature confiscated. The publications of the Watchtower Society were prohibited and the movement itself was banned in 1935. The movement was persecuted to an extent out of all proportion to its sise and importance: thousands of Witnesses were imprisoned in concentration camps, a thousand were executed and another thousand died awaiting sentence. The persecution intensified in the late 1930s and especially during the war. During the first year of the war 96 per cent of all death sentences passed by the Supreme Court Martial in Berlin for refusing to fight were imposed on Jehovah's Witnesses.[50] In general, however, there was less pressure on the churches after the outbreak of war as the regime sought to avoid open conflict in the interests of domestic stability.

Revolutionary Rhetoric and Social Reality

Despite the ambitious rhetoric of its propaganda, Nazism did not bring about a revolution in Nazi Germany, either in terms of real social change or in the way social reality was perceived.[51] The suppression of the political left and its organisations reversed the gains made by the working class since the First World War, left the labour movement weaker than at any time since industrialisation, and considerably strengthened the position of the employers: this restoration of 'management's right to manage' was one of the regime's most pressing priorities and – in its own terms – one of the most important achievements. The effect was to reinforce rather than transcend or overcome class divisions in German society; the working class was contained rather than integrated into a putative 'national community'. For their part the middle classes generally welcomed the restoration of a social authority that they felt parliamentary democracy had undermined. In practical terms this meant a freedom from the irritations of accountability, not only for the civil servants who might otherwise have had to take public opinion into account when devising and implementing policy, but also for a range of professionals whose authority derived from an expertise which they were happy, on the whole, to place at the disposal of the new regime. One or two further points can be made about German society under Nazism. First, much of the social change that is discernible is broadly compatible with long-term social and economic developments: there are very clear continuities from the 1920s to the 1950s and beyond in the way family life and work life developed, in the growth of personal consumption and leisure activities, however shoddy the goods or facilities. The breaking down of communal identities and solidarities in working-class communities continued and accelerated after 1945, and while the Nazi agenda seemed to epitomise modernity to many managers and professionals, modernisation continued, more successfully, in the Federal Republic. The clearest and most dramatic impact of Nazism on German society came not directly, but as a consequence of war, defeat and the division of Germany.

Chapter 5: Culture, Leisure and Propaganda

The Nazis' approach to culture is associated with a handful of telling images illustrating their barbaric anti-intellectualism, such as the burning of books in Berlin in May 1933, the ransacking of the Bauhaus later the same year, the flight abroad of hundreds of Germany's leading intellectuals and creative artists, or the exhibition of 'degenerate art' in Munich in July 1937, where the works of modernist artists were ridiculed with racist jibes. Beyond the first glance, however, the picture is more complicated.

The burning of books in 1933 was not carried out by uneducated stormtroopers, 'the unfettered masses' of popular representations, but by students, along with their professors, and in some cases the rectors themselves, albeit inspired by the propaganda ministry, and guided by party officials. It was a symbolic gesture against the culture of the Weimar Republic, and it took place not just in Berlin, but in university towns across Germany. Similarly, not all German intellectuals and artists were victims of Nazism by any means. To be sure, many of Germany's leading artists, writers and performers left the country, and not all of them were Jewish intellectuals who had lost their jobs, or left-wing opponents of the regime; many liberals and conservatives also left, including, for example, the Nobel prize-winning novelist and erstwhile nationalist Thomas Mann. But the Weimar Republic had not been short of right-wing intellectuals and conservative revolutionaries who were broadly sympathetic to the new regime; and although many of them, particularly on the straightforwardly *völkisch* right, were quick to denounce artistic modernism as degenerate, many right-wing artists and intellectuals in Germany positively supported modernist experimentation (as they did elsewhere).[1]

This meant that there was not one simple, unreconstructed Nazi view of culture within the new regime, but a range of diverse attitudes and approaches, and the spring of 1933 did not see the straightforward reckoning with 'cultural bolshevism' that many might have hoped for. While Jews, Communists and Social Democrats were sacked and, if they had the foresight, left the country, the regime was also keen to recruit those whose reputations were not irredeemably compromised to lend some respectability to the new cultural order. Some of the most prominent figures in the arts agreed to serve the new regime. Richard Strauss, for example, was appointed president of the Reich Chamber of Music, and Wilhelm Furtwängler agreed to be his deputy. Stefan George, hero of the conservative revolutionaries, expressed his support for the regime, but prudently left for Switzerland (where he died then shortly afterwards). Fritz Lang, courted by Goebbels, left immediately for Paris when he was offered a leading position in the Reich film industry. Some admirers, on the other hand, were spurned nevertheless by the regime. The expressionist artist Ernst Nolde, for example, became a party member, but his work was condemned as degenerate.

The New Cultural Order

Culture was important to the regime. Gaining control of culture was not only an end in itself; it was also indispensable in order to achieve the ideological revolution of which Hitler spoke in 1933. Leading figures in the regime, not least Hitler himself had very strong opinions on the subject, and there was some tension between a conservative faction of anti-modernists and a pragmatic tendency that was more open to some kinds of modern art.

The interests of the former group were represented by Alfred Rosenberg, the veteran party ideologue, whose approach to the arts reflected the thinking of an old, hard-core *völkisch* right: these were cultural *alte Kämpfer*, loyal to the aesthetic values of the early Nazi Party, and Hitler, with his sentimental provincial nostalgia for the Biedermeier days of 'old Vienna', was instinctively one of them. Rosenberg himself was an anti-Semitic émigré from the Baltic who had exercised considerable influence over Hitler in the early 1920s, and over the Nazi movement generally as editor of the *Völkischer Beobachter*.[2] In 1929 he had founded the Combat League for German Culture (*Kampfbund für deutsche Kultur*, KfdK) as a vehicle for his anti-Semitic cultural nationalism, and it became one of a network of dozens of *völkisch* pressure groups campaigning against modern art.[3] Rosenberg recruited other party leaders, such as Himmler and Darré, in support of his organisation, along with well-known right-wing intellectuals such as Othmar Spann; he also founded a journal (*Deutsche Kulturwacht*) and a newsletter to promote a conservative aesthetics both within and outside the party. In addition, *völkisch* critics were recruited to the staff of the *Völkischer Beobachter*, where the campaign against modernism culminated in a series of articles by Rosenberg himself in 1933, directed in particular against the party's student wing, which was more sympathetic to expressionism.

By the time the Nazis came to power, however, Rosenberg's star was on the wane. His main work, *The Myth of the Twentieth Century* (1930), went down badly with his colleagues, including Hitler who disapproved of its mysticism. They found it difficult and obscure and, as he was to find out from their evidence at the Nuremberg war crimes trials, none of them bothered to persevere with it. Moreover, Rosenberg was an inefficient administrator, who lacked focus. His energies were dissipated among a number of responsibilities, and he could not give his full attention to any one of his portfolios. As a consequence his standing within the party was in decline. For those in the art world who thought like Rosenberg, however, the establishment of the Third Reich created something of a career opportunity. With the dismissal of Jews and Social Democrats from museums and galleries, new curators were appointed who were more sympathetic to the *völkisch* cultural lobby, energetically organising 'exhibitions of shame' (*Schandausstellungen*), ridiculing modern artists in ways that anticipated the 'degenerate art exhibition' of 1937. The confidence among the anti-modernists was illusory, however, with the establishment of the Reich Ministry of Popular Enlightenment and Propaganda, Goebbels had already won the struggle for control of German culture. The future lay with his new 'cultural bureaucracy', headed by a small core staff of relatively young officials at the new Propaganda Ministry. These were educated people who recognised the danger of politicising culture to the extent that it would damage the image of the regime and the country by promoting second-rate work that was ideologically uncontroversial at the expense of genuinely creative material.[4] In practice the ministry did little to counter the proliferation of mediocre, politically correct culture, and there was little genuinely creative art in the Third Reich.

Hitler himself announced the creation of the new ministry in cabinet on 11 March 1933 and Goebbels, who had been responsible for propaganda in the party since 1928, was appointed minister two days later.

Departments within the ministry mirrored the sections of the party's
Central Propaganda Office, which continued to play an important role
in supporting activities of the ministry, and leading party functionaries
were appointed to the same responsibilities in the ministry, so that
party and state overlapped in terms of activity and personnel at both
national and regional level. In addition the new ministry took over a
number of responsibilities from other portfolios: the press office, for
example, which had been under the auspices of the Reich chancellery;
broadcasting from the ministry of posts and the control of censorship
from the interior ministry. These responsibilities and others were divided
between seven sections within the propaganda ministry. Department I
dealt with legal and administrative matters and Department II with a
range of activities from the 'popular enlightenment and propaganda' of
the ministry's name, to sport and travel. The rest dealt each with a more
or less clearly defined cultural portfolio: radio, the press, film, theatre
and music and the fine arts. Goebbels wanted a manageable, efficient
organisation rather than a rambling bureaucracy and started with a staff
of 350. His preference was for young, well-educated men, preferably with
doctorates, and the average age (about 39) of the ministry's employees
was 10 years lower than that of the political class generally. The sharp
increase in radio ownership during the 1930s proved a lucrative source
of income for Goebbels, who managed to finance most of his ministerial expenditure with the revenue from licences, and the new ministry
quickly established itself as, by far, the most important institution in Nazi
cultural policy.[5]

Goebbels also presided over the Reich Chamber of Culture, an
umbrella organisation established in September 1933 that brought
together a number of professional bodies in the arts and media in
separate chambers for film, literature, theatre, music, the fine arts, broadcasting and the press. As an overarching body for co-ordinating the
day-to-day business of Germany's cultural industries and institutions, it
was the main instrument through which the country's artists and intellectuals were 'Nazified' (*gleichgeschaltet*) and their activities brought into
line with the regime's cultural policy. Membership of one of the seven
chambers was compulsory for practising artists, writers and performers
in the Third Reich, and the denial of a work permit on racial or political grounds was effectively a prohibition from working. Jewish artists
and intellectuals were excluded from the outset, and many of them
went into exile immediately, along with prominent political opponents of the regime from the intelligentsia, and many of those whose
work was considered too abstract or experimental. But while leading

figures with international reputations were assured of a welcome abroad, lesser known artists and writers found it more difficult to leave, and many simply could not afford to anyway. Thousands of people worked in Germany's cultural institutions and industries, as minor performers, often in local orchestras or theatres, as museum or gallery curators, as editors in publishing houses or in newspapers, and as administrators in all kinds of institution. Most of these people had to stay and – if they kept their jobs – had to find their own accommodation with the new regime.[6]

Goebbels' strong institutional position did not mean that he got all his own way. Hitler made clear his continuing hostility to modern art during the debate that came to a head in the summer of 1933, and this meant that some of the more pro-modernist voices in the Goebbels camp were restrained. In addition, Rosenberg's defeat in the struggle for control of German culture was softened when he was charged by Hitler the following year with 'overseeing the entire intellectual and ideological schooling and education of the party and co-ordinated organisations'. His responsibilities were wide-ranging and covered culture in the broadest sense, including education and the churches; but his remit involved more ideological supervision than engagement with issues of aesthetics.[7] Finally, two other senior figures in the regime played a role in the development of cultural policy. The first of these was Robert Ley, the Labour Front leader, who was involved in the setting up of Rosenberg's new office and the second was Bernhard Rust, who was appointed Reich minister of science and education on 30 April 1934. Ley collaborated with Rosenberg, and the KfdK was merged with a Labour Front theatre organisation to form the National Socialist Cultural Community (NS-Kulturgemeinde) which was destined to be little more than a glorified booking agency for theatre and concert tickets. Rosenberg also took over control of the Labour Front's ideological training and cultural activity, but there was no clear division of authority between his jurisdiction in cultural matters and that of Ley, and this gave rise to tension when the Strength through Joy organisation (KdF) tried to encroach on Rosenberg's territory. Rust was in a rather thankless position from the outset. As an education minister he was threatened on all fronts by the other leading Nazis' constant self-aggrandisement, including attempts by the Propaganda ministry to take over control of museums and galleries. Finally the foreign office organised external cultural policy, including travelling exhibitions, musical and theatrical performances and cultural exchanges.[8]

Nazism and the Mass Media

This new cultural order was perceived to be under continuing threat from two sides. On the one hand it was undermined by 'degenerate' experimentation with abstraction, streams of consciousness and twelve-tone music. Degenerate (*entartet*) literally meant 'alien to the race' and such work was rejected as 'un-German', and thereby dismissed in the most damning terms of the age – despite the unambiguously modern nature of the work of creative artists who were revered by the right, including Richard Wagner. At the same time German culture was felt to be threatened by a torrent of popular culture, in the form of pulp fiction, cinema and the mass-circulation press. Right-wing cultural critics were not against popular culture in itself, and recognised that the 'masses' would find classical culture inaccessible, and encouraged a sentimental folk culture with an emphasis on traditional values, much of it invented. Their hostility was directed against *commercial* culture, such as the instalments of genre novels (horror, romance, crime) that were hawked from door to door, and increasingly during the 1920s against the perceived Americanisation of German culture by the emergent entertainments industry. Although the real cultural changes brought about by the regime were in the relatively new fields of propaganda, popular culture and organised leisure, the high-profile cultural battleground remained high culture: fine art, literature, music and theatre.

The centrepiece of the regime's policy was the degenerate art campaign of 1937, which saw the removal of thousands of works of art from German art galleries and museums, and culminated in two exhibitions in Munich. The first, organised by Goebbels and Adolf Ziegler, president of the Reich Chamber of Fine Arts', was the 'Degenerate Art' exhibition itself, which opened on 19 July 1937 and went on to tour Germany. The artists whose work was exhibited, among them Max Ernst, George Grosz, Ernst Ludwig Kirchner and Paul Klee, were widely held to be some of the finest German artists of their generation. Their work was displayed alongside pictures of the disabled, and contextualised as the product of sick minds, no less a symptom of debility than the physical disfigurements of the handicapped, or the racial and ideological shortcomings of Jews and Communists, and these connections between art, politics and racial hygiene were made explicit in the explanatory material that accompanied the exhibition. The second exhibition was the 'Great German Art Exhibition', which had opened the previous day at the new House of German Art, also in Munich. The building was designed in the monumental neo-classical style favoured by the Nazis by Paul Ludwig

Troost (1878–1934), who had also worked on buildings for the Nazi Party and Hitler (the *Führerbau*). A competition was organised to find work that met the exacting new standards of racially hygienic (*artrein*) art, and the entries were judged by Ziegler and Hitler's favourite sculptor, Arno Breker (1900–91). Both Hitler and Goebbels were also involved in the selection, and Hitler opened the exhibition with a prepared speech, in which he expounded the principles of a true German art. In place of the international modern art of the early twentieth century, a true German art with roots in the nation and indifferent to voguish taste:

> Art can in no way be a fashion. As little as the character and the blood of our people will change, so much will art have to lose its mortal character and replace it with worthy images expressing the life-course of our people in the steadily unfolding growth of its creations. Cubism, Dadaism, Futurism, Impressionism etc. have nothing to do with our German people. For these concepts are neither old nor modern, but are only the artifactitious stammerings of men to whom God has denied the grace of a truly artistic talent, and in its place has awarded them the gift of jabbering or deception.[9]

The Nazis campaign against 'degenerate' culture extended to other creative fields, including architecture, design and above all music, and the Munich exhibition of degenerate art was followed in 1938 by an exhibition of 'degenerate music' in Düsseldorf. The Reich Chamber of Music promoted a canon of great German composers, in a tradition from Johann Sebastian Bach to Wagner, Bruckner and Richard Strauss, the chamber's first president. Contemporary composers and musicians who found favour with the Nazis flourished, among them Hans Pfitzner and Carl Orff. Others were condemned, either for the nature of their music or for their Jewish origins – or both. Among these were Gustav Mahler, Alban Berg and Arnold Schoenberg. Jazz was also naturally beyond the pale, on both musical and racial grounds. A particularly irritating work for the guardians of pure German music was the avant-garde jazz opera *Jonny spielt auf* by Ernst Křenek, whose central character was a black musician.[10] Hundreds of gifted composers, performers and teachers left Germany, either to escape racial persecution, avoid imprisonment for their political beliefs, or simply in order to continue with their work. Among them were the Austrian composers Erich Korngold (1897–1957), who won Oscars for his film scores (including *The Adventures of Robin Hood*, starring Errol Flynn), and Ernst Goldner, who wrote music for the TV western series *Wagon Train*. One of the best-known musical exiles was

Kurt Weill, who had composed music for Brecht's plays including *The Threepenny Opera*. Not all of those who found themselves in difficulties with the regime were able to leave, of course, and were compelled to stay in Germany and make the best of things. Thousands of musicians and music teachers were employed in bands and orchestras, or in schools and universities, and as in other professions employment prospects improved somewhat during the 1930s, not least as a consequence of the Nazi preoccupation with parades, ceremonies and rituals.

Nazi cultural policy involved much more than the campaign against modern painting and music. Goebbels was determined to exploit the new media of the day, radio and film, for the regime's purposes. Radio was an important medium for propaganda, and the Nazis had found it difficult to gain access to it before 1933. Taking control of the medium was straightforward, as it was jointly owned by the Reich Ministry of Posts and nine regional broadcasting companies. There was some initial opposition from Goering who, as Prussian interior minister, defended the interests of the regional companies, but the issue was resolved by a decree from Hitler in June 1933, and a Reich Chamber of Radio was established in July under 'Reich Broadcasting Leader' Eugen Hadamovsky. Over half of German households had a wireless set in the 1930s, and the figure was higher among the middle classes and in large cities. The regime set out to increase the radio audience by organising and subsidising the manufacture of cheap wireless sets (*Volksempfänger*), which were designed to make it difficult to receive foreign broadcasts.[11] Sopade reporters estimated that the number of sets had more than doubled between 1933 and the end of 1938 from 4.3 million to more than 10 million, and the SD reported that the number of listeners had grown by 1.7 million in 1938 alone, an increase attributed to the political events of the year.

The importance of radio for the regime's propaganda was held to be incalculable. Speeches by Hitler and other party leaders were broadcast regularly, and local party branches and other Nazi organisations were encouraged to organise communal listening. Radio speakers were mounted on pillars in cities, and portable radios were provided for smaller communities, to ensure that even the most stubborn non-listeners could be reached. There were limits to the efficacy of radio propaganda, however. Hitler himself found it difficult to speak as effectively in the studio as in front of a live audience, and in any case people gradually grew indifferent to the endless speeches made every day and paid less attention to the news. The weariness set in before the outbreak of the war. A Sopade report of December 1938 noted that people increasingly had the radio switched on without really listening to it, and paid attention only when they could get hold of foreign radio broadcasting. Although the regime's own observers expressed their satisfaction with the contribution made by German radio during the Sudeten crisis, for example, Sopade reporters claimed that even Nazi party members had preferred to listen to British and French broadcasts for reliable news, and it was estimated that some 80 per cent of all radio owners listened to foreign radio broadcasts regularly. It was a mistake to think that you could not get foreign radio with a *Volksempfänger*, according to a reporter from Silesia: in fact, if you knew what you were doing you could even get Radio Moscow, despite the attempts of authorities to jam the signal.[12]

Radio was particularly important during the war, and the popular reception of broadcasts was closely monitored by the regime. Popular entertainment broadcasts with light dance music or folk music were among the most popular programmes, along with request shows for the armed forces, although there were sometimes complaints that the inclusion of foreign songs and foreign performers was uncalled for and out of place, or that some types of music were in questionable taste.[13] Direct complaints from the public, at least during the early days of the war, were generally less to do with the content of broadcasts than with poor reception, the unavailability of certain popular programmes in peripheral regions, and not least the difficulty in getting spare parts. Even from the beginning of the war, however, there were complaints about the lack of choice between programmes, and the constant repetition of certain songs or pieces of music. Reports from the front conveyed the individual experience of war: a night in the bunker at Tobruk, or the awarding of a medal to an officer after the battle of Mechili, for example, or the report of a naval officer who sank three tankers in five minutes.[14] Such reports were generally popular, and followed attentively, but there were also complaints that current affairs programmes repeated material from the press and news broadcasts. As a result there was an increasing tendency to ignore radios in public places when the news was on, and such displays of indifference during communal listening were considered bad for morale: in October 1940 the SD reported an 'increasing lack of discipline among the public during news broadcasts' particularly in bars.[15]

There was greater interest after the invasion of the Soviet Union. Popular responses to the news from Russia followed the pattern that was familiar from other campaigns: initial uneasiness, followed by relief when the German armies swept across the western Soviet Union. As campaign faltered, and the tide of the war began to turn, people looked to the radio bulletins for reassurance. It was felt, for example, that a programme on the 'psyche of the Soviet soldier' had helped explain the Russians' resistance.[16] By the autumn of 1942, however, there were complaints that reports on the military situation at Stalingrad and in the Caucasus were unclear, and that it was difficult to form an overview of what was happening, and the defeat at Stalingrad marked a turning point in popular morale that was reflected in an increased interest in bulletins and a pessimistic response to the news from both the eastern front and north Africa. The regime responded by acknowledging the gravity of the situation (albeit indirectly) and (less convincingly) by presenting the war in the East as a defence of Europe against Bolshevism. People responded well to the straight talking of military experts like Lieutenant General Dittmar, who broadcast regular commentaries on the military situation. He acknowledged the strength and successes of the enemy, and the achievements of the Soviet system, and was not afraid to refer to setbacks. His talks were followed attentively by a wide audience, and he was considered one of the most honest commentators.[17]

Many looked for greater objectivity by listening to foreign radio stations, which had been forbidden at the beginning of the war by decree of the Ministerial Council for the Defence of the Reich. Passing on information from foreign broadcast was punishable by imprisonment, or death in 'severe cases'. Even so, the authorities felt that the punishments were deemed lenient by the public. A 2-year sentence in 1940 for 'weeks of listening to foreign radio broadcasts' and passing on the contents was held to have been too little, and a report from Bavaria seemed to confirm that there was popular support for such punishments.[18] In the autumn of 1941 local Nazi functionaries attempted to reinforce the widely disregarded prohibition by organising the distribution of notices to hang on wireless sets. The initiative was a disaster. People thought they were being singled out individually or as a community, and refused to believe that Hitler or the Reich government could have had anything to do with it: the whole business confirmed the popular perception of the 'little Hitlers' of the local branches as interfering busybodies.[19] Despite this rather prickly reaction, it is clear that the practice was very widespread, particularly among members of former left-wing parties and among the educated middle classes. Men were more likely to listen to radio than women. Of a group of 666 people from Hessen-Nassau questioned by US military personnel after the war, just over half (51 per cent) claimed they had listened to foreign radio stations, and almost half (43 per cent) of these said they had done so even before the war, while almost a quarter (23 per cent) had not done so until after Stalingrad. The most popular stations were Radio Luxembourg and the BBC, while Radio Moscow was relatively unpopular. Catholic priests openly admitted to listening to Vatican Radio.[20]

Film, like radio, combined the transmission of propaganda and high culture with popular entertainment. Unlike radio, film production and distribution had been largely in private hands during the 1920s. The state had had an interest in 'Ufa' (Universum Film AG), Germany's most important film company since its establishment in 1917, when it was used to make patriotic films and propaganda. The company had been bought up by the German nationalist media tycoon Alfred Hugenberg – one of Hitler's leading political allies. (He already had extensive interests in publishing, advertising and the press.) Ufa's importance increased during the Depression when the advent of talkies, at a time when receipts were falling, forced a further concentration of film production. Film producers and cinema owners were quickly 'co-ordinated', and the Reich Chamber of Film regulated the industry as a whole. A Reich Cinema Law was introduced on 16 February 1934, which established the principle of pre-censorship to ensure films were free of politically unacceptable content before they were cleared for release. Many people involved with the industry left Germany as victims of racial or political persecution, and Berlin's loss was Hollywood's gain as directors, scriptwriters and performers found work there in the 1930s. Goebbels continued to extend his control over the industry, compelling Hugenberg to sell Ufa in 1937. By 1943 German film production dominated Europe, as occupied countries and allied states alike were compelled to take German rather than British or American films, and a state-owned company (Ufi) took control of the industry and its subsidiaries in 1942.

Goebbels was not interested in propaganda alone, however, and recognised in any case that films with a heavy-handed political message could be counter-productive. Most films were feature films of one kind or another, whose chief purpose was to entertain. About a sixth were more or less political, among them Leni Riefenstahl's monumental documentaries *Triumph of the Will* (1935), which covered the previous year's party rally, starting with Hitler descending from the clouds accompanied by the music of Wagner; and *Olympia* (1938), which documented the Berlin Olympics of 1936.[21] Others made their political points by drawing historical analogies: Veit Harlan's film Der grosse König (1942), for example, showed Frederick the Great on the point of defeat in 1759. His advisers recommend capitulation, but he insists on fighting on to victory, albeit at the cost of enormous losses, and changed the political map of Europe. Similarly *Kolberg* (1945), at 8.5 million Reichsmarks the most expensive film made under the Nazis, depicted the last stand of the Prussian army against Napoleon in 1807 at Kolberg (Kolobrzeg in present-day Poland). The message was clear: the townspeople preferred to die fighting rather than surrender and although they were eventually defeated, the conquering enemy was forced to withdraw.

The authorities were just as interested in the reception of film as in that of radio broadcasting, and the SD provided detailed analyses of popular responses to individual films. *Der grosse König*, was generally well received, but not without some criticism. Austrians on the other hand – including audiences in the formerly Austrian towns of Karlsbad, Reichenberg and Troppau – were only too quick to recognise the glorification of an enemy of the old Austria, and objected to the emphasis on 'Prussiandom'; audiences in Berlin had found that the analogy between the eighteenth-century Prussia and the present too heavy-handed. Nevertheless, it was considered a success on the whole, and if some audiences failed to recog-nise the 'old Fritz' of popular tradition in Otto Gebühr's portrayal of the king, then all the better, this was a re-interpretation for the times.[22] Particular attention was paid to the reception of explicitly propagand-istic films. *Der ewige Jude* (The Eternal Jew), for example, a documentary illustrating the 'uncivilised' nature of the Jews, by filming the squalid conditions created by the German themselves in Polish ghettoes, was one of a series of anti-Semitic films whose impact was closely monitored. The population had been prepared for the release of the film with a propa-ganda campaign, and it had been an enormous success when it opened. Audiences had found the visual presentations, including maps and tables, much more 'enlightening' than the anti-Semitism of the pamphlets and the press, according to SD reports, and the juxtaposition of images were particularly striking: the Jewish ghetto, contrasted with the march of the Hitler Youth at a party rally, for example. There had been great interest, it was noted, in the extent of Jewish influence abroad (as presented in the film), particularly in the United States where the openness of Jewish domination had caused some surprise. And yet, although the film had initially attracted extraordinary interest, audiences had melted away very quickly in many places, including Frankfurt, Munich and Dortmund. Only the 'politically active' part of the population seemed to be inter-ested, perhaps because the film had followed so quickly after *Jud Süss* (the first and best known of a series of anti-Semitic propaganda films), but also because people had found it distressing.[23]

The reception of such films required particular attention. A similar case was '*Ich klage an*', a film intending to justify euthanasia – a policy which had caused some controversy, and had led to sharp criticism of the regime from the Bishop of Münster. The plot of the film bore little resemblance to the realities of the Nazi 'euthanasia' programme initiated in 1939. In the context of a love story the beautiful wife of a doctor voluntarily seeks a 'mercy-killing' from her husband as a response to her condition. Analysis of responses, particularly from the churches and the medical profession, was correspondingly cautious. The principal theme of the film was held to be 'killing on demand in the event of an incurable illness', while the 'disposal of valueless life' was a 'subsidiary theme'. Reporters discerned agreement with the general argument, albeit with some reservations, for the notion that 'it should be possible to bring about death more quickly, for those who were suffering severely, and for whom there was no hope of a cure'. The response of the churches, on the other hand, was almost entirely negative, as was to be expected, and that was true of both confessions, although less emphatically among Protestants than Catholics. According to the SD, Catholic priests had told their parishioners that it was an attack on the Catholic Church and a state propaganda film which justified the murder of those with hereditary handicaps. Reporters nevertheless claimed to discern some disagreement among the Catholic clergy, with some priests prepared to accept the justifiability of euthanasia if it was agreed by a panel of doctors that the patient was incurable and that death would be a mercy. If this was true, it meant that the film had already been extraordinarily successful in shifting opinion (and loyalties) among a particularly intransigent section of the population. Doctors themselves, it was reported, had responded positively to the issues raised by the film, especially the younger generation, who were all for it – apart from a few religious ones.[24]

Although propaganda films have done much to determine our perceptions of German cinema under the Nazis, it should be remembered that the films most Germans went to see most of the time (and far fewer Germans went to the pictures than their British contemporaries) were light entertainment of one kind or another: comedy, music or *Heimat* films set against the background of country or small-town life. In addition there were regular newsreels, whose reception the authorities followed as keenly as they did radio broadcasts, and not least countless educational and documentary films (*Kulturfilme*) which reinforced the leitmotifs of Nazi ideology. Themes included science and technology (e.g. the new ways in which synthetic materials were being produced), education and the arts. Geographical documentaries celebrated the 'diverse character and peoples of German landscapes' – not least those landscapes recently incorporated into the Reich, such as Carinthia and the Wachau in Austria.[25]

Such celebrations of recently reclaimed territory and ethnically mixed border areas as 'truly German' were a recurrent feature of both film and press propaganda, which celebrated the German history of cities such as Prague and Strasbourg, and the German landscapes and people of Silesia, Alsace-Lorraine and Carniola. Film was especially important in the cultural integration of such border areas into the Reich, and new picture houses were opened, or older ones renovated in order to encourage the local population – rather than just Reichswehr soldiers or German civilians – to watch more German film. Great efforts were made during the autumn and winter of 1940, for example, to educate people in the recently annexed territories of the West in German film culture.

German film production also catered increasingly for the rest of Europe, particularly in areas such as the Balkans, where there was little indigenous film production, and local people had depended on imports from Germany certainly, but also from the West, and to a lesser extent from the Soviet Union. By 1940 the German film industry had displaced its rivals in quantity and – it was firmly believed – in quality. German observers of the cultural life of south-eastern Europe believed that people there were unimpressed by the cheap effects of American film and were looking for something more substantial, for films that spoke directly to them as Europeans. German films, which raised serious social and political issues, would be able to provide what was lacking.[26] Audiences abroad were less convinced, and the educated elites of Europe's capitals, who had exhibited a demonstrative interest in German culture – whether cinema, theatre, music or literature – rejected and even boycotted it as the defeat of the Reich loomed closer.[27]

Access to radio and film as propaganda tools really came only after 1933. Before that the Nazi propaganda had had to rely on public appearances, posters and their own press. The party had bought its official newspaper from the Thule Gesellschaft in 1920: *Der Völkischer Beobachter*, originally founded in 1887 as the *Münchener Beobachter*. It was edited by Dietrich Eckart until 1923 and then by Rosenberg. In addition the party had a range of other titles, most of them regional or local, such as *Der Stürmer*, the viciously anti-Semitic magazine founded in 1923 by Julius Streicher – the *Gauleiter* of Franconia – and Goebbels' Berlin paper *Der Angriff* founded in 1927. By 1932 there were 59 Nazi newspapers with a combined circulation of nearly 800,000. A year later the circulation of the Nazi press had leaped to almost three and a half million, and by the outbreak of the Second World War there were 200 titles with a circulation of more than 6 million. Both before and after the establishment of the Nazi regime many of these copies were taken by individuals who felt compelled to do so.

In Germany, as a whole, there were over four and a half thousand newspapers in 1932. Authoritarian measures against the press had already begun under Brüning, when there were nearly three hundred newspaper suspensions, over half of them involving Nazi or other right-wing publications. During von Papen's brief chancellorship there were fewer than a hundred but half of these now involved Communist or Social Democrat publications. Further restrictions were placed on the press after the Reichstag fire in February 1933, when the Decree for the Protection of People and State suspended civil liberties, including the freedom of expression and the freedom of the press. The nazification of the press in 1933 threatened to be a more complicated business than the 'co-ordination' of other media, where ownership was more straightforward or at least more concentrated. In practice, however, the newspaper publishers, like so many other groups of businessmen, proved very obliging, and the publishers' association effectively 'co-ordinated' itself. Left-wing publications were suppressed and the properties of the KPD and the SPD party presses, including the buildings and machinery, were seised by the state and acquired by the NSDAP. (The value of the SPD publishing business alone has been estimated at over 100 million Reichsmarks.) Eher, the party publishing house, then began to acquire ownership of the remaining non-Nazi publications.[28]

Far-reaching control of the press had been established by the summer of 1934, and was consolidated by further measures later in the year. The Reich Editors' Law of 4 October officially excluded Jews, thereby formalising a de facto ban on the presence of Jewish journalists at press conferences, and imposed a degree of self-censorship on editors, albeit in rather vague terms. It also brought editors directly under the control of the Propaganda Ministry by a process of registration under the Auspices of the Reich Association of the German Press. Goebbels was empowered to remove editors from the register if he deemed it in the public interest.[29] A Reich Press Chamber was established in November 1933 under the leadership of Max Amann, the head of Eher Verlag, which regulated the press with and through the publishers' association, and began by forbidding the establishment of new newspapers or periodicals, provisionally for 3 months (13 December 1933). In the following months the independence of the remaining non-Nazi press was rapidly eroded, beginning in the spring of 1934 with the takeover of the Jewish-owned Ullstein publishing house, which published the prestigious liberal daily *Vossische Zeitung* and the popular Berlin paper *B-Z am Mittag*. Goebbels and Amann arranged to buy the firm, but the Ullsteins received only a fraction of the true value of their assets. Other individual newspapers were the targets of specific campaigns organised by local party branches. Control was further tightened with a series of decrees in 1935. One of these purported to clamp down on scandal and sensationalism in the press; another provided for the closing down of newspapers if it was felt there were so many newspapers that the competition was bad for business as a whole and a third, which purported to guarantee the independence of publishing, made it obligatory to disclose ownership of the press and required evidence of 'Aryan' ancestry. It also prohibited societies and organisations from ownership.[30] As a consequence both the overall number of newspapers and their combined circulation declined dramatically, and the proportion of the press owned, a more or less directly controlled by the party increased. In an extensive report on these developments in 1936, Sopade analysts calculated (on the basis of figures from newspaper catalogues) that 43 per cent of all newspapers published in 1932 had been lost by the end of 1935 and that despite the establishment of some new papers, there were still nearly a thousand fewer, including a hundred fewer in the Rhine province alone and 54 fewer in Berlin. It was also estimated that the average combined circulation had fallen by almost half between 1932 and 1935. The print run of the Nazi press in 1935 was given as 3,758,250, and that of the Völkischer Beobachter put at almost half a million. By 1944 fewer than a thousand newspapers remained, and over four-fifths of them were controlled by the party.[31] The effect on the quality of the German press was incalculable.

Supervised Leisure: Strength through Joy

The Ministry of Propaganda and Popular Enlightenment and the Reich Chamber of Culture managed to extend their authority over traditional cultural institutions and established cultural industries such as film and publishing, but many of the new developments in organised leisure remained largely outside their direct control. The most important institution in this new area was the German Labour Front's Strength through Joy (*Kraft durch Freude*) organisation, which was founded on 27 November 1933. It was inspired by the Italian Fascist organisation *Dopolavoro* (and was originally called *Nach der Arbeit* – both terms mean 'after work'). Its formation was announced in November 1933 by the Labour Front Leader Robert Ley, who stressed that work and leisure were not separate but complementary spheres. Strength through Joy was intended to structure the leisure time of the working public, not least in order to transform class warriors into fully integrated members of the national community.[32] The organisation was divided into a number of subordinate departments accordingly, dealing respectively with after-work activities, holidays and hiking, sports, working conditions (Beauty of Labour), and educational classes. Each of these departments was further sub-divided into separate sections. The *Feierabend* office, which was responsible for after-work activities, dealt with much of the routine cultural work handled by Strength through Joy. On the one hand this meant organising theatre tickets, concert bookings and trips to Bayreuth, and on the other it meant rebuilding a Nazified version of the working-class associational life that had been destroyed in 1933, by organising chess clubs, photography groups and the like, while at the same time trying to promote interests in folk culture through music and dancing groups. It also dealt with the special events in the Nazi calendar of festivals and anniversaries, such as May Day and harvest festival. The popular education section (*Volks-bildungswerk*) supplemented these entertainments with more edifying pursuits such as language and music courses and public lectures.[33] By the regime's own reckoning the number of participants in KdF cultural events – concerts, theatre, films and light entertainment – increased from just over 9 million in 1934 to over 54 million in 1938, and popular entertainment, cabaret and variety shows accounted for over a third of the total.

No less important was the KdF's programme of sports activities. Until the early twentieth century, sport had been associated with the leisured classes, who could afford both the time and the equipment, but it now began to emerge as a mass phenomenon as millions of ordinary people had enough free time to engage in sports as either participants or spectators. The KdF became a vehicle for the promotion of sport, an initiative which reinforced the regime's emphasis on the eugenic value of health, fitness and hygiene for the well-being of the race. In addition the training and discipline involved were seen as a preparation for military service. Twelve million people participated in KdF factory sports activities during 1938, the overwhelmingly majority of them men, and another 10 million or so, again mostly men, took part in a range of other sports activities. The propagandistic centrepiece of the regime's sports policy was the 1936 Olympics, which were held in Berlin. The decision had originally been taken to stage the 1936 Olympics in Germany before the Nazis came to power, and the party had been against the idea. Hitler and Goebbels had been persuaded of the propaganda value of the event, however, and once they won over no expense was spared in the preparation and although an American-led boycott was only narrowly avoided, the games opened in the new Olympic stadium on 1 August 1936 with all the disciplined festivity that was to come to characterise the games. The convergence of sporting and military purposes was epitomised here by the Olympic village, which was built by the Wehrmacht and later used as a barracks. Despite the Nazis' obvious discomfort at the success of black athletes, lip service was paid to the internationalism of the event with the inclusion of two German participants who were of partly Jewish extraction. Anti-Semitic activity, including the publication of *Der Stürmer*, was suspended for the duration of the games, but members of the Sinti and Roma minorities were removed from the streets. Strength through Joy built cheap accommodation in order to enable Germans to attend the games themselves.

Perhaps most dramatic in propaganda terms were the organisation's travel offers, and above all the foreign cruises. Strength through Joy effectively became the country's largest travel agency, accounting for a tenth of all travel and tourism in Germany. Most people took short excursions of one or two days, to Bavaria, Lake Constance or the Harz mountains, and these accounted for the overwhelming majority of trips – just over 2 million in 1934 and 6.8 million in 1938, according to the regime's own statistics. Longer trips, of three to fifteen days, were under-taken by rather fewer people – fewer than half a million in 1934 and 1.4 million in 1937. Mass tourism within Germany was held to be a force for the further integration of the nation; it was hoped that visiting other parts of the country – especially to the border regions – would help break down the strong regional particularism that was characteristic of Germany. It would also help stimulate the economy in depressed rural areas. Very few people were able to take advantage of the foreign holi-days, including the much-vaunted cruises to Madeira or Norway: 3000 visited the Canary Islands in 1935 and 8000 in 1936. An arrangement with *Dopolavoro* saw the number of trips to Italy double between 1937 and 1938, and more than double the following year.[34]

There were less successful projects too. Famously, none of the few much-vaunted people's cars (Volkswagen, but originally 'KdF-Wagen') that were produced were made available to the general public, justi-fying the scepticism that accompanied the widespread enthusiasm for the project – and even the sceptics recognised the potential: it would be half the cost of cars produced by other exporters, and Germany would be able to flood the emerging markets in eastern Europe, South America and Asia;[35] and even in the absence of the cars themselves the projected image of a nation on wheels, and the symbolic status of motorway construction remained for many Germans lasting positive images of the Third Reich.[36] On the whole Strength through Joy was one of the more successful Nazi organisations in its own terms, and contributed to the positive appeal of Nazism even among those for whom its entertainments remained a very rare treat and its pleasure cruises a distant promise. And perhaps this was not the point: both the liberal *Frankfurter Zeitung* and the Social Democrats reporting for the *Deutschland-Berichte* emphasised the large element of participation by amateurs and enthusiasts in the organisa- tion's popular 'educational' activities – 'dilettantes from all branches of the arts, amateur photographers, stamp-collectors, apprentices in graph- ology, model-makers etc.' – nothing was too complicated; and at the same time there were new courses in comparative art criticism according to racial criteria, racial hygiene and colonial policy.[37]

While many in the old guard fought ideological battles over culture, those with more technocratic inclinations had harnessed elements of popular culture, not necessarily towards modernising ends (if by that we understand modernity as rational and progressive, the creation of a free and open society based on genuine popular participation in politics), but certainly by employing modern techniques of management and manipulation.[38] Consumerism, albeit of a modified and circumscribed nature, was necessary in order to achieve a relatively consensual domestic stability, and was more effective than political browbeating: oppositional critics of the regime recognised that the particular efficacy of Strength through Joy was its ability to mobilise without compulsion. People could be forced to join organisations such as the Labour Front, compelled to work for nothing, even to part with 'voluntary' contributions to charity, but 'it is not possible to force people against their will to go to cinemas, operettas and variety shows, or to order them to undertake an excursion at their own cost.'[39]

Culture – in the broadest sense – was not only an important element in achieving domestic stability in the Third Reich, however, it was an important dimension of the way in which the Nazis understood them- selves and their objectives. For many policy-makers in the regime, *Kultur* had a clearly anthropological and ethnological meaning, and cultural issues were inextricable from racial issues. The nation consolidated at home could expand and absorb irredenta and their inhabitants, who could be Germanised or dispensed with. German culture would shape occupied Europe, and even the very landscape was to be re-modelled to accommodate German tastes and expectations.

Chapter 6: Consensus and Opposition in the Third Reich

Nazi Germany was not merely a police state: it was the police state against which police states have been measured, and the image of a society terrorised by fear of the Gestapo dominates popular understanding of the relationship between society and political authority in the Third Reich. That relationship was far more complex and ambiguous, however, as we now know. The Nazis did not rely on coercion alone to maintain order, but sought to win acclamation and even approval, relying on propaganda as much as censorship, and attempting – albeit unsuccessfully – to manufacture an inclusive consensus around the ideal of the 'national community'. This is not to diminish the extent to which the Nazis relied on terror, however: if the *Volksgemeinschaft* always remained a fond hope, the apparatus of the police state was a constant reality and threat.

The Political Police

The political role of the police was already well-established in central Europe in the nineteenth century, and although the political fragmentation of Germany held back the development of a centralised security police, forces were set up before 1848 whose remit extended beyond fighting crime to include political surveillance and dealing with threats to public order.[1] The centralisation of attempts to combat 'political criminality' began in Prussia in the second half of the nineteenth century under the auspices of the *Polizeipräsidium* in Berlin, and during the Weimar Republic Department I A of the Berlin Police Praesidium was the centre of domestic political intelligence gathering for Prussia (and informally for the Reich as a whole). Its role had already become explicitly partisan with the exclusion of 'republicans' in the wake of the Papen coup in Prussia of 20 July 1932, and Prussian police officials. From the summer of 1932 the infiltration of the political police by Nazis and Nazi sympathisers accelerated rapidly.[2]

With the appointment of Hitler to the chancellorship, responsibility for the Prussian police passed to the new Prussian interior minister, Hermann Göring, who lost no time in deploying the political police against the movement's enemies alongside 'auxiliaries' from the SA and SS. On 24 February a decree was issued establishing an independent criminal police office for Prussia. Four days later the Reichstag Fire Decree (Decree of the Reich President for the Protection of People and State) not only suspended civil liberties and allowed for the interception of mail and telephone calls, but from 3 March also allowed police to enter and search private premises, confiscate private property and detain 'suspects' in protective custody. This was one of the most dramatic and important developments in the early history of the Third Reich, enabling the regime to terrorise the opposition by recruiting SA, SS and *Stahlhelm* members into an auxiliary police force. The spring and summer of 1933 saw the establishment not only of 'legitimate' concentration camps for the left-wing political opponents of the new regime, but also of illicit or 'wild' concentration camps, where even the notional legalities of the emergent dictatorship were ignored, and where prisoners were beaten, tortured and murdered with impunity. The political police found it difficult in such circumstances to assert their own control and authority over the situation against the claims of the stormtroopers.

On 26 April the secret state police office (*Geheimes Staatspolizeiamt* or *Gestapa*) was established, and quickly became a vehicle for Göring's empire-building. Under the direction of Rudolf Diels, a civil-service lawyer, it quickly established an organisational network across the whole of Prussia, based on state police offices (*Staatspolizeistellen*) at local level, but dependent on the local political authorities, the *Regierungspräsidenten* in the Prussian provinces (*Provinzen*), to take any action. This situation was transformed in the autumn by Göring's response to an attempt by Reich Interior Minister Wilhelm Frick to absorb the police forces of the *Länder* in a Reich police force. Instead the Gestapo law of 30 November 1933 created the Gestapo as a quasi-autonomous agency, making the '*Stapostellen*' in the provinces independent of either the local police and political authorities or the Prussian interior ministry. Instead they were directly responsible, through Diels, to Göring as Prussian minister president (since 11 April). This was an important step in centralising the political police in Germany, but it did not mean that the struggle for control was resolved: it now shifted its focus.

Göring's next antagonist in the battle for control of the police was Heinrich Himmler, Reich leader of the SS since 1929. In March 1933, Himmler was appointed provisional president of the Munich police, which already had its own political section (Department VI). In April he became 'political police commander of Bavaria', a role in which he was directly accountable to the Bavarian interior ministry, and this meant that a Bavarian Political Police, independent of the jurisdiction of the Munich police headquarters, was established more quickly than in Prussia. Himmler also assumed responsibility for the concentration camp at Dachau. Himmler's position meant that there were close links in Bavaria between the police and the SS. Reinhard Heydrich, head of the SS counter-intelligence service (SD), was also head of the political police in Bavaria. Between the autumn of 1933 and the spring of 1934 Himmler and Heydrich had managed to assume control of the political police in all the German states except Prussia. But in April 1934 Himmler was appointed deputy chief and inspector of the Prussian Gestapo (in place of Diels, who was 'promoted' to a local government post in Cologne), while Heydrich became director of the Gestapo office. Himmler's hand was further strengthened by the role of the SS in the suppression of the stormtroopers, and despite Göring's attempts to retain even nominal control of the Gestapo (as minister president in Prussia), he had effectively conceded authority to Himmler by the end of 1934.

This resolved the major conflict for control of the country's police forces, but other frictions continued between Himmler's emergent SS-Gestapo police apparatus and Frick's interior ministry. Again the wrangling was settled in Himmler's favour. A new Prussian Gestapo Law was enacted in February 1936, and although it seemed to subordinate local police offices (*Stapostellen*) to the local political authorities, it also gave ultimate authority over the *Stapostellen* to the Gestapo office in Berlin. In addition Himmler was appointed head of the German police in June 1936. His formal accountability to Frick was now meaningless in practice, and all Germany's police forces were effectively now subject to Himmler's control.[3] This was a turning point, at once the culmination of the struggle for control of Germany's police forces, and the beginning of the closer integration of police and SS as a force independent of state authority which could be used for direct intervention as an instrument of Führer power. Himmler immediately merged the Gestapo and the criminal police (*Kripo*) in a new security police force (*Sipo*) (26 June 1936) under the command of Heydrich, who also remained head of the SD.

Given the organisational integration of the Gestapo and the SD, and the similarities between their operational tasks, some clarification was needed of the roles of the two organisations in domestic policing. The SD had been created in 1931 as an intelligence service within the SS, responsible for surveillance of the political enemies of the NSDAP. It also gathered intelligence on oppositional activity within the party. In the summer of 1934 Himmler designated the SD, the party's sole intelligence agency, responsible for investigation of the regime's political enemies, and an extensive network of SD agents reported regularly on the impact of government policy and eventually on popular morale in general, in the manner of the 'reports from the Reich' that were circulated internally among the regime's institutions and personnel. Practical measures against the regime's enemies were the responsibility of the Gestapo. The SD also had a foreign intelligence network independent of that of the military. As resistance to the regime receded during the late 1930s, the SD concentrated more on systematic research. Historical studies were undertaken and the confiscated libraries of Masonic lodges and Jewish organisations were examined for the purposes of research. Alongside courses on oppositional groups such as the churches, freemasons and Jewish organisations, in 1936 trainees at the SD school in Bernau were instructed to look at the press and analyse economic developments.[4] The SD was effectively an intelligence service for the Gestapo, and later for the Sipo.

The Gestapo's role was more practical: its officers made the arrests, and concentrated largely on specific oppositional groups – clandestine resistance organisations such as the cells of the underground Communist Party or forbidden religious organisations; dealt with opposition and dissent of a less organised kind, such as outbursts against the regime and its policies and other forms of non-conformity, and with failure to comply with specific prohibitions that were introduced or extended by the Nazis, ranging from abortion and homosexuality to spreading rumours, listening to foreign radio stations and handling forbidden publications. Although the Gestapo was perceived as ubiquitous, it actually had a very small staff. In 1934 the Gestapo office in Berlin had 645 staff, and all the 33 regional offices together had 1025 officials. The administrative district (*Regierungsbezirk*) Düsseldorf (one of the best documented Gestapo offices) had a population approaching 4 million and encompassed a broad swathe of the industrial Rhineland, including several of the industrial cities of the Ruhr. The predominantly Roman Catholic Rhine Province, of which it formed a part, had returned some of the lowest Nazi votes in Germany, and in the last provincial elections in 1933 the Communist Party had outstripped the SPD. In short this was relatively hostile territory for the Nazis. Nevertheless, in 1937 the local Gestapo office had only 291 staff, over half of them (126) in the city of Düsseldorf itself: Essen and Wuppertal, with populations of over 650,000 and over 400,000 respectively, had 43 officers each, Duisburg 28 and Oberhausen 14. The number of Gestapo employees was similar in other cities: Hanover, an administrative district with a population of over 800,000, employed 42 people in 1935, the majority of whom had been employed there and involved in the surveillance of left-wing groups since before 1933.[5] There were only 32,000 officers across the Reich in 1944.

How did the police state function with such a small staff? How did it manage to convey the impression of a pervasive police presence? Recent research has suggested that the police state was based on popular consensus to a greater degree than had been assumed. Nazi propaganda worked because it built on popular opinion rather than working against it. The concept of the 'national community' was founded on strict social, racial and political criteria for inclusion, but ones which nevertheless embraced the overwhelming majority of Germans. The regime exploited popular prejudices against social outsiders and anxiety about crime and social non-conformity, building on a decade of scare-mongering in the right-wing press about the criminality, sexual depravity and political subversion encouraged by the lax moral standards of the Weimar Republic. Moreover the punishments meted out to the regime's victims were regularly reported in the press as a deterrent to other potential miscreants. Whether they met with horror, approval or indifference, it seems beyond doubt that the brutal and repressive measures taken by the regime against its opponents were well known. Dictatorship does not work by coercion alone, and the Nazi regime set out to build a consensus among this majority of 'national comrades' for a social cleansing of Germany. (Although racial anti-Semitism was central to the Nazis' own preoccupations, it has been argued, it was played down initially because it did not find a similar resonance among the general public.)

In practical terms this meant that for many kinds of 'misdemeanours' the Gestapo relied as much on denunciations of suspicious behaviour of individuals from the general public as on its own network of agents.[6] The extent of this complicity is debatable, however; and in any case the police did not merely react to all denunciations, as many of them were so clearly motivated by revenge or personal animus that it would have been pointless to do so. Nazi Germany was unambiguously a police state, and the Gestapo acted on their own initiative, relying on existing information about known criminals and political activists, and information from within the police service or the broader Nazi movement. This was supplemented by information from searches, police raids and confessions. The behaviour of some victims made their job easier. Communists persisted in disseminating propaganda that was easily traced, and building and rebuilding networks of underground cells that were easily infiltrated. Jehovah's witnesses were quite open about what they were doing, and posed no problem of detection. For their part, Gestapo officers left most Germans in relative peace, despite their minor political peccadilloes, and concentrated on clearly defined oppositional groups, along with racial or social outsiders. Most of the Germans who worked towards this consensus did so by compliance and self-censorship rather than active collaboration.[7]

The Reich Security Head Office (RSHA)

One of the most important aspects of the development of a police state in Germany was the centralisation of political control of the police. On 20 September 1936 the country's separate regional police forces were brought together for the first time in German history and, finally, after the outbreak of war in September 1939 the Sipo and SD were merged, under Heydrich's continuing leadership to form the Reich Security Head Office (*Reichssicherheitshauptamt*, RSHA). This measure came into effect from 1 October 1939, and fused together state and party within a single organisation: The RSHA was both an office within the interior ministry and one of the principal offices of the SS. The SD continued to be financed by the NSDAP, and its personnel remained private employees (*Angestellten*) of the party, while the Gestapo and Kripo retained some of their identity and functions as departments of the state, and their staff remained public officials (*Beamte*). In practice there was good deal of cross-over, and state officials and party employees often worked in the same office. Similarly, party employees were appointed to positions in state departments, as in the famous case of Eichmann. Following the assassination of Heydrich in 1942 the new head of the RSHA was Ernst Kaltenbrunner. The son of an Austrian lawyer, Kaltenbrunner had studied law himself at Graz University, and joined the Nazi Party in 1932. He had organised the Gestapo in Austria after the German invasion, and was involved in the setting up of the concentration camp at Mauthausen near Linz. He then took over the SS in Vienna in 1939, and was appointed Heydrich's successor on 30 January 1943.[8]

All the offices of the RSHA were involved in some way or another with aspects of the state terror used by the Nazis against their victims.

Office (*Amt*) I, which dealt with personnel matters, was responsible for
the preparations for the deployment of the special units (*Einsatzgruppen*)
in Poland and the Soviet Union. Office II dealt with organisational,
administrative and legal matters, including the provision of resources for
specific objectives, such as the transport of Soviet POWs to Auschwitz,
and the development of gas vans to murder Jews at Chelmno. Office
III was responsible for domestic intelligence, and it was here that the
'reports from the Reich' (*Meldungen aus dem Reich*) were written, based
on local intelligence from all over Germany. Office III also involved in
the regime's Germanisation policies in the East. Office IV was responsible
for the taking into 'protective custody' and incarceration in concentration camps of the regime's political opponents. It was in Section IVB 4
that the mass murder of European Jews was organised. Office V was the
old head office of the criminal police, and remained largely unaltered.
Nevertheless it was involved with the incarceration of habitual criminals,
'asocials' and homosexuals in concentration camps, and the imprisonment of members of oppositional youth groups. It also oversaw the
criminological institutes which specialised in technology and biology,
including the development of poisoned ammunition. Office VI was
responsible for foreign intelligence, which meant that it also provided
lists of those to be imprisoned by special units following the invasion of
enemy territory. Office VII had taken over the more academic interests
of the SD, and was involved in the plundering of cultural objects from
Jewish organisations and Masonic lodges in the occupied territories.
Together, these RSHA offices constituted the central bureaucracy of the
SS state.

The SS

The SS itself had its organisational origins in 'guard units' (*Schutzstaffeln*)
that were originally a part of the SA, and were established in the 1920s
to protect leading Nazis. They were under Hitler's direct command and
functioned as guards for meetings and as bodyguards for leading party
personnel. Under Himmler (Reich Leader of the SS from 1929) the
organization grew rapidly from a membership of 280 in 1929 to some
240,000 a decade later. Nevertheless it remained an exclusive order,
with strict rules for admission based on racial origin and political reliab-
ility. It was intended to constitute the kernel of a 'new aristocracy' for
a German-dominated racial new order in Europe, and its ideology and
self-image drew extensively on the idea of the Teutonic 'orders', but also

suggested comparisons with other elite organisations, such as the Jesuits or the Japanese Samurai. Although Himmler's ambition for the SS was to provide a new ruling class for Germany and Europe, its values frequently tended to be expressed in terms of conventional middle-class masculine virtues: discipline, comradeship, loyalty, achievement and even chivalry. These values reflected those of traditional – and traditionally authoritarian – Prussian institutions, above all the army and the bureaucracy, and they were directed towards Nazi objectives through their subordination to the over-arching principle of obedience to authority.

Despite these influences the SS differed from traditional instruments of authority. Unlike the armed forces, the civil service or the churches it was outside the control of the state and its laws; its loyalty was not to 'normal' state authority but to the 'exceptional' authority of the leader ('*Führergewalt*') which was held to transcend 'conventional' legality, and thereby provided a sanction for the routinely criminal acts of the SS. To this extent the ethos of the organisation was anti-bourgeois. Its ideology had revolutionary implications: it dictated that membership of the racial community created an imperative to dominate, and one which was also unchecked by Christian morality. Himmler was resolutely hostile towards the churches, and tried to encourage a culture of neo-paganism that was organised around pre-Christian festivals for the changing seasons, but one which both drew on Christian liturgy and made reference to faith in a supreme being, thereby providing a reasonably familiar framework of belief for the middle-class youths recruited to his 'order'. This was supplemented by a re-interpretation of history in which the role of the individual was subordinate to the racial community and its leaders.[9]

The rise of the SS to the level of a 'state within a state' has been attributed to its ability as an organisation to seize opportunities at times of general crisis for the regime.[10] Its first decisive intervention as an instrument of coercion was during the Röhm purge of 1934, and it subsequently became the most powerful affiliated organization of the NSDAP, gradually, under Himmler, establishing its authority over the state police forces as we have seen, until it formed the basis of a police state. It exploited the political shifts within the regime during the late 1930s to expand its influence in relation to the armed forces and the foreign office on the eve of war, and the war itself provided further opportunities in occupied Europe. Task forces (*Einsatzgruppen*) of the Security Police (Sipo) and the Security Service (SD), at this point still legally subordinate to the armed forces, were deployed during the Polish campaign for 'special duties', euphemistically described as the suppression of elements hostile to the

Reich. In practice this meant the systematic mass murder, on Hitler's orders, of the Polish elites, but the task forces and members of the armed forces were involved in atrocities against the Jews, including the systematic mass shootings of Jews from 1939 within the context of Heydrich's implementation of a 'Jewish policy' in Poland. The task forces were also deployed behind German lines during the invasion of the Soviet Union in 1941, this time independently of the armed forces.[11] The war zone in the east never developed into the 'living space' envisaged in Nazi ideology, but it did provide a vast laboratory for the implementation of SS racial policies. Even as the tide of the war turned against Germany, the SS managed to consolidate its position, and Himmler's appointment as interior minister (25 August 1943) opened new avenues at the centre of power in the Reich itself.

The SS was not one straightforward organisation, but a complex of related agencies that exemplified the manner in which Nazi institutions proliferated for the purposes of self-aggrandisement, staking claims to the political territory of Reich ministries and rival party organisations. At the centre of its operations, as we have seen, was the RSHA which brought together the state police forces and the internal party intelligence service founded by Himmler in 1931, later the *Sicherheitsdienst* (Security Service, SD). The SS guards who had formed Hitler's bodyguard expanded to become the special duty troops that would form the basis of the *Waffen-SS*. Some were designated special guard groups for concentration camps, the Deaths-Head units. By 1939 there were about 9000 of these, and they too were incorporated into the Waffen-SS, and replaced by men of the general SS. In addition there were a number of departments that reflected the particular goals of the SS as a distinct organisation within the regime. Among these was the Race and Settlement Head Office (*Rasse- und Siedlungs-Hauptamt*, RuSHA), headed by Walther Darré. This office was responsible for the racial purity and 'nordification' (*Aufnordung*) of the Germans, but in practice this meant establishing the racial credentials of SS men and their prospective wives, a policy which became increasingly impractical during the war. It was also responsible for the settlement of newly conquered living space in the east, which meant in practice the eviction of local people and their replacement by SS men and their families. The Reich Commissioner's Office for the Strengthening of Germandom (*Reichskommissariat für die Festigung des deutschen Volkstums*, RKFdV) dealt with the resettling of ethnic Germans in the Reich and the occupied territories on a much larger scale.[12] The Economic and Administrative Head Office (*Wirtschafts- und Verwaltungshauptamt*, WVHA) was formed in 1942 under the leadership of Oswald Pohl. It was responsible for running the concentration camps and managing the internal economy of the SS, including the economic administration of the death camps.

The Concentration Camp System

The SS was responsible for running the concentration camps set up outside major German cities for the internment of the regime's political opponents in 1933. The first was set up in Bavaria, in March 1933, to cope with the increase in numbers of political prisoners following the appointment of Adolf Wagner as *Gauleiter* of Upper Bavaria on 9 March. Wagner wanted to establish special quarters, separate from those of the police and judicial system, for political opponents detained under the 'special custody' regulations, and a disused gunpowder factory outside Dachau, near Munich, was used for the purpose. The justice ministry welcomed this development as a solution to the over-crowding of conventional prisons during the state terror that accompanied the establishment of the new regime. The majority of the first wave of political prisoners had been Communists, but increasingly during the spring and summer Social Democrats, trades unionists, Jewish intellectuals and political leaders of the bourgeois parties also found themselves in the concentration camps that had now been set up around the country. By the end of July there were 26,789 people incarcerated in 'protective custody' according to the interior ministry's own reckoning.[13] The mistreatment, torture and murder of inmates was routine in concentration camps; they stood outside normal legal jurisdictions, and were an important constituent in the development of a parallel 'exceptional' state outside the rule of law.[14] Nevertheless they had been established by agencies of the new state and were regulated to some extent; the so-called 'wild' concentration camps, erected on their own initiative by rank-and-file Nazis, were subject to no regulation and stood entirely outside the law. These were sites of unlicensed brutality and murder, and although the uncontrolled behaviour of the perpetrators brought them into conflict with the police, they nevertheless went unpunished: on 25 July the Prussian justice minister ordered all charges against stormtroopers and SS men incurred as a result of their dealings with political opponents to be dropped. On 2 August Prussia disbanded its auxiliary SA police force.

The concentration camp system survived the 'national revolution', however, and became institutionalised. Revised protective custody regulations issued by the Reich interior ministry in April 1933 provided a framework for an institutionalised system of camps based on the 'Dachau

model'. Dachau had originally been like one of the 'wild' camps: there
was widespread mistreatment of prisoners and a number of murders.
This arbitrariness was superseded in May 1933 following the intervention
of the public prosecutor in Munich, and although the terms and regulations introduced were draconian in the extreme, they at least constituted
some attempt by Himmler to regulate the camp. More permanent camps
were set up on the Dachau model during the 1930s: Sachsenhausen in
1936, Buchenwald in 1937 and Neuengamme in 1938. In May 1939 a
concentration camp for women was opened at Ravensbrück to the north
of Berlin. The first group of about a thousand prisoners were mainly
Jehovah's Witnesses and Sinti and Roma women. During the war Polish
and Soviet women were also imprisoned there, including prisoners of
war. Around each of these in turn was a further network of subsidiary
camps. From about 1938 there were important changes to the function of
the camps. They ceased to be used more or less exclusively as internment
centres for the political opponents of the regime, and came to be seen as
a potential economic resource for the SS. After the annexation of Austria
in March 1938 plans were immediately made for a new camp outside Linz,
close to granite quarries which were then bought by the SS-owned quar-
rying company Deutsche Erd- und Steinwerke (DESt), with the intention
of using camp labour to extract stone for the rebuilding of Berlin. The
company already had brickworks near Sachsenhausen and Buchenwald.
A new camp was also established near Flossenbürg in the Palatinate, and
DESt began to quarry granite here too during the summer. The exploit-
ation of labour from concentration camps quickly became an important
contributor to the war economy.[15]

In 1938 too, changes were made to the procedures for protective
custody, extending its definition to include non-political opponents of
the regime, and restricting the authority to issue custody orders to the
Gestapo office in Berlin. (Regional government and police authorities
had hitherto also been able to issue such orders.) Finally, protective
custody was to be used to cover long-term imprisonment in concentration camps. 'Protective custody' had become a means of imprisoning
those whom the regime sought to persecute, but could not prosecute
under existing law. Communists who had served gaol sentences, for
example, were frequently transferred to a concentration camp rather
than being released. Alongside the political prisoners at Sachsenhausen
there were increasing numbers of so-called 'asocials': habitual criminals,
homosexuals, gypsies, the homeless, alcoholics, prostitutes, pimps, and
'the work-shy'; some 10 thousand 'asocials' were arrested and interned
in concentration camps during the 'work-shy campaign' of June 1938,

over half of them at Sachsenhausen. The criteria for 'asocial' behaviour were arbitrary and overlapping, but these were all groups of people who 'did not, could not, or would not perform their duties to the *Volksgemeinschaft*' – who were not only targets for persecution by the regime, but often unpopular too with the communities in which they lived. Nazi policy towards such 'anti-social elements' in the community reflected rather than led popular opinion. (These were also categories of victims for whom there was relatively little sympathy *after* 1945.)[16] The persecution of Jehovah's Witnesses also increased in the mid-1930s, particularly after 1935 when young members were imprisoned for refusing to serve in the armed forces because they were pacifists. From 1937 Jehovah's Witnesses serving prison sentences (often for trivial offences such as refusing the Hitler salute) were transferred to concentration camps when their sentences were up.[17] The number of prisoners from all categories increased following the annexation of Austria and the Sudetenland, and in November 1938 some 35,000 Jews were arrested in the immediate wake of the pogrom, and the number of prisoners more than doubled within a few days from 24,000 to 60,000. Many Jews were subsequently released, provided that they were able to emigrate, and the numbers in the largest camps declined again, but the episode demonstrated the way in which the regime was creating a Jewish 'problem' that would lead to mass deportations to the death camps in Poland.

The outbreak of the war brought further changes to the 'protective custody' system. New offences were created, within the provisions of the War Economy Decree, for example, and as a consequence of special measures related to broadcasting, sabotage and behaviour likely to undermine morale. Most importantly, legal and judicial procedures were changed to extend the jurisdiction of the 'special courts' (*Sondergerichte*), of which there were 55 by the beginning of the war, and they now encroached more and more on the business of the regular courts. Measures were taken to speed up court procedure (at the expense of the defence), sentences were more severe and there were more death penalties, including an increasing number of opponents of the regime who were 'executed' without recourse to legal procedure at all. The concentration camp system also grew dramatically: 22 new camps (with additional associated satellite camps) were built between 1939 and 1944. Although the number of camp inmates quadrupled during the first half of the war (from 25,000 to 100,000), the growth of the system remained relatively slow until the camps were subordinated to Oswald Pohl's WVHA in 1942.

New camps had been set up in the occupied territories since the beginning of the war, including a 'transit camp' for 10,000 prisoners at

Auschwitz as a solution for the overcrowding of local prisons following the arrest of large numbers of Poles by the Security Police. It became the main concentration camp for the occupied Polish territories, and various categories of prisoners, mainly Polish, but also German, were imprisoned there. Plans for expansion began in earnest in 1941 following a visit from Himmler in the company of senior managers from IG Farben, who wanted to establish a subsidiary there, a major industrial enterprise that was to be built by Soviet prisoners following the invasion of the USSR. The main camp was able to accommodate 18,000 prisoners by the end of 1941 and 30,000 by 1943.[18] Eventually the camp consisted of three sections: Auschwitz I, the main camp, Auschwitz II (Birkenau) and Auschwitz III (Monowitz), the IG-Farben slave-labour camp, also known as Buna. Rudolf Höss, formerly commandant of Sachsenhausen, was placed in command. Construction of the Birkenau camp began in October 1941, and was accelerated when the main camp became congested with the arrival of Soviet POWs. The building work, overseen by Karl Bischoff, resulted in high mortality rates among the Soviet prisoners, and with the faltering of the Russian campaign, the survivors were redeployed in the German arms industries. Instead the camp became an extermination camp for Jews, under the command of Josef Kramer. It comprised 300 prison barracks, four gas chambers along with storage cellars for corpses and crematoria. Some 1,600,000 people were murdered at Auschwitz, of which it is believed around 300,000 were non-Jewish victims. Other death camps were built across Poland, at Chełmno, Belzec, Sobibor, Treblinka and Majdanek, but more than any other site Auschwitz has come to symbolise the singular criminality of the holocaust.

By the middle of the war, Himmler's SS empire had acquired such enormous power within the Nazi political system that it was outside the jurisdiction of either state or party. It controlled the police state within Germany, and was able to operate relatively free of constraints in the occupied territories – a freedom that was used to force the implement-ation of a racial new order that resulted in the murder of millions of Jews. In addition the SS organisation had a bureaucracy which paralleled that of the state, the camp system developed its own economy, based on slave labour, and the Waffen-SS had effectively broken the monopoly of the armed forces and was in a position to challenge their authority. It developed a quasi-autonomous existence within the Third Reich, which gave the impression that it was a 'state within a state'. It was not at home in Germany but in the occupied territories, however, and above all in eastern Europe, that the most extreme excesses of the embryonic SS state occurred, where legal and political constraints were weaker or absent than in the Reich. More radical attitudes and practices were exported back to the Reich – a foretaste, arguably, of what might be to come in the event of a German victory.

Resistance

The development of the police state did not go unchallenged by the regime's opponents. Resistance to the creeping authoritarianism afflicting Germany in the early 1930s had begun to take shape even before Hitler was appointed chancellor, and the first and most obvious organised resistance on any significant scale came from the left. Illegal political organisations and resistance groups sprang up fairly quickly after the Nazis came to power, and there was a tendency to believe that the regime would be short-lived. Fritz Henssler, a Dortmund Social Democrat, forecast that the Nazis would remain in power only a few weeks, and that the party would be able to continue working, albeit illegally, within the same institutional framework.[19] His attitude reflected a degree of self-deception among the opposition generally, and there was a fond belief among many 'politically schooled' workers that the regime could be ousted in a matter of weeks by a short all-out battle on the streets. They were more prepared for such a confrontation than for clandestine resistance, and as a result many early resistance groups were easily detected by the Gestapo, and most of the opposition from the left had been stamped out by 1936.

The Communist Party had been planning for the possibility of a Nazi government since the end of 1932 and aimed to replace party cells with small groups of five members (*Fünfergruppen*) who worked in isolation and would be less easily detected by the authorities. The imprisonment of thousands of Communists in the wake of the Reichstag fire – 1500 in Berlin alone – meant that the transition to illegal work did not go as smoothly as planned. In the absence of leading functionaries the rank and file was initially disorientated, but with some 300,000 members the KPD had become the country's third largest political party and recovered sufficiently to maintain a coherent existence. But although the KPD was numerically by far the most significant resistance movement the Nazis confronted, it was caught in a contradiction: the main objective was to demonstrate to its constituency that the party had survived, by collecting contributions and organising the distribution of propaganda – but both of these activities exposed members to easy detection by the police. Any run of Gestapo case logs (*Tagesberichte*) clearly demonstrates that

Communist opposition was the main preoccupation of the secret police: the organisation was infiltrated with relative ease, and its members were arrested and imprisoned. Finally, the party was also ill served by the strategy dictated to it by the Comintern. Moscow believed that the Nazi regime was unstable and could not last, and party leaders continued to speak of an 'incipient crisis of German fascism', throughout 1933 and 1934, with apparently little sense of the extent to which the regime was consolidating its position. From the perspective of the Comintern there was no need for the KPD either to correct its strategy or to make its peace with the 'social fascists' of the SPD. This policy was modified quite radically at the seventh world congress of the Comintern in Moscow in July 1935, which declared its support for the 'popular front' solidarity that had recently characterised anti-fascist demonstrations in France.[20] The membership gradually drained away as political and economic circumstances changed, and as the supply of willing activists dried up. The final blow for many of those who remained loyal throughout the 1930s was the Hitler–Stalin pact: 'The Communists feel betrayed, and during discussions on the shop floor they frequently make the point that the Hitler–Stalin agreement is a dreadful disappointment for them'.[21]

The Social Democrats had longer to come to terms with the new situation than the Communists, and long after the KPD had been suppressed. Otto Wels, the SPD leader in the Reichstag, spoke against Hitler's Enabling Law on behalf of the only remaining opposition party. The speech was a courageous one, given the threats of violence from Nazi members, and clearly a moving one for the Social democrats themselves: one party member recalled it as 'a valediction to the principles of humanity'. Even so, some party leaders persisted in trying to negotiate a legal opposition to the government, concentrating on attempts to lift the prohibitions against party publications.[22] All this changed with the events of 2 May. After the attacks on party and trades union offices most of the leaders who had not already done so fled abroad, in the first instance to Saarbrücken, and then on to Prague, where a leadership in exile was established: the Sopade. The majority of the SPD activists withdrew from politics and adopted a cautious approach to resistance; mindful of the weakness of the labour movement after several years of mass unemployment, they were realistic about the personal danger that open confrontation with the new regime would mean for its supporters and their families. At the same time it was made clear that everything possible should be done to maintain communal solidarity and political contacts within working-class communities. In some instances well-placed Social Democrats could score minor victories against the Nazis. The

Germania bakery in Duisburg, for example, was owned by a Social Democrat who sacked all the Nazis in the workforce for 'poor performance', and concealed for over a year a network of illegal SPD activists that extended as far as Mönchengladbach and Düsseldorf, and which was led by one of his bread-delivery men, Hermann Runge. The group was denounced to the Gestapo by a minor Nazi in Moers and the first arrests were made in June 1935. During the course of 18 months of beatings and interrogations the whole network was wound up, and the conspirators were sentenced in 1936: Runge was sentenced to 9 years penal servitude and 17 others to prison terms between 2 and 8 years.

Conflict between regime and oppositional groups during the first years of the Third Reich was generated as much by the Nazis' own drive to eradicate its political rivals, particularly on the left, as by any spontaneous resistance. Communists and Social Democrats resisted not only because they were more fundamentally opposed to the principles and objectives of the new regime, but also because they were its first political victims. They were not the only political activists who were excluded and marginalised, however, and there was opposition of one kind or another from across the political spectrum. Compromises, concordats and coalitions notwithstanding, the establishment of the Nazi regime represented a disaster for many Catholics, liberals and conservatives, including some of those who had been dissatisfied with the Weimar republic or worked towards a new authoritarian political settlement. It was some time, however, before any significant opposition emerged among people within the country's political class, although the establishment of the 'confessing church' in 1934 was a striking example of the way in which the nazification of German institutions could be effectively blocked if there was sufficient political will. In the spring of 1934, some conservatives still clearly thought it was possible to express criticism of the regime from within. In a speech at Marburg on 17 June – written by the 'conservative revolutionary' Edgar Jung – Franz von Papen quarrelled openly with the Nazis. (The speech was banned, Jung was shot and Papen was sent to Vienna.)[23] Similarly the purge of the SA at the end of June was prompted by concerns in the armed forces. Despite concerns and differences of emphasis the country's elites remained generally sympathetic to the regime throughout the 1930s, and in most cases beyond. It was only with the sharp radicalisation of policy in 1938 that the first stirrings of fundamental opposition began to emerge.

Several strands of resistance to the regime now began to emerge very clearly. For the most part, senior members of the armed forces were only too enthusiastic about rearmament, revisionism and the restoration of

German greatness. Eventually, however, the breakneck speed of preparations for war, combined with Hitler's nerve-rackingly risky foreign
policy, began to prompt some concern among senior military personnel.
Military resistance crystallised for the first time following the dismissal
of Blomberg and Fritsch in 1938, and the forced resignation of General
Beck following his reservations about Hitler's foreign policy strategy.
Generals Beck, Halder and Witzleben, in collaboration with Admiral
Canaris and his chief of staff, Hans Oster, began to plan for the even-
tuality of a military coup as a means of restraining Hitler. Their plans
were scotched by the Munich Agreement and the appeasement policy
of Neville Chamberlain (dubbed 'J'aime Berlin' among oppositional
circles). Although further conspiracies would have been unrealistic in
the context of national euphoria and popular acclaim for Hitler that
followed the victories in Poland, the West and the Balkans over the next
3 years, an 'emergent' military resistance to Hitler is discernible among
those who opposed Hitler.[24]

The centrepiece of German resistance came much later, at a time
when the Reich's military misfortunes – at Stalingrad, in Africa, in Italy
and finally in France – had given a far wider circle pause for thought
about the future. It culminated in the failure of the 1944 bomb plot,
an attempt to assassinate Hitler at his East Prussian headquarters (the
'Wolf's Lair) in July 1944. The leader of the conspiracy, Claus Schenk,
Graf von Stauffenberg, was a member of one of Germany's oldest aristocratic families, and his fellow conspirators were for the most part arch-
conservatives who had worked with the regime for much of its duration,
and whose vision for a post-Nazi Germany made few concessions to liberal
democracy, and even fewer to the frontiers of 1937.[25] The plotters were
in contact with broader resistance circles, including a nominal handful
from the political left, but there was little sense of any need for popular
support, which was taken for granted among some of the conspirators,
or of a realistic assessment of Germany's present position. Certainly the
Allies were unconvinced that it was worthwhile or appropriate to support
the coup, or indeed any internal attempt to change the political system
at this stage in the war.[26] In the event, of course, the bomb failed to
explode with sufficient force and the planned putsch in Berlin was also
easily suppressed. The chief conspirators were shot immediately, and
there followed some fifty trials in the *Volksgerichtshof*, and over a hundred
death sentences were passed. Hundreds more were arrested in the immediate aftermath of the failed coup including, eventually, the extended
families of the conspirators. Hitler and Himmler also acted against other
potential sources of opposition, and all prominent politicians from the

Weimar Republic were now arrested, including former Reichstag deputies belonging to the Communist Party, SPD and Centre Party, although many were subsequently released. Other trials, against the Kreisau circle and the group around Klaus Bonhoeffer, went on into 1945. The regime had survived, but was shaken by the attempted coup, as was Hitler personally.[27]

Resistance in Nazi Germany needs to be seen in the context of a broader understanding of the relation between regime and society. Attitudes to the regime and its policies were not entirely clear-cut, even among its staunchest supporters or those who came to be its most resolute opponents and organised resistance with the clear political intention of otherthrowing, undermining or damaging the regime. Although only a tiny minority were involved in active resistance, it seems that opposition to the Nazis occurred on a number of levels ranging from industrial sabotage in factories and on farms, to small principled acts of defiance, such as refusing the Hitler salute, and many of these acts were both intentional and political. Popular opposition was often a temporary and limited response to specific policies. Small businessmen and farmers, for example, were often vituperative about details of economic policy, especially where the state attempted to restrict or control their activity, but were among the most vociferous supporters of other aspects of government policy. Attitudes were selective, temporary and shifting. Some groups, arguably, preserved a higher degree of immunity (*Resistenz*) to the regime and its ideology, but the responses of individuals shifted with events and developments. As often as not, people were defending their individual or collective self-interests; but frequently such opposition was on a point of principle.[28]

The existence of such popular opposition or resistance from below long remained unacknowledged, and as a historiography of resistance to Nazism within Germany emerged it came to be dominated by accounts that emphasised the role of institutions and influential or articulate social groups, such as 'the military, church and bourgeois youth' as Detlev Peukert observed in 1979.[29] East German historians on the other hand emphasised working-class resistance, but only in relation to the leadership of the Communist Party. Since then our understanding of conformity and opposition, resistance and collaboration has been transformed, as historians have taken into account the importance of mobilisation, acclamation and the manufacture of consensus as important elements in the political strategies of modern dictatorships.

Chapter 7: Reproduction, the Family and Racial Hygiene

Racism was the fundamental guiding principle of Nazi ideology, and the effects of racial ideology on policy-making were pervasive. The focus of the regime's obsessive racism was the relentless persecution of the country's Jewish population, which culminated in the mass murder of European Jews; but the regime was also preoccupied with the improvement of the German race itself, and it was a preoccupation that underpinned its approach to the whole spectrum of Nazi policy from culture, education and health policies to the conduct of war. The nation itself was defined in racial terms, and its destiny was held to be dependent on good racial health, and that in turn required high standards of 'racial hygiene': only the fittest would survive and prevail.

This essentially biological vision of social well-being had a particularly profound effect on the way the regime thought about gender: the nature of masculinity and femininity, and the respective roles of men and women both in the household and in society. The Nazis went some way towards endorsing traditional gender roles: in the party's propaganda, from the early days to the end of the war, women were routinely presented as mothers, housewives and carers, whose sphere of activity is in the home, while men confront the wider world in the workplace, in public affairs and, ultimately, on the battlefield. Yet the Nazis' apparent conservatism was qualified by an insistence on the state's right to intervene on behalf of the interests of the race. Nazi population policy encouraged large families if the parents were 'Aryan' and considered capable and free of hereditary diseases or other forms of debility. The births of 'worthless' children were prevented by compulsory sterilisation and abortion. Miscegenation – marriage or sexual intercourse with partners from races considered inferior – was discouraged and then prohibited, and severe penalties were introduced for homosexuality. The German people – the 'racial body' – was to be purified and regenerated within a few generations by means of policies to evaluate the relative worth of individuals, rooting out the bad or 'diseased' elements and promote the healthy; and the resources of the bureaucracy, the police and judicial systems, social policy and health services would be directed to this objective: the improvement of the race from within ('*Aufartung*').[1]

Women, Wives and Mothers

Nazi attitudes towards women were not formed in a vacuum: they were responses to changes – and just as often *perceived* changes – in the role of women in the wake of urbanisation and economic change. The experience and expectations of German women changed dramatically in the space of just over half a century, but traditional attitudes, led by conservative public opinion and influential institutions, above all the churches, were much slower to change. Women's organisations were formed, and women's rights were promoted by the Social Democratic Party and enshrined in the Weimar constitution. But while women's labour played an increasingly important role in the German economy, and women's health and life expectancy improved, real changes in the position of women were few and limited. Despite the widespread images of the 'new woman' of the 1920s, the law, which affirmed a husband's authority within marriage, remained more or less unchanged until after the Second World War. Women were expected to run the household, and could be prevented from taking paid employment outside the home or family business. For most women very little changed, except that of course the increasing numbers were now wage-earners as well as housewives.

Hostility to feminism had long been an important component of the ideology of the radical right, and a German League to Combat the Emancipation of Women (*Deutscher Bund zur Bekämpfung der Fraueneman-zipation*) had been formed in 1912. Nazi leaders were largely agreed that most German women should be good wives and mothers, producing healthy Aryan children for the national community: this was their biological destiny, and images of strong, noble German women as housewives and mothers dominated Nazi propaganda. Conversely, women were not expected to become involved in public affairs, although they were not straightforwardly excluded either. Since the advent of female suffrage in 1918, conservative nationalist women had established a presence, if not a major role, in party politics, and had gained a measure of acceptance among right-wing men. While the Nazis acknowledged women's presence in the public sphere up to a point, they sought to roll back – along with democratic rights across the board – the political rights of women in particular.

The NSDAP allowed women to join, but they were not accepted as candidates for election or allowed to take on leading positions within the party hierarchy, and they never accounted for more than 8 per cent of the membership before 1933. Working women were members of the Labour Front, although this meant little politically. Middle-class women's organisations were then absorbed into the *Deutsches Frauenwerk*, which had 4 million members by the end of the decade. An elite Nazi women's organisation, the *NS-Frauenschaft*, was led by the Nazi women's leader Gertrud Scholtz-Klink, who explicitly rejected the claim that women were excluded from politics (albeit in a qualified way):

> It is the first time that women are responsible for women in this way, responsible to the national community for their development, their way of life, their human decency and the fulfilment of their duty. It is also the first time that women have placed their trust in the leadership of women with such complete willingness and discipline.[2]

Nevertheless, a woman's place was very firmly held to be in the home. 'In the really good times in German history', Hitler declared in 1934,

> women had no need to emancipate themselves [. . .] If the man's world is said to be the state, his struggle, his readiness to serve the community, then it might also be said that the woman's world is a smaller one. For her world is her husband, her family, her children and her home. Where would the greater world be, if nobody were prepared to look after the smaller world? How could the greater world survive if there were nobody to make the cares of the smaller world their own lives' work? No! The greater world is built upon this smaller world.[3]

This was a message that was reinforced by the *Bund deutscher Mädel* (BdM) and through the values transmitted to girls in school. Girls were expected not only to be more emotional than boys, but also to be more docile, though not entirely passive. The finishing school model of the cultivated young lady was dismissed rather peremptorily for producing 'geese, educated geese'; and the glamorous contemporary images of femininity were also frowned upon, and self-reliance, discipline and self-sacrifice valued more highly than a femininity based on luxury and self-regard. Boys on the other hand were expected to evince manly, soldier qualities, proof of their preparedness for a life of struggle, and the building of state and culture (or indeed destruction of the states and cultures of others).[4]

The BdM encouraged physical fitness for girls just as the Hitler Youth did for boys, in the form of highly disciplined and structured sessions of sport, gymnastics and dance. Free expression was frowned on. Apart from sports, typical BdM activities were singing, handicrafts and political training. For older girls there was great attention to dress, manners and personal hygiene, and to the domestic duties for which girls would be expected to take responsibility after marriage: laundry, sewing, and making arrangements for meals, festivals and entertaining. The BDM's 'Faith and Beauty' (*Glaube und Schönheit*) organisation produced prolific domestic advice for young women between the ages of 17 and 21, much of which amounted to a training in good bourgeois rules of etiquette. The table must be laid properly on all occasions; neither lack of time nor lack of money was an acceptable excuse. Detailed guidelines are given for behaviour at the table, and during the course of an evening with guests: everybody should have enough room; eating should not begin until everybody has been served. Similarly, for one's own behaviour as a dinner guest: 'the bunch of flowers is given directly to the hostess, without paper [. . .] when you leave you must not forget to thank the hostess for the invitation and for her trouble'. There are rules for introductions, and visiting a café with a male companion. Simplicity is emphasised as a great virtue, whether for clothes, furniture or even crockery. National Socialists preferred the term 'clothing culture' (*Kleiderkultur*) to the more international term 'fashion', and showiness and vanity were to be avoided. Ornament (in dress) was only considered pretty, when it had a purpose: everything else has an insincere, ugly effect. The clutter and plush of the previous 50 years was dismissed as 'painfully ugly and petty bourgeois' (*spiessbürgerlich*), while crockery and cutlery was to be plain and functional (except for coffee and cake, where more colourful cups and plates were allowed).[5] BdM schools trained girls in housecraft and childcare, including gardening; and school textbooks for girls reinforced traditional family values, extolling the rural family in particular, and idealising motherhood. Further courses were offered for adult women at the Women's University, set up by the *NS-Frauenschaft* in 1934, and by the Reich Mothers' Service.

Discussion of sex and sexuality was restricted to impressing on girls the importance of restraint and the virtue of monogamy; promiscuity was strongly disapproved of, and although boys and girls were frequently together during youth movement activities, they were expected to show camaraderie rather than flirtation, still less lust, and exercise and fresh air were expected to dispel any temptation. Sex was for reproduction within a healthy 'Aryan' marriage, and girls were warned against infecting the race through sexual intercourse with non-Aryans, particularly with Jewish men, and despite suggestions that all procreation was valuable, in or out of wedlock, the BdM was very firm in upholding the traditional ideal of marriage and family. Otherwise, the whole approach to sex was rather coy.[6]

If women were to be active outside the home, whether they were in paid employment or involved in voluntary work, the roles permitted them were carefully circumscribed, and reflected the rather genteel image of women's work that was widespread on the right. Catering, needlework, childcare, nursing, teaching, social work and charity were all acceptable forms of occupation, and farm work was also thought to be acceptable by some leading Nazis – indeed young women were more or less forced into farm work during the war. In practice of course, these were already occupations where women were generally a majority of the workforce, as they were in certain consumer industries, such as textiles and confectionery. There were also one and a quarter of a million female domestic servants, over 98 per cent of the total. Despite the Nazi stereotypes, women were needed in the workforce, and legislation was introduced during the war that sought to compel mothers of young children to work in industry, albeit not without encountering some resistance.

The most direct way in which the Nazi state intruded in the lives of women was in the sphere of reproduction and the family. Healthy German women were expected to marry and have children, and a range of incentives was provided to encourage them to do so. The state offered loans to young couples when they married, and these were written off in instalments with the birth of each child. The cult of motherhood was reinforced by the appropriation of Mother's Day, which had been introduced in the United States in 1914, and celebrated in Germany for the first time in 1923 – on the initiative of the Federation of German Florists. Mother's Day not only reinforced Nazi ideology, but served too as a symbolic occasion for the promotion of policy. The Reich Mothers' Service (*Reichsmütterdienst*, RMD), for example, was established on Mother's Day, in 1934 to offer training courses for wives and mothers, thereby performing a service hitherto provided largely by the churches and private organisations. The following year Mother's Day was accompanied by an exhibition by the *Deutsches Frauenwerk* in Düsseldorf. During the war it was the occasion on which the Mother's Cross (*Ehrenkreuz der deutschen Mütter*) was awarded. This was a party medal, introduced in 1938 in order to honour the mothers of large families. Mothers of four or five children received a bronze medal, those with six or seven a silver one, and mothers of eight or more were rewarded with gold.[7] Incentives, rewards and distinctions for mothers of large families were not restricted to Germany, of course. There were anxieties about falling birth rates and population loss across the industrialised world, and pro-natalist policies of one kind or another were also introduced in Fascist Italy, the Soviet Union and the Western democracies.[8]

Along with the positive incentives to have children the state also intervened to restrict access to birth control and tightened the law on abortion. The most widely practised method of contraception between the wars was the interruption of sexual intercourse, which was unreliable but less expensive for most couples than condoms or other forms of mechanical contraceptives. The hostility of the churches to contraception undermined attempts to make access to safe, reliable forms of contraception more difficult, and placed practising Christians, particularly Catholics, in a moral dilemma. The Social Democrats and Communists on the other hand disseminated knowledge about contraception as widely as possible, and helped further the establishment birth control clinics. These were closed down by the Nazis, but the use of contraceptives was not prohibited until 1941, when production was halted. Even then the army was exempted, so that condoms could be used to prevent the spread of venereal disease.

The left-wing parties had also campaigned for reform of the abortion law during the Weimar Republic, and the pros and cons of the debate were transmitted to a wider audience through popular culture.[9] Abortion was illegal in Germany, but the inaccessibility of safe reliable contraception compelled many women to seek abortions, often with the help of an older friend or neighbour. It has been estimated that there were half a million abortions a year during the 1920s, and up to a million a year during the Depression, as many large families came under greater economic pressure. The law was reformed in 1926, reducing the penalties for the aborting woman, but increasing them for paid abortionists to a maximum of 15 years penal servitude. From 1927 legal abortions were permitted. The reforms in the abortion law were repealed by the Nazis, and Himmler's Central Office to combat Homosexuality and Abortion compiled information about women who had undergone abortions.

Abortionists were sought out by the Gestapo and prosecuted, and the incidence of such prosecutions increased in the later 1930s.[10] The *Lebensborn* (Spring of Life) organisation of the SS – much misrepresented in popular writing on the Third Reich – sought to provide maternity care for unmarried mothers, provided that they met the racial criteria of the SS.[11]

In fact, it is unlikely that the regime's pro-natalist policies had much impact on the birth rate, which recovered from the low of the Depression years from 14.7 live births per thousand in 1933 to 20.4 live births per thousand in 1939. It never reached the levels of the early 1920s (around 25 live births per thousand), however, still less than those of imperial Germany, and it fell again during the war, to 14.9 live births per thousand in 1942.[12] The broader context of economic circumstances, war and peace determined people's decision (or opportunity) to have children rather than the regime's incentives.

In Germany, however, unlike the other countries which tried to boost the birth rate through pro-natal policies, there was also a significant element of *anti*-natalism in the regime's population policy. The objective was a regeneration of the race ('*Aufartung*') according to eugenic principles, and not all mothers were equally favoured by the regime. In the course of reforms to the public health system in 1934–35, public health offices, hitherto available only in urban areas (above all in Prussia), were now introduced on a nationwide basis. Such offices oversaw public health issues in the broadest sense, dealing not only with food hygiene and the purity of air and water, but also with public health programmes, including maternity and child welfare, and initiatives to deal with tuberculosis and venereal diseases. Programmes for the physically or mentally disabled, including alcoholics, also fell within their remit, and counselling centres for 'genetic and racial care' (*Erb- und Rassenpflege*) collected data about the hereditary health of the population on a systematic basis, for a database which could then be used to judge the racial value of a patient and his or her family. It was here that the responsible official issued approvals for marriage (which were necessary to obtain a marriage loan), and this approval was withheld in the case of racially mixed marriages – that is those between Jews and 'Aryans' – and in cases where partners were found to be 'unfit' according to Nazi eugenic criteria. Candidates for the Mother's Cross were also examined by health officials.[13]

In addition the public health offices dealt with the cases of compulsory sterilisation which became routine procedures from the very beginning of the dictatorship. In June 1933 Wilhelm Frick, the Nazi interior minister, drew attention to the degeneration of the German people in an important speech which set the agenda for population and race policy in the Third Reich. Over a million Germans suffered from hereditary diseases, he announced, and should be prevented from passing on their physical and mental debility to another generation, and a further 11 million were also unfit to be parents. Frick was not alone in considering not just a handicapped minority but a substantial proportion of the German population incapable of reproduction that would serve to strengthen and regenerate the race. Other leading Nazis felt that many of the people, who were not to be directly prohibited from breeding, should not be encouraged to do so either. Walther Darré divided the population into four categories of racial quality, and thought only the first should be positively encouraged to reproduce.[14] In order to secure a healthy racial future, 'biologically inferior hereditary material' must be eliminated from the racial stock, in the first instance by preventing them from 'breeding', and a law was introduced providing for compulsory sterilisation.

The new law did not suddenly appear from nowhere as a radical Nazi initiative, however. There had been considerable interest in legislation for sterilisation on eugenic grounds during the 1920s. In 1925 the Reichstag had rejected draft legislation proposed by a local health officer who had announced 2 years earlier that the mentally handicapped were being sterilised without legal provision in his district. It was followed by similar proposals, both in Prussia and at Reich level, the most recent of which had been drawn up in 1932. These were submitted to the Reich government for consideration at about the time of Hitler's appointment as chancellor.[15] The Law for the Protection of Hereditary Health of 14 July 1933 provided for compulsory sterilisation of the 'congenitally feeble-minded' and those with hereditary blindness or deafness. It also covered a number of other mental and physical conditions, including schizophrenia, manic Depression, congenital epilepsy, Huntington's Chorea and a category of 'serious inheritable deformities'. In a separate provision, chronic alcoholics could also be sterilised.

The initiative for sterilisation could now come not just from prospective patients or their relatives or guardians, but could also be instigated by the authorities – whether a doctor or the officer in charge of a sanatorium or prison. Such requests were dealt with by an 'hereditary health court' (*Erbgesundheitsgericht*), which was attached to a municipal court. Decisions were made by a local judge, a medical examiner and another doctor, and their deliberations were secret. Voluntary sterilisation was effectively forbidden, in so far as sterilisation could henceforth only be carried out subject to the procedures embodied in the law: choices were now to be made by medical professionals, including psychiatrists and geneticists, academics and lawyers, according to criteria set out in the law.[16] It has been estimated that almost 400,000 men and women were sterilised over the next 10 years, and in many cases the police were used to enforce the decisions of the professional panels. The 1933 law did not include race as a criterion for sterilisation, but Jews, Gypsies and black people were sterilised both within and outside the law.

The Nuremberg Laws of 1935 institutionalised racial segregation. The detailed definitions of mixed race which created the categories of first and second degree *Mischling* were incorporated into marriage law and family law, and included a prohibition against marrying Gypsies and Negroes as well as Jews. The Marriage Health Law of 18 October 1935 prohibited marriages on eugenic grounds, and the onus was on couples to provide a certificate of proof, issued by the public health office, that they were able to marry (*Ehetauglichkeitszeugnis*). From 1936 couples were obliged to report their intention to marry to the public health office, which would then undertake a search for possible impediments to the marriage. Only if one of the partners was infertile or if the woman was over childbearing age would the provisions of the law be waived and a marriage permitted where the bride or groom had a hereditary illness. The objective was to prevent reproduction rather than marriage per se. The message was reinforced by state publicity and propaganda. A brochure published by the Reich Committee of Public Health gave ten commandments for the choice of marriage partner, encouraging healthy Germans to marry, but to bear considerations of hereditary health and physical purity in mind. The fifth commandment was to marry only other Germans or those of Nordic blood, and the sixth recommended interrogating a prospective spouse about his or her ancestors. Without any obvious irony the eighth instructed couples to marry only for love.[17]

The law regulating marriage was revised several times during the short life of the dictatorship, particularly during the war, when new regulations were introduced forbidding soldiers to marry foreigners (except women of Nordic blood), prostitutes and women with hereditary disorders. Finally, in 1943, various proposals were put forward to restrict age differences between married couples in order to ensure that those men capable of reproducing married women of childbearing age. (During the war of course, staff shortages and the increasing chaos and upheaval of the last year of the war ensured that corners were cut in any case.) Reform of the marriage law also entailed a new approach to divorce. The Marriage Law (6 July 1938) made it easier to end marriages deemed undesirable from the perspective of Nazi racial policy. 'Racial error' had long been accepted as grounds for divorce in the case of mixed marriages between Jews and gentiles; the 'marital hygiene law' (Law for the Protection of the Hereditary Health of the German People, 18 October 1934) enshrined in law the right to contest such marriages, and also legalised divorce on grounds of hereditary health. The Marriage Law of 1938 also made it possible to obtain a divorce on grounds of mental disturbance or contagious disease. It also made it possible to apply for a divorce on grounds of refusing to procreate, the use of illicit methods of preventing birth, and even on grounds of premature infertility. Attempts by Himmler and the interior ministry to dispense entirely with traditional grounds for divorce and to replace them with criteria derived from racial policy were blocked by the justice ministry and opposed by Hitler himself. Gabriele Czarnowski's research has suggested that while the total number of divorces under the new regulations was not large, men were shrewder in using the new legislation to obtain divorces more easily, claiming their new rights in order to escape from responsibilities to their wives and families, and that they were assisted in converting adulterous relationships into 'fertile' second marriages. Women on the other hand were more dependent on marriage economically, and stood to lose further from the new marriage legislation, which enabled judges to free men of the obligation to pay maintenance. In practice, the new marriage laws had shifted the balance sharply in favour of husbands.[18]

Family Policy

German political leaders, like those in many other parts of the industrialised world between the wars, were actively seeking to increase the birth rate, and that meant encouraging large families, but here too this aim was qualified by the perceived need to improve the quality of the race as a whole, and a discriminatory distinction was made between 'racially valuable' families, which were designated 'child-rich' (*kinderreich*), and those that were merely large. Child-rich families had been promoted by pressure groups concerned with the nation's slowing birthrate since the end of the First World War. The foremost of these, the Reich League of Child-Rich Families (*Reichsbund der Kinderreichen*, RdK) – defined as four children or more – became a vehicle for Nazi family policy after 1933, and was affiliated to the party's Racial Policy Office (*Rassenpolitisches Amt*) in 1934.[19]

The distinction between 'child-rich' and 'large' families was more often than not based on class. Wealthier, better educated, middle-class families made a more favourable impression on officials, doctors and other professionals, and it was precisely such families that were reluctant to have large numbers of children, while large families were more likely to be found among the industrial working class or among poorer sections of the rural population, where poverty, poor health and a perceived lack of social responsibility were all more frequent problems. The professionals who made these judgments, a self-selecting company of the 'racially valuable', proved nevertheless most unwilling to do their bit for the improvement of the race. Doctors in particular, the most enthusiastically Nazi of all the professions, tended to have just one child. Similarly, almost half of all Nazi party functionaries married in the mid-1930s had only one child, while 18 per cent had none at all, and most of the rest had only two. Two-thirds of SS men – the new racial elite – were unmarried in 1942, and those who were married also tended to have only one child.[20] 'Racially valuable' members of society were beset with pleas and propaganda, but could not be coerced into having more children in the way more unfortunate members of society could be prevented from having them, not least since the government was unwilling to offer substantial financial and practical help to help parents raise and, most importantly, to house large families.

Unlike middle-class Germans, members of 'asocial' families seemed only too willing to marry young and have lots of children. Wolfgang Knorr, the leader of the Racial Political Office in Saxony, divided 'asocials' into five categories based on observations of their behaviour. In the first were those families who were frequently in trouble with the police. The 'work-shy' were in the second category, and the third comprised those who could not manage their household or bring up their children properly. The fourth consisted of alcoholics, drug addicts, gamblers, vagrants and beggars, and the fifth was reserved for those who were 'hostile to the community' or immoral. Although those in the first, and especially the last category were inclined to have few or no children, most of the families in the other asocial categories had six or more children. Since the regime's racial policy experts believed that 'asocial' behaviour was hereditary, the problem was exacerbated by the fact that 'asocial' men married 'asocial' women and thereby perpetuated the problem. In preparation for the physical elimination of this entire underclass, proposals were made to extend the sterilisation legislation to cover 'asocial' types who could pass standard tests for mental debility, but conflicts between the various agencies and individuals delayed its implementation until 1945. They remained excluded from all the honours and distinctions accorded large 'healthy' families, and it was felt that welfare was wasted on them.

Asocial families were seen as a problem by both the authorities and their more respectable neighbours, and proposals to isolate them in separate communities were supported by local councils and welfare agencies. One such settlement, effectively an internment camp, was established at Hashude by the authorities in Bremen, in order to establish whether it was possible for the workshy and the indigent, former Communists and neglectful parents, to be educated for re-integration in the community. Those who infringed the strict rules of the camp were threatened with more draconian conditions at a nearby forced labour camp. It was closed down in 1940 and converted into an open estate for 'healthy' child-rich families.[21] More serious 'asocial' offenders against the social norms of the Volksgemeinschaft faced more punitive treatment. The criminologist Robert Heindl had argued in 1926 that professional criminals – rather than small-time habitual crooks – were responsible for a great deal of the organised crime in Germany and should be imprisoned indefinitely. Others were in favour of the idea, but wanted to see the principle extended to a wider group of offenders. In November 1933 a new kind of security confinement (Sicherungsverwahrung) was introduced for such habitual criminals, and hundreds of offenders already in prison were more or less immediately condemned to indefinite terms of confinement as incorrigible crooks, without being heard themselves, on the basis of the recommendation of prison governors. Although the sentence was reviewed periodically, early release was a remote possibility and the chances diminished further as policy towards criminals became more radical. From 1940 the courts were instructed to reject all requests for release, and from 1941 certain kinds of habitual criminal could be sentenced to death: Hitler thought it was necessary to exterminate such people as a group for the greater good of the nation in wartime, and made this clear to the new Justice Minister Otto-Georg Thierack on his appointment in August 1942. In September the new minister agreed with Himmler on the transfer of all surviving asocial prisoners to the police for annihilation through labour. Deteriorating conditions and harsher treatment in prisons during the war had already reduced their survival chances considerably, but illness was not regarded as a reason for exemption from transfer to the camp system, and this meant that death rates among those already weak from the effects of security confinement were greater than those of other inmates. Of those who survived the system, many remained imprisoned after the end of the war, eliciting as they did less sympathy than other victims of the Nazis. Moreover, the legal provisions survived for two decades after the war, and were repealed only in 1970.[22]

Criminal Sexualities

Quite apart from the threat of uncontrolled reproduction among the nation's physically and mentally 'less valuable' racial stock, certain kinds of sexuality posed a direct threat to the country's racial hygiene.[23] Prostitution, although tolerated and even exploited in certain circumstances, carried with it the threat of venereal diseases associated with 'frequently changing sexual partners' or 'alternating intercourse' (häufig wechselnder Geschlechtsverkehr). It had been effectively decriminalised in Germany in 1927, with the Law for Combating Venereal Diseases (Reichsgesetz zur Bekämpfung der Geschlechtskrankheiten) which abolished state-regulated prostitution (Reglementierung) and the power of the 'morality police', which supervised registered prostitution, and arrested women outside the official system. This reform provoked hostility from the political right, the churches and the police themselves, and provided the Nazis with a moral meeting point for collaboration with Christian conservatism, and representatives of both denominations welcomed the Nazis' new morality.[24]

From 1933 there was increasing emphasis on the unacceptability of deviating from the sexual norm in principle, and an influential section of medical opinion favoured the Nazi emphasis on healthy sexuality and eugenic policies. Prostitutes were rounded up and imprisoned in concentration camps, and women could be classified as asocial if they were judged to become too easily aroused, or to create too erotic an impression – whether they were prostitutes or not, and this might make them candidates for sterilisation. Despite the early onslaught against illicit or promiscuous sex, however, prostitution could not be dispensed with. Himmler saw it as a way of preventing young men drifting towards homosexual behaviour, prostitution was accepted as a necessary outlet for men, and military brothels came to be seen as a necessity: the regime accepted regulation as a lesser evil against advice from the medical profession and in the face of hostility from the churches. After the outbreak of the war, the regime effectively stopped trying to accommodate conservative opinion on the matter. In 1939 an interior ministry directive issued instructions for the construction of brothels for the military, and brothels for civilians were effectively legalised by changes in the law in 1940, and set up in Berlin during the war. Himmler gave instructions in 1942 for brothels to be established in concentration camps in order to improve the labour productivity of the inmates. To this extent sex (for men) was a reward for service. Nazis shared with conventional opinion the belief that the sexual drive of men was more or less uncontrollable; but they also shared with Italian Fascists the belief that racial superiority could be demonstrated by the sexual prowess and stamina of the nation's men. In the fascist conception of 'militarised masculinity', men drew strength and renewed energy from their sexual encounters with women, and prostitutes were necessary to invigorate soldiers for the fight. Promiscuous *female* sexuality was associated with asocial behaviour and the threat of disease, and the extension of state controls did little to reduce the regime's paranoia on this issue. The health authorities intruded increasingly onto the intimate life of individuals, exercising the power to examine those suspected of promiscuity. Official decisions about the extent and nature of sexual deviancy could have serious consequences for the individual concerned, including confinement to a state-run brothel. Promiscuous *male* sexuality on the other hand was seen as positive. Despite the Nazis' rationalisation of sex as a functional way of ensuring the healthy reproduction of the nation, men's sexual behaviour was divorced from the simple imperative to procreate for very subjective reasons: in fact Himmler believed that those soldiers most in need of prostitutes – the most masculine in his view – would also make the best husbands in civilian life.[25]

Of all the anxieties about promiscuity, one of the greatest was that of miscegenation. This was the 'racial disgrace' (*Rassenschande*) of sexual intercourse with those of inferior races, especially Jews, but also foreign workers and prisoners of war. Miscegenation was criminalized by the Law for the Protection of German Blood and German Honour of 15 September 1935, one of the Nuremberg race laws, and various other measures were introduced that reflected Nazi anxieties about the allegedly sexually predatory behaviour of Jewish men. The application of the law varied, and initially the number of cases brought far exceeded the number of successful convictions. It was interpreted with increasing harshness in the later 1930s, especially by the higher courts, presumably as a consequence of pressure from above. The term 'intercourse' was extended far beyond the legally accepted definition of penetration, and lewd acts and lascivious glances were interpreted as threats to German blood by some of the (supposedly) finest legal minds in the Germany. The insistence on this threat was an important point, of course, because it meant that the offence was not treated as an individual lapse, but as an act which endangered the whole racial community, and one which therefore excluded the possibility of mitigating circumstances. It also made it logical to prosecute in the case of liaisons that took place outside Germany.

Although anti-Semitism prompted the legislation forbidding miscegenation, the concept of racial disgrace or defilement did not remain restricted to marriage or intercourse between Germans and Jews. A court in Kassel sentenced a Hungarian Protestant to death as a habitual criminal in 1943. There were seven counts of racial defilement against him, but he also had a sexual relationship with the daughter of a district judge whose husband was at the front.[26] The Nazi Party in Upper Silesia requested the revocation of ethnic German status in 1944 for a single woman who had just given birth to the child of a German soldier. This was her fourth child, and the woman was stigmatised as a 'downright whore' and a poor mother, an example of the way in which wily and promiscuous non-Aryan women could entice German men and threaten the purity of the race.[27]

During the war foreign workers and POWs introduced a new threat to the purity of the German race, and by the last year of the war there were some 5.7 million of the former (a third of them women) and almost 2 million of the latter, and relationships of all kinds developed between Germans and foreigners. The regime discouraged all forms of fraternisation, even the most innocuous social relationships that developed between German farmers and the Polish agricultural labourers who worked their land. Farmers were not to be condemned for accommodating good workers in the farmhouse rather than outbuildings such as barns or stables if there was room, but a clear line should be maintained and too much familiarity was to be avoided – Germans speaking Polish to their workers at home, for example – otherwise foreigners would become insolent.[28] Alongside the casual friendships more intimate relationships developed, and the regime responded with a number of laws and regulations, which not only superseded, overlapped and contradicted each other, but were also virtually unenforceable in the sense that the way in which relationships with foreigners were regulated in practice on a day-to-day basis often had little to do with the legal provisions. Regulations had to address the different 'racial' status of the various types of foreigners. A new offence of 'forbidden contact' (verbotener Umgang) with prisoners of war was introduced on 25 November 1939, but in practice prisoners were treated very differently according to nationality, and this was reflected in inconsistent sentencing when cases came before the courts, not least when there was a conflict of interest between hanging or imprisonment and preserving the life or liberty of a healthy productive worker. To the chagrin of the SD there was no universal prohibition of sexual relations with foreigners, nor were any reliable figures kept on the number of relationships with foreigners.

For the most part, those involved in such relationships were punished with disproportionate severity. For the German women involved in cases of adultery with foreigners, there was frequently not only imprisonment or financial loss, but public humiliation as well. This sometimes back-fired on the regime, however, prompting adverse reactions and even solidarity among other women, who questioned whether, for example, the same treatment would be meted out for a man in a relationship with a Frenchwoman in France as for a woman involved with a Frenchman in Germany. In any case neither regulation nor punishment seemed to deter those involved in such relationships, and as the demands of the war economy for productive labour increased rather than diminished some officials were also increasingly apt to take a pragmatic approach. In a long analysis of the reasons for relationships with foreigners, the SD came up with a whole range of ideologically predictable reasons, including the poor example of the elites, the fickleness and superficiality of women and the degeneration of a culture in which the life presented in films was excessively eroticised. But the main reason was felt to be the dura-tion of the war and all that it entailed in terms of social uprootedness, loneliness and the ever-present risk and danger caused by bombardment. In short the authorities themselves recognised that people wanted such little pleasure as they could get.[29]

Unlike the other categories of illicit sexuality, male homosexual rela-tionships were already criminalized when the Nazis came to power (and remained so long after 1945). 'Unnatural sexual acts' (*Unzucht wider die Natur*), a category which included sexual intercourse between two men, was punishable under the provisions of Paragraph 175 of the Reich penal code of 1871 – which in turn was based on an earlier Prussian law. (There was a similar provision in Austria, dating from the time of Maria Theresia.)[30] A sub-culture of bars and other meeting places had existed in imperial Berlin and other large cities, and there had been attempts by Magnus Hirschfeld, and a number of leading intellectuals and Socialist politicians to have the law reformed. Although Paragraph 175 itself was not repealed or liberalised, the political climate of the Weimar Republic had encouraged a more relaxed attitude towards homosexuality, and this in turn had provoked a backlash as early as 1925, when civil servants had drafted an amendment to the law for the governing conservative coali-tion (Centre Party, DVP and DNVP). It was intended to tighten up the law and was presented to the Reichstag in 1927, where it was vociferously supported by the Nazis. This was based on the notion that a number of 'original homosexuals' were using the liberal climate to proselytise and convert heterosexual men – pre-empting the Nazi characterisation of homosexuals as a threat to the community. By the time the law came to its committee stage in 1929, there had been a shift to the left in the general election of 1928 and the conservatives were outvoted on the issues by the Communists, Social Democrats and liberals (DDP). The Criminal Law Committee of the Reichstag recommended the deletion of Paragraph 175 within the context of a general reform of the criminal law. There was no resolution to the question before 1933, except in so far as it was generally agreed that practical solutions required medical opinion, reflecting a climate of expert opinion which had seen homosexuality transformed from sin or deviation to clinical condition during the course of the nineteenth century.[31]

Homosexuality clearly represented a threat to the nation in terms of Nazi ideas about racial hygiene too, and the regime's declared aim was to eradicate it. Homosexuals failed in their duty to produce children, and the Nazis could draw on support from medical opinion that identified homosexuality – and masturbation – as threats to the birth rate, characterising them as 'an adverse influence on national reproduction', deviations which could be cured by 'educational measures, strength of will and physical exercise.'[32] As with other aspects of 'race science', the results of academic research were too inconclusive to support the pseudoscientific conclusions of the Nazis, and hostility towards homosexuals was based on a number of other premises, above all popular prejudice (the 'healthy instincts of the people'), which also characterised homosexuals as secretive, cliquey and therefore potentially conspiratorial and oppositional. Not least they constituted a threat to young people – and here the left-wing press clumsily tried to outdo the Nazis on their own territory by publishing alarmist stories warning parents of the threats to their sons of 'physical preparation' in the Hitler Youth.

The Nazis' own hostility to homosexuality was perhaps more muted than it might have been during the early 1930s because Ernst Röhm, the leader of the SA, was relatively open about his own sexuality. Nevertheless, the new regime began with the spectacle of Hirschfeld's Institute for Sexology being ransacked and its contents burned. The SA was purged the following year and Röhm was murdered in the 'night of the long knives'. This incident was the prompt for an intensified campaign of police terror against individuals, clubs and meeting places and for changes in the law. In the wake of Röhm putsch,

Himmler proceeded to register all known homosexuals, heralding a new phase in the campaign against homosexuality. The Reich Office for the Combating of Homosexuality and Abortion (Reichszentrale zur Bekämpfung der Homosexualität und Abtreibung) was established in 1936, in the course of the reorganisation of the criminal police, and the number of men arrested and sentenced under the provision of paragraph 175 increased sharply. Some 50,000 men were sentenced during the 12 years of the Third Reich. Of these many were sent to concentration camps after serving their sentences, where they were treated with extreme brutality not only by the guards, but by the other prisoners as well. In 1941 the death penalty was introduced for homosexuals in the SS and police. The regime's measures against homosexuals were generally approved of by the German public, and the Nazi framework of legislation was not repealed until 1969.[33]

The treatment of lesbians differed in a number of respects: above all Paragraph 175 did not include female homosexuality. The same anxieties were expressed by experts about the possibility of heterosexuals being converted, but female homosexuality was not perceived as a direct political threat in the same way as male homosexuality, not least because women were excluded from influential positions in public life; instead it was constructed in a way similar to other kinds of behaviour in which women determined their own sexuality, and associated with the perceived 'masculinisation' of modern women. There was also considerable pressure on women to conform to the Nazi ideal of wife and mother, and some of the 1 million or so lesbians estimated to have been living in Germany in 1933 married homosexual men and embarked on a life in disguise. Even so there was continued pressure on couples in childless marriages to reproduce for the Reich.

There are relatively few known cases in which women were persecuted specifically for their homosexuality. Some cases of 'dependent' relationships between teachers and pupils or labour service recruits and their supervisors were treated as paedophilia (under Paragraph 176 of the Reich penal code); other lesbian women were persecuted as asocials, or ended up in concentration camps for political reasons or on account of their ethnicity. There was no separate category in the camps for lesbian women: only men wore the pink triangle badge that designated homosexuality, while the issue of 'deviant' sexuality among women continued to be treated with some coyness even here, and lesbians were placed in one of the other categories (e.g. political, Jewish or asocial). For this reason alone it is almost impossible to know how many women ostensibly imprisoned for other reasons were in the camps largely or wholly as a consequence of their sexuality.[34]

'Life Unworthy of Life'

A great deal of the discussion about racial hygiene was as much about cost as about eugenics: money could be saved by ridding society of the 'burden' of its hereditarily ill or asocial members. The most extreme manifestation of the regime's drive to purge the nation of the unfit was a euthanasia programme which involved the mass murder of the incurably sick and disabled from the autumn of 1939. 'Mercy killing' and the release from suffering of the interminably ill had been discussed in Germany, as it had in other industrial countries, long before 1933, and in the case of eugenics, the issue drew supporters from a range of moral and political positions, including those such as Karl Binding, a former president of the national criminal court, and Alfred Hoche, professor of psychiatry at Freiburg University, who questioned the value of lives – for the patients themselves and for society – not only of those who were terminally ill and able to make their own wishes known, but of those who were mentally ill and incapable of making such a decision themselves, and of those who were either permanently unconscious or so intolerably physically crippled as to make their lives unbearable.[35] Even among circles otherwise opposed to such ideas, such as Catholic intellectuals, there were dissidents who advanced arguments in favour of medical intervention. The theologian (and editor of the Catholic journal *Caritas*) Joseph Mayer published a work on the compulsory sterilisation of the mentally ill in 1927, with the consent of the church authorities, and later supplied the SD with a paper on euthanasia, which was inconclusive but provided the regime with arguments to counter those of opponents in the church.[36] Although the medical and psychiatric professions rejected euthanasia as an option during the Weimar Republic, cuts in public expenditure during the Depression had made more of them more receptive to the Nazis' arguments about cost, particularly in the context of the climate of opinion after 1933, when more radical solutions to the problem of these 'burdensome existences' (*Ballastexistenzen*) became increasingly acceptable.

Hitler's own views were very clear and – at least in terms of generalities – were well known to the public. In *Mein Kampf* he had argued very strongly in favour of intervention to prevent the 'propagation of the defective', and in 1929, in an address to the party rally at Nuremberg, he advocated 'doing away' with thousands of the weakest children in each generation: the result would be to strengthen the race as a whole. Sentimentality and humanitarian values, he argued, served only to protect the weak at the expense of the strong. Neither consent nor patients' welfare was a consideration in what the Nazis' euphemistically termed 'euthanasia': the chief attractions of such a programme were the improvement of the race, and apart from that the sheer cost savings that could be achieved by murdering the weakest members of society – an argument which the party's propagandists were clearly confident would find some resonance in the 'healthy instincts of the people'.

Although the issue of euthanasia opened up differences of opinion within the political and professional elites of Nazi Germany, the arguments in favour of killing the incurably sick or deranged specifically for the benefit to society became more explicit in party and state propaganda, and in 1937 the SS magazine *Das schwarze Corps* used the story of a farmer, who had murdered his handicapped son and nevertheless been treated leniently by the courts, as the introduction to a public discussion of 'mercy killing'. Films produced by the Reich Office for Educational Films were used to support the case for sterilisation and euthanasia in schools and universities.[37] At the same time the public was allowed to see conditions in asylums and hospitals, and group visits were organised by the party and its affiliated organisations with the intention of demonstrating that here were lives that were genuinely not worth living. There is relatively little evidence on how the public responded to such visits, but the testimony of a psychologist who visited one such institution in 1939 makes clear that the director was frank about the issue: the patients were a burden on the nation, and although they could not be straightforwardly murdered for fear of inciting foreign 'hate propaganda', they were already being allowed to perish by slow starvation.[38]

The children's euthanasia campaign ostensibly began with the case of the Knauer baby. The child had been born blind and deformed, and his parents had petitioned Hitler, through the Führer Chancellery, requesting that the child be killed. Hitler's doctor, Karl Rudolf Brandt, testified after the war that he was sent to Leipzig to examine the child, ascertain the facts of the case, and authorise the local doctors to 'carry out euthanasia'; any legal consequences would be over-ruled by Hitler himself. It seems that the Leipzig case provided a prompt or starting point to the children's 'euthanasia' programme, but there are several versions of the sequence of events that accompanied Hitler's response to the petition, and most of the files relating to the case are missing.[39] According to the post-war testimony of Hans Hefelmann, the Leipzig case prompted Hitler to authorise Brandt and Philip Bouhler, the head of the Führer chancellery, to deal with similar cases in the same way – effectively an instruction to begin the systematic killing of the incurably sick and the mentally ill.

It is clear, however, that this was no spontaneous radicalisation of policy. The road to the ostensible trigger for the programme had been well prepared, and Hitler's own role was indispensable. After coming to power he had confided plans for the systematic killing of the handicapped first in Hans Heinrich Lammers, the head of the Reich chancellery, in 1933, and later in Gerhard Wagner, the Reich Doctors' Leader in 1935, when he suggested that such a programme might be best carried out in war time when opposition would be less effective. In 1933 the Prussian Justice Minister Hans Kerrl had been equivocal about whether euthanasia could be legal, but Reich Justice Minister Franz Gürtner ruled it out in 1935. In any case Hitler was reluctant to legislate, and only in October 1939 did he take the exceptional step of committing his instructions to Brandt and Bouhler – backdated to 1 September – to paper. Although the authorisation for the murders had no real legal authority, it was sufficient to persuade Gürtner that this was indeed the Führer's will rather than the work of ambitious subordinates, and he ceased all attempts to stop or regulate the killings.[40]

Bureaucratic preparations for the programme had begun long before the outbreak of the war. The Reich Committee for the Scientific Registering of Serious Hereditary and Congenital Diseases had met to discuss the issue of euthanasia in the Führer chancellery several times during the spring of 1939, and Hitler was briefed by his doctor, Theo Morell, on the material discussed by the committee. Compulsory registration of all 'malformed' newborn babies was introduced on 18 August (without any legal provision), and a committee of three specialist paediatricians was set up in Berlin to decide on the children's fate on the basis of reports from midwives and doctors, but without actually seeing them. The killings were carried out in one of the thirty or so clinics designated for the purpose around the country, either by starvation or through lethal overdoses of drugs. Parents under pressure sometimes consented to their children being taken into care in such clinics, where their admission was quickly followed by 'sudden' death. Others were talked into admitting their children to such institutions by doctors or health visitors, who emphasised that the institutions would provide the best possible care. It was theoretically possible for parents to refuse, and accept responsibility for care of the child themselves, but the authorities reserved the right to remove the child at a later stage. Very few parents openly acknowledged what was happening, so that it is difficult to ascertain how many gave their consent to 'euthanasia' rather than admission to an institution.[41]

During the summer of 1939, at the time of the Knauer case, Hitler separately instructed Leonardo Conti to implement a programme of 'euthanasia' for adults who were incurably mentally ill, but Bouhler and his subordinate Viktor Brack, anxious to retain and extend their own control over the 'euthanasia' programme, pressed for it to be carried out under the auspices of the Führer chancellery, thereby prompting Hitler's belated but retroactive written authorisation. A team of academics and asylum directors was recruited and met in Berlin in July 1939 to discuss the practical implementation of the programme, and not least the issue of how exactly large numbers of people could be killed. The solution adopted was poison gas, specifically carbon monoxide, which was acquired by the Criminal Technical Institute – one of a number of cover organisations – from the Mannesmann steel concern. Forms were sent out to asylums for the purposes of registering patients, and it was estimated on the basis of a very rough calculation that up to 75,000 cases could be expected in which 'euthanasia' was appropriate. It was also necessary to recruit doctors to the programme, and although many refused to be involved, ideological commitment or the promise of rapid promotion attracted others. The programme's burgeoning bureaucracy moved in April 1940 to the house at Tiergartenstrasse 4 that gave the programme its name: T4.

It was estimated that 70,273 people had been killed by gassing by September 1941, and that over 93,000 had probably been killed altogether. Refusal to participate was permitted, but overt criticism was prohibited. Although the programme of mass murder was carried out in secret, news of it escaped in a variety of ways, and insensitive administrative blunders – including the sending of urns with ashes to the wrong families – aroused wider suspicions. As well as the medical and ancillary staff who were directly involved, administrators, academic specialists and many of those with an interest in the running of asylums knew what was going on, including the clerical and lay representatives of both Christian denominations, who enquired, complained and negotiated with the authorities throughout the programme. Outspoken criticism came only belatedly, however, for example in the sermon by Clemens von Galen, bishop of Münster (3 August 1941), and it is likely that by that time the 'euthanasia' programme had more or less achieved its central objectives. Moreover, although the mass gassings of the mentally and physically handicapped largely came to an end, decentralized euthanasia programmes continued throughout the war.[42]

Those who had been involved in 'Aktion T4' were also recruited for 'Aktion Reinhardt', the best-known example is probably Franz Stangl, who went on to become the commandant of Treblinka.[43] Many, but by no means all, of the perpetrators were brought to trial after the war, at Nuremberg, where leading figures in the 'euthanasia' programme were tried by an American military tribunal, along with some of those who had carried out medical experiments on camp inmates. Bouhler committed suicide in 1945; Brandt, Brack and a number of others were executed. Others were given sentences of life imprisonment (many of which were reduced to 15 or 20 years following successful appeals).

The involvement of medical and other professionals in the Nazis' racial hygiene policies – long understood either as a 'slippery slope' of tiny concessions to the regime's plans or as a 'sudden subversion' of medical ethics under pressure from a 'totalitarian' regime – has more recently given way to an understanding of these developments in which the professions involved were less victims than pace setters, whose enthusiasm for measures such as compulsory sterilisation the government had to 'rein in'. The economics of such projects was also a constant consideration, whether in terms of the growth of new medical industries, or in terms of the projected 'savings' that were to be achieved as a consequence of the T4 programme.[44] The regime's regulation of reproduction, racial hygiene and sexuality was proposed, planned and enforced not by the stereotypical street-fighting thugs of the Nazis' popular image, but overwhelmingly by university-educated professionals working in some of the finest research institutions and hospitals in the world, and with the best equipment German industry could supply. Nor were proposals and plans couched in the terms of a primitive and irrational racial ideology: the framework of reference was relentlessly positive and progressive, and the aim was always improvement, whether of individual health or of society – to that extent Nazi eugenics reiterated in extreme form the respectable values of cleanliness, order and industry.

Chapter 8: Anti-Semitism and the Holocaust

Anti-Semitism was widespread in Europe from the Middle Ages, and was characterized by social, political and cultural discrimination, pogroms and expulsions. Jews were progressively emancipated in the wake of the Enlightenment, but anti-Semitic prejudice re-emerged strongly – in Russia and eastern and central Europe in particular – during the second half of the nineteenth century. Anti-Semitism in Germany was stimulated by the work of radical right-wing publicists at home (such as Wilhelm Marr, founder of the Anti-Semitic League) and abroad (notably Arthur, comte de Gobineau and Houston Stewart Chamberlain) and found organizational form with the foundation of associations and political parties such as the Anti-Semitic League and the Anti-Semitic People's Party. Explicitly anti-Semitic parties had little political success in Wilhelmine Germany; however, their candidates won 3 to 4 per cent of the vote in Reichstag elections during the 1890s and 1900s, and 16 anti-Semites sat in the parliaments of 1893 and 1907. Such groups were vocal and unpleasant, but remained marginal to the political culture of the empire, and although discriminatory measures were enacted first against Catholics and then against Socialists, there was no serious suggestion, beyond the marginal fringe of racial anti-Semites, that the emancipation of Jews should be reversed.

'Scientific' Racism

The imperial period marked something of a turning point in attitudes, however, in that long-standing popular prejudice was now re-invented as 'scientific' racism. The term 'anti-Semitism' itself first appeared in

173

German at the end of the 1870s with the formation of Marr's Anti-Semitic League and the publication of his journal *Antisemitische Blätter*. It was supposed to lend the movement a scholarly air, thereby giving it more authority than earlier, similar forms of xenophobia, despite the fact that the supposedly 'scientific' criteria for assigning racial identity amounted to little more than the old cultural indicators and subjective observations of physical appearance, and this remained the case right down to the Nazis' anti-Semitic legislation, which incorporated religious observance as a final determinant of race. Similarly, European races were more or less equated with the different linguistic groups – Germanic, Slavonic, Celtic and so on – in the Indo-European (or 'Aryan') family of languages described by philologists.[1]

Many scientists also took the idea of race seriously. Anthropologists rationalised human diversity by constructing ethnic categories and seeking to establish objective criteria for racial difference based on physical characteristics. This idea originated with the German anatomist Johann Friedrich Blumenbach, who established the existence of five races descended from a single human origin. Scientists took these ideas further during the course of the nineteenth century in the attempt to establish a correlation between physical characteristics, such as skull shape or hair and eye colour, and mental qualities, between racial origins and cultural difference. Approaches to such issues were invariably determined by political considerations: for liberal anthropologists who thought in terms of a single human race culture was used to explain diversity, while those ethnologists who thought in terms of several archetypes used cultural evidence (including language and history) to support their argument that racial difference was permanent.

Similarly Darwinism, originally a progressive ideology, was reformulated in a manner which reflected changes in political ideology. For early Darwinists, evolution could be applied to the development of society in an optimistic way, and they suggested a natural evolution from primitive communities, warfare, religion and superstition to the establishment of nations and the promotion of reason and science through education. This outlook proved very acceptable to a generation of liberal (and anti-Catholic) German nationalists. Some, like the zoologist Ernst Haeckel, conceptualised this development in terms of a hierarchical order, in which 36 racial categories were identified, and organised in 12 groups, with primitive 'woolly-haired' races at the lower end (along with children and the mentally handicapped). Although the highest stage of development had not yet been attained, Europeans had achieved a medium level among the cultured, who in turn outranked the mere 'civilised', the barbaric and the wild – Haeckel's four levels of cultural development. Liberal individualism lost favour as a political doctrine in the late nineteenth century, and in a parallel intellectual development the concept of 'natural selection', particularly in so far as it suggested free competition between organisms was rejected by some scientific thinkers. Instead the notion of an original source of immutable genetic material gained support, an idea that enabled 'social Darwinism' to converge more easily with racial politics: 'racial fitness' came to be seen as necessary for the survival of the group. The nation itself came to be represented metaphorically as an organism or body, which had to be kept free from 'infection'. The 'racial stock', by extension, should not be contaminated or diluted by miscegenation (inter-racial marriage or sexual relations), and this meant that assimilation into German society by Jews was neither possible nor desirable for the new 'scientific' racists of the fin-de-siècle anti-Semitic movement.[2]

Anti-Semitism in Germany

Although explicitly anti-Semitic parties remained on the margins of politics in imperial Germany, a more diffuse anti-Semitism was adopted, as Shulamit Volkov has argued, along with anti-feminism as a kind of 'cultural code' among certain kinds of nationalists and conservatives: 'Professing antisemitism became a sign of cultural identity, of one's belonging to a specific cultural camp.'[3] Jews on the other hand were instinctively associated with liberal values: rationalism, internationalism and increasingly with socialism. In this way anti-Semitism made inroads among politicians, journalists and intellectuals beyond the fringe activists, and thereby acquired a respectability which made unreflecting everyday prejudice uncontroversial, and Jews going about their everyday business were routinely confronted with prejudice and bullying that was no less malicious for being trivial and mundane. The Düsseldorf art dealer Jakob Sander, for example, was driven off the holiday island of Borkum, which described itself as 'free of Jews' (*judenrein*) in advertising for prospective holidaymakers that contained thinly veiled threats of intimidation. Sander went there in the summer of 1905 to organise an exhibition but was forced to leave after repeated threat and taunts, an experience that reflected that of many Jewish people at the seaside or at country spas.[4]

The Jewish community in Germany was relatively small, certainly in comparison with those of Austria–Hungary and the Russian Empire. In 1871 Germany had about half a million Jewish citizens (1.25 per cent) of the population, most of whom lived in big cities such as Berlin, Hamburg and Frankfurt, or in the eastern provinces. There were almost 54,000 Jewish Berliners in 1880, and just over 90,000 in 1910 (144,000 in 'greater Berlin'). This was just under 5 per cent of the city's population, a smaller proportion of the population than in Vienna (8.6 per cent) or Budapest, where nearly a quarter of the population was Jewish.[5] Although there was a wealthy, educated and influential Jewish elite, which included high-profile figures in finance and in the country's intellectual life – universities, publishing, music, the stage and the art world – most German Jews were poor, and this was even more true of Austrian Jews, particularly in the eastern provinces of the Habsburg Empire.[6] The Jewish proportion of Germany's population declined consistently from the 1890s. In 1933 there were still around half a million Jews in Germany, but this now accounted for less than 1 per cent of the population: 160,564 lived in Berlin, and that was now less than 4 per cent of the population. Despite this a myth of 'Judaiziation' gained ground, which propagated the idea that in the wake of emancipation Jews exercised disproportionate influence and were about to occupy important positions of power.[7]

The political radicalisation of the German right that came with the First World War provided a vehicle for the dissemination of anti-Semitism, first through the Fatherland Party and then through the proliferation of right-wing splinter groups that flourished in the early years of the Weimar Republic. Nationalist propaganda depicted Jews as cowards, war profiteers and traitors, an image that was reinforced by the propagation of the 'stab-in-the-back-myth'. In more muted tones the DNVP committed itself to the struggle against the dominance of Jews in public life: the anti-Semitism of the German Nationalists was not the obsessive preoccupation that it was for Hitler and the Nazis, for whom the old threat of the Jewish usurer (turned capitalist or 'plutocrat') was now complemented by the new threat of the Jewish Bolshevik. Despite the post-war political crisis and the economic hardships of the inflation, the anti-Semitic parties, whether conservative or radical, were scarcely more successful with the electorate than their Wilhelmine predecessors. It was not until the election of July 1932, in the context of a virtual collapse of the Protestant middle-class parties, that the anti-Semitic right succeeded in winning more than a quarter of the vote. Until 1930 most of this went to the DNVP, whose electorate was probably voting primarily against Versailles, fulfilment, parliamentary democracy and a host of other conservative demons rather than against the Jews; and even in the elections of 1932 it seems unlikely that anti-Semitism was the main pull for new Nazi voters.

The Persecution of the Jews under the Nazi Regime

Nor were anti-Semitic measures the first priority for Nazi leaders when the party finally came to power in 1933. Jews were certainly victims right from the outset, and were immediately dismissed from all branches of the civil service along with Social Democrats. Although the main thrust of the initial terror was against the party's political opponents on the left, individual Jews were attacked and beaten by Nazi stormtroopers, and there was an escalation of anti-Semitic violence.[8] In Hamburg, for example, cemeteries had been desecrated, and violent attacks had made parts of the city dangerous for Jews even before 1933. The new regime licensed all kinds of criminality. The homes and community associations of Jews were looted with impunity by stormtroopers, shop windows were broken and individuals were beaten up following the so-called 'Jew hunts' in the Grindel area. Middle-class Hamburgers threw Jews out of their professional and business associations, and boycotts of Jewish businesses – not uncommon, even before 1933 – were organised under the auspices of the Nazi Party and the Combat League for the Commercial Middle Class. Such initiatives came from below and needed no legislation or instruction. Ideological motives were reinforced by material ones: whereas SA men stole directly from Jews, their more respectable colleagues improved their lot by eliminating business competition. This was made transparent by the boycott organised by the non-Jewish rivals of the largely Jewish pharmaceutical firm Beiersdorf AG (producers of Nivea) and the anti-Semitic campaign against the 'Detuv' fabric company by the Association of North German Dressmakers – despite the co-opting of 'Aryan' partners by the former precisely in order to prevent anti-Semitic attacks. For the educated middle classes, 'Aryan clauses' resolved the problem of the over-supply of lawyers – a particular problem in Hamburg – and improved university students' career opportunities as doctors and civil servants.[9]

To this end a national boycott of Jewish businesses, medical practices and lawyers was organised for 1 April 1933 and advertised as a defensive measure against Jewish 'atrocity propaganda', by which was meant reports in the foreign press of acts of violence against Jews and their property. (In fact such reporting was subdued, and calls for boycotts of German goods were rejected by Jewish organisations on the grounds that the Nazis would simply take their revenge on Jews in Germany, as Goebbels later confirmed in a speech in May.) The 'Committee for Combating Jewish Incitement to Boycott and Atrocity Propaganda', led by Julius Streicher, appealed for German businessmen to finance the boycott.

On the day – and sometimes the day before as well – stormtroopers were posted outside businesses to prevent people from entering. (The fact that English translations were added to the anti-Semitic slogans they carried suggests that the organisers expected to attract foreign attention themselves.) Those who protested or who persisted in entering Jewish premises were photographed in order to be shamed in the local press. In Annaberg in Saxony, customers had abusive slogans stamped on their faces and elsewhere there was violence. If the aim was to intimidate the foreign press, it backfired in so far as there was now more extensive reporting of German anti-Semitism, and serious attempts were made for the first time – by British trades unions – to boycott German goods.[10] Although there was no particular popular enthusiasm for the boycott, many people complied. Hertha Nathorff, a Jewish doctor in Berlin (and niece of Albert Einstein), recorded the response among her patients in her diary: 'of course some patients who had appointments do not turn up. One woman rang to say that of course she couldn't come today, and I said it would be better if she didn't come at all. [. . .] But people are a cowardly lot.'[11]

The boycott enabled the Nazi leadership to channel the undisciplined anti-Semitism of the rank and file in specific action, while at the same time it was a test of public reaction at home and abroad. Many non-Nazi supporters of the regime, both in the political class and among their broader constituency in the country were broadly in favour of reversing the emancipation of the Jews, but quibbled over the details.[12] President Hindenburg, for example, was not against the dismissal of Jews from the civil service in principle, but he insisted that war veterans be exempted. The pursuit of a more radical anti-Semitic policy remained the preoccupation of a small number of committed activists for the time being, and the number of sporadic attacks and boycotts receded somewhat during 1934.

There was a resurgence of uncoordinated anti-Semitic incidents during the summer of 1935, including demonstrations in Berlin, Munich, Cologne, Düsseldorf and other city centres, which were followed by 'copycat' incidents in suburban shopping centres and small towns and villages. Shop windows were painted with anti-Semitic slogans (or simply broken), and display cases for Julius Streicher's *Der Stürmer* were mounted everywhere. As the weather got warmer public swimming baths were a particular focus for anti-Semitic demonstrations. Jews were banned from the magnificent Herschelbad – so named after its Jewish bene-factor – in Mannheim on 10 June, and SS men drove Jewish bathers (still in their costumes) from another pool into the shrubbery of a nearby park. Baden's *Gauleiter*, Robert Wagner, described such incidents as acts of self-defence in response to Jewish 'provocation'. Confident in the knowledge that they would not be punished, stormtroopers took little trouble to establish the identity of their victims. In July they attacked traders and customers at the cattle market in Fulda indiscriminately, and a Gestapo officer from Berlin was beaten up along with Jewish bathers at a swimming pool in Kassel. Elsewhere non-Jewish businesses were attacked and ransacked.[13] The increasingly indiscriminate nature of the violence prompted a meeting of ministers on 20 August, where Schacht argued that such behaviour was damaging the economy, while Adolf Wagner, *Gauleiter* of Munich, responded on behalf of the party that the government should legislate in order to regulate anti-Semitic activity. The government responded with the 'Nuremberg laws', which were announced at the party rally in September. Hitler had intended to make an important speech on foreign policy, and the Reichstag had convened in Nuremberg for the occasion, but the speech was dropped at the last minute and had to be replaced by a policy announcement of an equally weighty nature and officials were brought to Nuremberg in some haste to assist in drafting the anti-Jewish legislation.[14]

Systematic Discrimination under the Nuremberg Laws

The Reich Citizenship Law and the Law for the Protection of German Blood and Honour, along with the supplementary decrees that followed, created the basis for the legal and economic discrimination that isolated and impoverished German Jews during the later 1930s. There had already been piecemeal changes to the law on citizenship, aimed at restricting the rights of Jews. The Law on the Revocation of Naturalisation and the Deprivation of German Citizenship (14 July 1933) had made it possible to revoke the nationality of naturalised German citizens of eastern European descent. The existing law on citizenship had been amended by Frick in May 1935, rendering legitimate claims for naturalisation void, and making future claims dependent on the discretion of the authorities. The Reich Citizenship law announced at Nuremberg now finally made ethnicity the fundamental criterion for citizenship, effectively revoking the German citizenship of all Jews, and thereby fulfilling one of the basic demands of the Nazi Party programme. A distinction was made between subjects (*Staatsangehörige*, with continuing legal obligations towards the state) and citizens – defined as subjects of German or kindred blood who demonstrated by their conduct that they were willing

and able to serve the nation and the state. This political qualification of
the racial definition of citizenship – although assumed to be met by most
Germans – made legal definition elusive, and facilitated the arbitrary
enforcement of the law. In practice the specific exclusion of Jews from
German citizenship was only made explicit in a supplementary decree
of 14 November, and for the time being only Jews and Gypsies were
intended to be excluded (although this was extended later to some east
Europeans).

The Law for the protection of German Blood and Honour (15
September 1935) forbade marriage and sexual relations between
Germans and Jews, but in order for this law (and the Reich Citizenship Law) to make sense the legal distinction between Germans and
Jews had to be clarified in terms of ethnicity. The first supplementary
decree to the Reich Citizenship Law set out to do this by defining a Jew
as the descendant of at least three Jewish grandparents, or somebody
who had two Jewish grandparents and was also either a member of the
Jewish religious community or was married to a 'full Jew' (*Volljude*) in
the stricter sense. Anybody with one Jewish parent was also considered
fully Jewish if the marriage of his or her parents had taken place after
the Law for the Protection of German Blood and Honour was passed.
A further two categories were also specified for those of mixed race
(*Mischlinge*): the first category, *Mischlinge* of the First Degree, had two
Jewish grandparents and the second, *Mischlinge* of the Second Degree,
had one. These were important distinctions that determined the level
and extent of discrimination. *Mischlinge* of the first degree initially had
a status between that of Jew and 'Aryan', and for the time being were
allowed, for example, to continue attending school and university for
longer. They were also entitled in principle to marry 'Aryans' with a
special dispensation from the Reich interior minister and deputy Führer,
but in practice such permission was hardly ever granted. Hundreds of
people were prosecuted.[15]

Once a basic legislative framework was established supplementary
decrees were used to exclude Jews from one occupation after another,
gradually isolating and impoverishing the entire community. The second
supplementary decree under the Reich Citizenship Law (promulgated
on 21 December 1935, with effect from 31 March 1936) demanded the
resignation of all senior Jewish doctors and consultants, and a number
of other proscriptive orders excluded Jews from a range of professions.
They could no longer be dentists, dieticians, vets, tax assistants, phar-
macists or chartered accountants, auctioneers, surveyors or policemen.
They could not hold public offices, be awarded doctorates, or apply

for game licences. With the Third Supplementary Decree to the Reich Citizenship Law (14 June 1938), Jewish films had to be registered as such, and the Reich minister of economics was empowered to introduce special trademarks for them. The Fourth Decree (27 September 1938) ended all Jewish medical practices, and the Fifth closed down all Jewish legal practices. Jewish lawyers were permitted to act only as legal consultants, only when absolutely necessary, and only where the case involved other Jews. Seventy per cent of the fees earned by such consultants were confiscated by the state in order to pay 'maintenance allowances' in lieu of pensions to Jews dismissed from positions in public service. Other provisions created difficulties for Jews in a range of private matters, including passports, adoption procedures, legacies and rights of succession.

Persecuting Jews was a full-time job for some civil servants. Virtually every government office had a division that dealt with changes in the law arising from the regime's anti-Semitic policies: the *Judenreferat* (Jewish section). Responsibility for 'Jewish matters' had been allocated to minor bureaucrats during the first months of the regime, and they had built up expertise and inter-ministerial contacts. Such people had a vested professional interest in the continuation and expansion of anti-Semitic measures, which they and their staff then oversaw, ensuring that anti-Semitic policy developed what has been termed a 'bureaucratic momentum'.[16] The edifice of anti-Semitic legislation is a veritable monument to the malice of the bureaucrats and party functionaries who created it. Changes to Jewish surnames, for example, had been an issue since 1933, when even non-Nazi civil servants – including Herbert von Bismarck – had fretted about the possibility of Jews changing their surnames in order to appear more 'Aryan', a procedure that had once been welcomed as a sign of assimilation. Similarly it was decided in 1935 'as an act of generosity' to leave the names of fallen Jewish servicemen on existing German war memorials (although they would not be added to new ones. In order to demonstrate their zeal, however, a number of officials took it upon themselves to erase the names of Jews anyway, sensing no doubt that as they did so they were 'working towards the Führer'. They were nothing if not pragmatic, however: no fuss was to be made about Jews in German sporting organisations until after the Olympic games.[17]

Yet there is little evidence that organised political anti-Semitism had much support among the general public during the 1930s. The boycotts and other isolated incidents that had spread during 1935 and prompted the leadership's decision to regulate anti-Semitic activity in the first place had generally been instigated by the party, and generated more antipathy than support among the public. Following two violent anti-Semitic demonstrations in Munich in May 1935 the police reported that people were 'wholly opposed' to such behaviour. Similar anti-Semitic incidents took place in Berlin, both on the Kurfürstendamm, in the middle of the city's affluent west end, and in the suburbs, particularly the working-class districts of Pankow, Wedding, Moabit and Neukölln. The Sopade reported that 'there was no resonance at all among the popula-tion' in the northern suburbs for such campaigns; the Jewish department store in Wedding was doing good business, and even small business people were not particularly anti-Semitic. The general feeling was that 'the Jews have done nothing to us'. Other reports from Berlin confirmed that there was no approval for the pogroms, even among people gener-ally sympathetic to the Nazis, and at one such incident a crowd had protested against the stormtroopers: 'louts with nothing better to do than cause trouble'. The public judged such obviously stage-managed events as diversions from real political problems, and mocked the stories of Jewish misdeeds that were published in the Nazi press to justify them.[18] Popular disapproval of Nazi intimidation could not protect Jews against the relentless tide of official discrimination, however, and it was little consolation for the private humiliations and increasing isolation of many ordinary Jewish people who just wanted to get on with their lives. The diary of the Jewish doctor Hertha Nathorff records an encounter in October 1935 with a former secretary: 'She fixed me sharply with her short-sighted eyes, and then turned away. I was so nauseated I spat into my handkerchief . . . I never go anywhere any more. I am so well known through my profession and my position; why should I make trouble for myself and others. I'm happy to be at home in peace.'[19] Any hopes that the Nuremberg laws would put an end to arbitrary violence and intimid-ation – and perhaps prove to be the final objective of Nazi policy – were quickly dispelled.

The Radicalisation of Anti-Jewish Measures

The purge of leading conservatives from influential positions in 1937 and 1938 marked the onset of a new, more radical phase in the development of the regime, and radicalism in one area of policy immediately had radical consequences elsewhere. Following the occupation of Austria, for example, Viennese Jews were robbed, beaten and humiliated in a pogrom that lasted for weeks. The plundering of Jewish businesses by men claiming to be stormtroopers quickly became a problem for the authorities themselves, who duly blamed the Communists in public, but took action behind the scenes against the Nazi rank and file, threatening both the men and their group leaders if discipline could not be restored.[20] A British journalist recorded the way in which Jews were made to scrub away the patriotic slogans and images stencilled on walls and pavements by the Schuschnigg regime:

> Now, day after day Nazi stormtroopers, surrounded by laughing mobs of 'golden Viennese hearts', dragged Jews from shops, offices and homes, men and women, put scrubbing-brushes in their hands, splashed them well with acid, and made them go down on their knees and scrub away for hours at the hopeless task of removing Schuschnigg propaganda. All this I could watch from my office window overlooking the Graben. (Where there was none available, I have seen the Nazis painting it for the Jews to remove.) [. . .] "Work for the Jews at last, work for the Jews!" the mob howled. "We thank our Führer for finding work for the Jews." '[21]

In the wake of the initial violence, a more genteel plunder was initiated. Economic experts moved into Vienna from Hamburg to advise Josef Bürckel, Reich Commissioner for the Reunification of Austria with the German Reich, on ways in which Jews could be eliminated from economic life – and opportunities opened up for Hamburg firms suffering the consequences of Germany's international economic isolation. In addition, the 'Aryanisation' of Jewish property in Vienna was to assist in stimulating the stagnating Austrian economy by 'rationalising' the small business sector. Many Austrian Jews had already left the country in March, and during the summer the pressure intensified to such an extent that some one hundred thousand left between May 1938 and the outbreak of the war, and it was estimated that some 12,000–14,000 Jewish flats could be made available to 'Aryans'.[22] The 'Vienna model' of expropriation and expulsion – co-ordinated by Adolf Eichmann's 'Central Office for Jewish Emigration' in Vienna – proved so successful that it was adopted both in the Reich itself and in other occupied countries.[23]

The situation was transformed in November 1938, when party leaders unleashed a full-scale pogrom against the Jews throughout the Reich. (The direct involvement of both Goebbels and Hitler in orchestrating the violence has now been established more clearly by the discovery of missing sections of Goebbels' diaries in Moscow after the collapse of the

Soviet Union.)[24] Known as the '*Kristallnacht*' (crystal night or the 'night of broken glass') on account of the extensive damage to Jewish property, the pogrom marked a further turning point in the regime's anti-Jewish policy. Ostensibly prompted by the shooting of a German diplomat, Ernst vom Rath, on 7 November in Paris, the pogrom was preceded by localised attacks on 8 November, which generally followed a rabble-rousing speech by a local SA leader. None of the local leaders claimed, at their post-war trials, to have been following orders from above, and most maintained that the riots were spontaneous. Although many non-Nazis did take part, however, most of the smaller riots on 8 November were in places where the local party leader was a radical anti-Semite. The following day was the anniversary of Hitler's failed 1923 putsch and the occasion of an annual reunion in the old town hall in Munich. The news of vom Rath's death from his wounds was brought to Hitler during the event and after a brief, urgent discussion with Goebbels (the principal instigator of the pogrom) he departed, leaving the propaganda minister to deliver a virulent anti-Semitic rant to the assembled stormtroopers, in which he mentioned that popular reprisals had already been taken in some parts of Germany. During the night a wave of terror was unleashed against Jews across Germany. Individuals were beaten and murdered, homes and businesses smashed and ransacked, and personal property looted on an unprecedented scale. Several hundred synagogues were burned down, over 8000 businesses were destroyed, and some 30,000 Jewish men were incarcerated in concentration camps.[25]

The pogrom was anything but a 'success', however, even in the Nazis' own terms. Goebbels' role as instigator irritated Himmler and Göring, the latter not least because of the economic implications of the material damage caused – and not all of it was to Jewish property, since many Jewish businesses rented their premises. The issue was addressed at a conference called by Göring on 12 November to co-ordinate responses to the 'Jewish question', at which Goebbels was also present along with Heydrich, Funk, the conservative finance minister, Schwerin von Krosigk, Kurt Daluege, head of the uniformed police, and a hundred or so officials and experts. Apart from a round of pedantic bickering between Göring and Goebbels about the best way to introduce anti-Semitic apartheid on the railways, the conference resolved to make the Jews themselves liable for the damage caused to property during the pogrom by imposing a collective fine of a thousand million Reichsmarks on the Jewish community. In addition a 'Decree excluding Jews from German Economic Life' was issued under the auspices of the Four Year Plan.[26]

The position of Jews in Germany deteriorated rapidly as effective control of anti-Jewish policy passed into the hands of the SS. Even as Göring reasserted his formal control over what he deemed to be an economic issue, Heydrich had insisted that the main problem was getting the Jews out of the country. On 24 January Göring instructed Heydrich to set up a central office for Jewish emigration on the Vienna model. Heydrich also oversaw the creation of a Reich Association of Jews in Germany, whose purpose to co-ordinate the emigration process from the Jewish side, just as Eichmann had used the Vienna *Kultusgemeinde* (religious community). Thousands of Jews emigrated, but those leaving Germany found it increasingly difficult to find foreign countries that would take them. Those Jews remaining in Germany were subjected to further restrictions and humiliations, and were progressively excluded altogether from public life. The existence of a corps of 'Jewish experts' within the German civil service ensured and reinforced the bureaucratic momentum behind the continuing stream of anti-Jewish measures, even as German Jews were emigrating and being deported to ghettoes in Poland.

The outbreak of war in 1939 had far-reaching implications for the development of the regime's anti-Jewish policy. The occupation of western and central Poland increased the number of Jews within Germany's jurisdiction by over 2 million, just as the outbreak of war simultaneously made emigration more difficult. (The remainder of Poland's Jewish population fell within the territories occupied by the USSR.) War not only changed the domestic political situation, freeing the regime from some of the remaining constraints on its radical impulses, it also provided a space outside the Reich altogether in which racial ideology could be implemented with less regard for legal and constitutional niceties or for public opinion. In a speech to the Reichstag in January 1939, Hitler had asserted that 'Jewish financiers within and outside Europe' were attempting to bring about another war, and threatened that if they succeeded the Jewish race in Europe would be annihilated.[27] Most historians now agree that it was unlikely there was already a specific intention behind the threat at this stage, but it certainly reflected a collective sense within the regime that the persecution of the Jews would escalate with the outbreak of war.[28]

Polish Jews suffered the worst of this radicalisation in the wake of the German invasion. Special units (*Einsatzgruppen*) followed the German army into Poland. (They had been deployed during the successive German invasions of Austria, the Sudetenland and Bohemia and Moravia.) These task forces were made up of members of the SD and the Security police (i.e. the Criminal Police and the Gestapo) and were led by educated men: over half of the leaders had doctorates in law or philosophy.[29] Although technically subordinate to the army, they received their instructions from the SS, and were charged with the suppression of 'elements hostile to the Reich' behind the lines as the German army advanced into Poland.[30] Jews were beaten up and murdered along with members of Poland's political elites. Those who survived were rounded up and herded into ghettoes. According to instructions from Heydrich in September, small Jewish communities in the countryside were to 'disappear' and their inhabitants were to be concentrated in urban ghettoes where they could be kept under surveillance and more easily moved on later. This operation was to be completed within 3 to 4 weeks, leaving behind only those Jews involved in supplying the German armed forces, and goods trains were to be used to move them systematically.[31] Pressure was increased on the timetable to deport Jews – and to 'clear' dwellings, land, business and jobs – in order to accommodate the arrival of some 440,000 ethnic Germans under agreements with the Soviet Union and Italy. To this extent, the envisaged resettlement of Jews in Poland was associated with the Nazi drive for the 'consolidation of Germandom' under the direction of Heinrich Himmler. The deportation of all Jews (and Poles) from the greater German Reich, the envisaged resettlement of ethnic Germans, in the first instance from the Baltic, Galicia and Volhynia, was part of a grandiose scheme for the demographic restructuring of eastern Europe by means of what has come to be known euphemistically as 'ethnic cleansing'.[32]

This meant that, for the time being at least, the solution to Nazi Germany's self-imposed Jewish 'problem' was conceived in territorial terms, and specifically the deportation of Jews first to urban ghettoes and then to a 'reservation' of some kind.[33] Once the new frontiers in occupied Poland had been agreed with the Soviet Union, plans were mooted for a large-scale 'Reich ghetto' or 'Jewish reservation' in the area around Lublin, but this policy encountered a recurrent problem in the regime's anti-Jewish policy in Poland: the tension between the ambition of local functionaries to deport as many Jews as possible from their own communities, and the reluctance of those in charge of the areas designated for reception to see very large numbers concentrated on their own territory. The deportation of large numbers of Jews to the *Generalgouvernement* from those territories to be incorporated directly into the Reich proved impractical not least because of the tensions it caused between Arthur Greiser, the *Gauleiter* of the newly created Warthegau,

and Hans Frank the 'governor general' of rump Poland, and by the
beginning of 1940 the SS had been forced to cut back its plans for
large-scale deportations and resettlements, not least on account of the
enormous practical problems they immediately generated.[34] 'Everybody
wants to dump his rubbish in the Generalgouvernement' Goebbels noted
in his diary in November 1940. 'Jews, the sick, the feckless etc. And
Frank resists. Not entirely without good cause. He wants to make Poland
a model territory. That's going too far. He cannot and he should not.
Poland should be an enormous reservoir of labour for us . . . and we'll
move the Jews out of this area later.'[35]

In the meantime the creation of ghettoes where the Jews already lived
seemed a more pragmatic policy, and plans were formulated for the
establishment of a ghetto in Łodz (which was set up in May 1940),
but here too the authorities were apprehensive about accepting large
numbers of deported Jews from smaller town. In practice ghettoes were
being established in smaller towns across the Warthegau, generally at the
instigation of local authorities or occupying forces responding to events
on the ground, while the official policy of the regime remained vague.
Many of the less fortunate, among them the weak and the elderly, were
taken to the woods and indiscriminately murdered. Ghettoization of the
Jews in the *Generalgouvernement* took place in the autumn of 1940 and the
Warsaw ghetto, the largest in Poland, was established in November, in
the face of all manner of practical objections – and despite the disruption
it would bring to the city's economic activity. At the same time Jews
were conscripted into forced labour programmes, often in camps or in
construction sites away from their families.[36]

With the defeat of France, and the prospect of peace with Britain,
an alternative 'territorial solution' emerged: the possibility of expelling
all the Jews from Europe to the French colony of Madagascar off the
coast of East Africa. The plan was supported by right-wing anti-Semites
in Britain and France and would not only mean an end to the accumu-
lating problems caused by the deportation of Jews to Poland, but also the
possibility of replacing Jewish economic influence with that of Germany
in one fell swoop with the confiscation of all Jewish assets by a bank
created for the purpose. The looting of Jewish property on a continental scale by German bankers would make the project self-financing. In
the *Generalgouvernement* Frank was immensely relieved and work ceased
on ghetto construction, while planning for the mass deportation forged
ahead under the auspices of Franz Rademacher, of the *Judenreferat* in
the foreign office. Simultaneously, Eichmann and his staff at the RSHA
drew up their own plans during the summer of 1940 to expel a million

Jews a year from Europe over 4 years. Germany's failure to defeat Britain in September 1940 meant that the plans came to nothing, however, despite the real preparations that had been made to suspend deportations from the incorporated territories and ghettoisation plans in the *Generalgouvernement.*[37]

The end of plans for large-scale deportations to Lublin or Madagascar meant that the concentration of Jews in urban ghettoes in Poland was now a long-term prospect. It was a situation that came about through failure rather than planning and was characterised by conflicting objectives. Some saw the ghettoes as a means of hastening the deterioration and death of as many Jews as possible in the quickest possible time; others saw them as potential labour camps that might contribute to the German war economy. Although the latter strategy prevailed in principle, the meagre rations (at 300 calories a day less than half of those accorded the Poles), lack of heating fuel and overcrowding meant that the health of those in the ghetto deteriorated rapidly in any case. Disease spread in the absence of adequate hygiene and health care, and to add insult to injury Strength through Joy organised coach tours, enabling tourists to gawp at, photograph, taunt and humiliate the inhabitants of the ghetto. Over 7000 people died in the Łodz ghetto in the second half of 1940, and the death toll rose to 2000 a month in the spring of 1941, and over 4000 in April. In the Warsaw ghetto the number of deaths rose from 1023 in January 1941 to over 5500 in July and August.[38] The establishment of the ghettoes marked a further step in the persecution of the Jews, but were more than a transitional stage on the way to mass murder. Gustavo Corni has argued that the ghetto constituted a 'distinctive moment' in the history of east European Jewish communities, and preserved something of a social structure in which elements of traditional Jewish society were able to survive. Appalling as conditions were in Łodz, Warsaw and other ghettoes, there was a clear dividing line between the treatment of the Jews there and what was to follow.

The regime did not abandon the idea of the mass deportation of Jews from those parts of Europe controlled by Germany. Jews from Alsace and Lorraine were deported into France in 1940, along with Gypsies and others from the various categories considered undesirable by the Nazis, including German Jews from Saarpfalz and Baden. Once the Vichy authorities realised what was happening, however, they resisted further deportations and refused to take them.[39] Moreover, German expansion in Europe meant that more Jews fell under German control and the pressure for a 'solution' increased both from Nazi officials in Poland and from Germany's Axis partners in south-eastern Europe, who also had large Jewish populations. Eichmann informed Himmler on 4 December that 5.8 million Jews would have to be resettled in a 'territory yet to be determined', presumably a reference to anticipated deportations to the Soviet Union. A fortnight later Hitler signed the directive for Operation Barbarossa.[40]

Operation Barbarossa and the Origins of the Holocaust

With the stalling of Germany's military campaign in the West Hitler had turned his attention to the East, and the invasion of the Soviet Union in June 1941 transformed and radicalised immeasurably the Nazis' understanding of the Jewish 'problem'. The Soviet campaign was conceived as a war of annihilation, a struggle of ideologies in the course of which the enemy, political commissars and 'Jewish–Bolshevik' intelligentsia alike must be annihilated, as Hitler put in an address to his generals in March 1941. To this end special units (*Einsatzgruppen*) such as those that had been deployed in Poland, but which had been conspicuous by their relative absence in the campaigns in western Europe, were to be sent into action again. In 1939 senior officers, fearing a general brutalisation of the armed forces, had complained about the activities of the *Einsatzgruppen*, but Hitler himself had intervened personally, to block any legal proceedings against the special forces by issuing a general amnesty, and on 17 October 1939 he had removed the police and SS altogether from any civil or military jurisdiction and placed them under exceptional jurisdiction. Since then, Hitler's own position had been immensely strengthened by the military successes in the West and it seemed there was now no question of opposition from the generals.[41] Moreover, Heydrich's orders to the higher SS leaders in Russia specifying those to be executed concentrated on Communist Party officials: 'all Comintern functionaries and in fact any career politicians, the senior middle-ranking and the more radical junior functionaries of the Party, of Central Committees, of regional and local committees, people's commissars, Jews in Party and state positions, other radical elements (saboteurs, propagandists, snipers, assassins, agitators, etc.)'. Little specific mention was made of Jews in the various instructions issued to the army and the *Einsatzgruppen* and – arguably – this made the instructions easier to accept.[42]

The German advance into the Soviet Union was accompanied by the indiscriminate mass murder of Jews, whether by shooting or by more barbarous methods, as in Bialystok where over 500 men, women and children were burned alive in a synagogue by German soldiers and policemen.[43] The invasion marked a transition from any lingering considerations of a 'territorial solution' to the practice of genocide both in practice and as a systematic policy. However unsystematic and dependent on local circumstances, the mass killings carried out in the Soviet Union in 1941 were on a scale unprecedented in Poland and elsewhere, and escalated further as the campaign continued. Within months of the invasion over half a million Jews had been murdered. Although there is continuing disagreement about the timing and nature of the decision to murder all the Jews of Europe, it seems that it was probably taken in the second half of 1941. A combination of developments indicated a radicalisation of policy. Pressure began to mount for the deportation of all European Jews to the East, particularly in the wake of Stalin's deportation of the Volga Germans to central Asia. In September Hitler decided to deport the remaining Jews in the Greater German Reich itself (including the Protectorate), and the emigration of Jews from Germany was halted by Himmler in October.

Accordingly, a number of leading historians of the Holocaust have located the decision to exterminate the Jews in October 1941, in the context of a series of discrete measures that collectively constituted an incremental move from persecution to systematic mass murder. More recently others have suggested that the turning point was in December, and was determined by the failure of the Soviet campaign to achieve a swift victory (thereby excluding the possibility of mass expulsions into the Soviet Union); and by the entry of the United States into the war, which seemed to mark the fulfilment of Hitler's prophecy of 1939.[44] The decision-making process that instigated the holocaust has been difficult for historians to determine, partly because the surviving evidence was uneven and incomplete, and partly because of the secretiveness of the perpetrators themselves. They obscured the record by avoiding direct references to what was happening, using coded or euphemistic language, and – in keeping with Hitler's own working practices – holding formal minuted meetings very rarely in any case. As a consequence local initiatives are well documented, but the furtiveness of the Nazi elites – who deliberately set out to prevent discussion of what was happening – has served to obscure any clear record of the overall planning for a large-scale genocide which required a high level of organisation.[45] That Hitler himself was ultimately responsible, however, is beyond doubt.[46]

This incremental decision-making process took place in the context of ever more radical initiatives from local Nazi functionaries in the East. Gas vans, which had already been used to murder victims of the 'euthanasia' programme, were tested on Soviet prisoners of war in Sachsenhausen in September 1941, and were used systematically by Einsatzgruppen in the Soviet Union from December. They were also used in the extermination camp at Chelmno, from December, to murder those Jews from the Wartheland who were considered unfit for work in the Lodz ghetto. 'Gas vans were used' to asphyxiate the victims slowly with carbon monoxide, a method considered less distressing for the perpetrators than the mass shootings, which had begun to cause symptoms of stress. Simultaneously pressure for the deportation of Jews from the *Generalgouvernement* intensified.

In January 1942 a meeting was held in Berlin at which Heydrich summarised the actions taken against the Jews so far, set out the number and location of Jews remaining in Europe, and outlined the regime's plans to deport them to the East. The meeting was attended by senior SS officers, civil servants and party members, who would have understood that deportation by now meant extermination, even if that could not be said explicitly in a meeting whose minutes – the 'Wannsee protocol' – were subsequently circulated to a number of government departments and SS offices. The conference itself was not the meeting that decided on genocide, nor did it produce a finalised programme of extermination in death camps, not least because neither Hitler nor any other Nazi leaders were present who were senior enough to make such a decision. But it confirmed that genocide was official policy, and it strengthened the hands of those running what was now very clearly a systematic programme of deportation and mass murder.[47]

Genocide

In the course of 1942 and 1943 the mass murder of the Jews was accelerated and intensified. Following the establishment of the first extermination camp at Chelmno, Himmler approved the construction of other death camps, first at Belzec, where work began in November 1941, and then at Sobibor and Treblinka. He put Odilo Globicnik, former *Gauleiter* of Vienna and now police chief in Lublin, in charge of 'Operation Reinhardt', the mass murder of some 1.75 million Jews in the *Generalgouvernement*. Staff were released from the euthanasia programme and arrived in Poland in the autumn of 1941 to take up their new duties. They were paid directly by Hitler's own 'chancellery of the Führer'.

The pace of the killing increased during the course of 1942 and 1943 in a single-minded drive to deport and murder all the Jews in Europe.

They were rounded up from occupied territories in the south and west and transported across Europe to the death camps in the East in an enormous undertaking which required correspondingly vast resources. The deportations deprived the regime of the labour of the victims themselves, and directed vital resources away from the war effort, including the time and energy of the collaborators who worked with the German authorities at local level; the ideological objective of ridding Europe of the Jews was deemed to be more important than the rational management of the war economy.[48]

In some parts of western Europe there was opposition to the deportations, whether from the authorities (as in Belgium) or the public (as in the Netherlands). In those parts of Scandinavia under German control (Norway, Denmark and Finland) there were scarcely 10,000 Jews altogether. Although the Quisling puppet regime in Norway was keen to do the Germans' bidding, Sweden not only opened its borders, but invited some of the Jews who had been arrested to apply for Swedish citizenship. In Denmark a tip-off from a senior German official made it possible to organise an operation to ferry the country's Jewish population across to Sweden.[49] In occupied France collaborators fuelled anti-Semitism from 1940 and measures were taken immediately requiring Jews to register with the authorities; the Vichy regime in the unoccupied south issued a 'Jewish statute' of its own in October 1940, and this formed the basis for a proliferation of restrictions and regulations, and although Vichy resisted some pressure from Germany it also introduced anti-Jewish measures of its own. Jews were arrested and imprisoned in camps in the occupied zone in 1941. The camp at Drancy, outside Paris, became the departure point for deportations to Auschwitz and remained in operation until a week before the liberation of the city. Over 75,000 Jews were deported, two-thirds of whom were foreign and a third French. Despite the active anti-Semitism among collaborators in the north and on the part of the Vichy regime in the unoccupied zone, a greater proportion of France's Jewish population survived than in many other European countries, not least because many Jews themselves resisted, and because French public opinion was turned from hostility indifference to sympathy and solidarity by the treatment of the Jews when arrests began in 1942.[50]

In the Nazi satellite states, pressure was put on the local population to introduce anti-Semitic legislation and eventually to assist the German authorities in deporting Jews to Poland. Such pressure was resisted most successfully in Bulgaria, where many of the country's Jews were saved, and in Hungary where the Horthy regime obstructed Nazi deportation plans until the country was occupied and the regime overthrown and replaced by a Nazi puppet regime in 1944. In Serbia the extensive participation of the Wehrmacht in local massacres, and the assistance it afforded the SS ensured that the mass murder of the entire Jewish population, including women and children, was completed by 1942, when the industrial genocide in Poland had scarcely begun.[51]

The victims were transported to Poland in conditions of unspeakable squalor and the casual brutality with which they were treated was frequently aggravated with calculated individual acts of violence and humiliation by the personnel charged with implementing the murder programme. The most chilling aspect of the death camps, however, was that unlike earlier stages of the persecution and even earlier murders, the planning, administration and implementation of the murders took place on 'an assembly-line basis'.[52] Most of the murders were carried out in gas chambers on the model of those used in the euthanasia stations, using the poison gas Zyklon B. Victims arriving at Auschwitz were given soap and a towel and herded into the chamber by SS men with dogs. A supervising doctor then gave the order to administer the gas, which was introduced through vents leading into induction shafts, or pellets were inserted through an opening in an antechamber. All the victims were usually dead within twenty minutes. Spectacles, artificial limbs, jewellery and even gold fillings and women's hair were all removed from the corpses, which were then burned in specially constructed crematoria in each of which 2500 corpses could be burned every day. When furnaces broke down through overload, corpses were burned in incineration pits.[53]

Much of this gruesome work was carried out by the prisoners themselves, who were assigned to special units (*Sonderkommandos*) charged with the various tasks. While such people were victims themselves acting under duress, the behaviour of the majority of perpetrators – from the relatively random violence of the pogrom and the apparently uncoordinated massacres of the German armed forces and the special units that accompanied them to the mechanised genocide of Auschwitz – seems to defy historical explanation (and has certainly attracted a range of *ahistorical* responses). There was no predictable route by which perpetrators came to be involved in the holocaust, and contingency played a part in the lives of both 'ordinary men' and 'real Nazis' involved in the mass murders in the east. While the process of 'brutalisation' that took place in Poland forms part of the explanation for the massacres and mass murders, it can never be wholly adequate; and nor can peer pressure, or fear of the consequences of a refusal to participate. We know that even when there was an option to withdraw from an operation, some did so and some did not.[54] For the senior officers, administrators and planners who played little or no direct physical part in the killing, it was perhaps easier to rationalise their role in the genocide in intellectual terms, as a 'necessary' service they performed for the notional greater good of the race. 'Pen-pushing perpetrators' (*Schreibtischtäter*) avoided confronting the grim reality of the holocaust, and frequently too the responsibility for their part in the killing.

Although the exact number of Jewish holocaust victims is difficult to determine, the evidence suggests that there were between 5 and 6 million, over half of them from Poland. In addition to those who were murdered, others committed suicide, died while fleeing from the Nazis, or of privations and sickness resulting directly from persecution. Apart from those gentiles who were mistaken by the Nazis for Jews, a range of other groups were victimised and murdered by the Nazis and their allies, above all Roma and Sinti, who were also persecuted on similar racial grounds.[55] In addition there were victims from a range of other groups of 'outsiders': homosexuals, 'asocials', political opponents.[56] The holocaust recruited collaborators from all parts of Europe, and particularly from eastern Europe.[57] Despite the secrecy surrounding the murders, knowledge of what was happening was relatively widespread, not only in the localities where massacres were taking place and death camps were situated, but also by many people in the communities across Europe from which Jews were being deported and among the civilian population in Germany.[58] Although the holocaust was a crime that originated with the Nazi dictatorship in Germany, it was one which was implemented on a European scale.

Chapter 9: Foreign Policy and the Second World War

Foreign policy, war and territorial expansion were absolutely central to Nazism as a political movement. Its ideological roots were in the radical nationalist milieu of the late nineteenth century, while the NSDAP itself grew out of war and defeat. The early Nazi Party was one of a number of right-wing paramilitary groups that recruited demobilised soldiers, among them Hitler himself, and it profited as a political party from the widespread indignation prompted by the peace settlement – and this was a feeling shared by millions of Germans, by no means all of them Nazis, or even nationalists. The Third Reich existed for barely 12 years and for half of that time it was engaged in an aggressive expansionist war. Even during its 6 years of peace, the reality of everyday experience in Nazi Germany was shaped by preparations for war, and by the economic dislocations that resulted from the headlong drive for rearmament. The combination of rearmament boom. Hitler's apparent success in restoring Germany's international greatness and the military victories of the early war years all did much to reinforce the stability of the regime and the authority of its leadership. Conversely, the removal of the dictatorship came only with total military defeat.

Defeat, revolution and the mythology of betrayal shaped the political climate in which the Nazi Party was established, and determined the course of politics throughout the Weimar Republic. The German people had been assured of victory by their military and political leaders, and when defeat eventually came it was such a shock that many people, especially on the nationalist right, refused to accept it, constructing for themselves the reassuring fiction that German's armies had not been militarily defeated but had been betrayed at home by Bolshevik revolutionaries led by Jews. General Field Marshall Hindenburg himself promoted this 'stab-in-the-back-myth' (*Dolchstosslegende*) in his self-serving testimony to a committee of Weimar's constituent assembly in November 1919: 'An English general said with justice: "the German army was stabbed in the back." No guilt applies to the good core of the army. [...] Where the guilt lies has clearly been demonstrated.'[1]

Hitler and Nazi Foreign Policy in the Weimar Republic

The shock of defeat was followed by humiliation at Versailles, where German responsibility for the outbreak of the war was enshrined in the so-called 'war-guilt' clause, which fuelled German indignation and served the interests of those seeking to undermine the legitimacy of the post-war settlement, domestic and international. For the radical right, the stab-in-the-back myth was a consoling self-delusion which persisted until the end of the Second World War. It is important to be aware that Nazi foreign policy – and Hitler's own thinking – developed in the context of an unusual level of public interest and popular engagement in questions of foreign policy. Positions were polarised, disagreements were shrill and accusations of treachery and betrayal were frequent, but the agenda was nevertheless determined as much by immediate events as by inherited ideological positions. Accordingly, Hitler's early speeches on foreign policy, like those of many other right-wing demagogues of the day, were dominated by hysterical tirades against the injustices of Versailles.

This is not to say that ideological influences were unimportant, and even among the radical nationalist groups of the time, Hitler brought distinctive perspectives to questions of international relations. His early ideas on foreign policy, like those on a whole range of issues, had been shaped by the Pan-German ideology of the *völkisch* movement. He demanded the return of Germany's lost territories both in Europe and overseas, and foresaw the creation of a 'Greater Germany' incorporating not only territory that had been lost to Poland and the Soviet Russia in the east or to France in the West, but the German-speaking territories of the former Habsburg empire as well. The proposed '*Anschluss*' of Austria and Germany was popular among the dispirited people of 'rump' Austria (as the new Alpine republic was called), almost all of whom were ethnically German. The union of the two countries was explicitly prohibited by the terms of the peace treaties, however. Germany could not be allowed to gain territorially from the outcome of the war, notwithstanding the widely

trumpeted Allied principle of the self-determination of peoples.[2] Naturally, then, France and Britain, rather than Russia, were cast as Germany's
arch-enemies at this stage of Hitler's thinking on international relations. This reflected the politics of the early 1920s, when the foreign
policy agenda was dominated by the issue of the 'fulfilment policy'
(*Erfüllungspolitik*) of Weimar governments who were compelled to accept
the real international situation and with it the conditions of the Versailles
treaty. The radical right – primarily, at this stage, the DNVP – refused to
be associated with the policy and exploited the issue politically in order
to undermine the post-war settlement.

Hitler's *Weltanschauung* was by no means unalterably set in stone by
the early 1920s, however, and under the influence of Alfred Rosenberg and Max Erwin Scheubner-Richter, both German refugees from the
Baltic, his ideas underwent important changes during the early 1920s.
The Baltic Germans were obsessed with the idea that Jews had brought
about the Bolshevik revolution, and Rosenberg convinced Hitler that it
had been the consequence of a worldwide Jewish conspiracy.[3] By 1924,
when Hitler was writing *Mein Kampf*, anti-Bolshevism and anti-Semitism
had become inextricably combined in Hitler's view of the world. This
did not mean that other elements inherited from Pan-German ideology
had to be abandoned: the peace settlement had been imposed by the
Western Allies in the interests of a Jewish 'plutocracy', which effectively
controlled the political and economic life of the democracies, and which
sought to make 'interest slaves' of the whole German nation with their
reparations demands. Many of these early ideas remained constant both
in Hitler's view of international relations and in Nazi propaganda, which
exploited the hostility to the Soviet Union and fear of Bolshevism that
were common across the spectrum of political opinion in both Germany
and abroad. At the same time it connected with a vein of cultural anti-
Americanism on the German (and European right) that was anxious
about the spread of popular commercial culture encouraged by 'Jewish'
publishers, entertainment managers and film producers.

With this anti-Semitic interpretation of foreign policy Hitler and his
mentors brought a specifically Nazi or *völkisch* perspective to international relations, but assumptions of racial difference had long characterised German foreign policy, particularly in relation to eastern Europe
(just as similar assumptions had characterised the imperialisms of western
Europe). It was something of a given conviction among many German
historians, archaeologists and ethnologists that the Slav nations in the
East were incapable of organising their states and economies independently to the same levels of civilised efficiency as the Germans themselves,

who were seen as historical bearers of culture in the region. These prejudices seemed to be confirmed by the experience of German soldiers on the eastern front during the First World War. They were shocked by conditions in the occupied western territories of the Russian empire, and senior officers responded with an experiment in authoritarian government that anticipated the characteristics of the SS state.[4] With the Treaty of Brest-Litovsk, which effectively made the Ukraine a puppet state of the Reich, the possibility of a much greater German presence in the East was opened up. These expansionist ambitions were thwarted by defeat and by the conditions of the Treaty of Versailles, which compelled Germany to withdraw not only from the newly acquired territories, but also from parts of Poland which had been Prussian for over a century.

This did not mean that the question of Germany's eastern frontier was considered as settled by any means. Gustav Stresemann, Germany's foreign minister for much of the 1920s, was nothing if not pragmatic, and with the Locarno Treaty aimed to regulate relations with the West, primarily France, by recognising the new frontier in the West. This was a step which prompted the formal withdrawal of the DNVP from the governing coalition, but which also ended Germany's international isolation and laid the basis for co-operation with the Western powers. He hoped to make a number of gains in the West, including the withdrawal of foreign troops from the Ruhr and the recovery of the Saarland, and hoped then to be able to negotiate a revision of Germany's eastern frontiers. Finally, he hoped to be able to achieve a state of affairs where all Germans could live together in one state (even if some foreigners had to be brought under German rule), an ambition that was also reflected in a memorandum of the *Truppenamt* from 1926.[5] This is not to suggest an inevitable continuity between Stresemann's revisionism and that of the Third Reich. Stresemann was realistic enough to recognise that Germany had far more to gain from co-operation with the West than from confrontation, and his strategy for the restoration of Germany's great-power status was cautious and gradual, and although he doubted it himself towards the end of his life, it was relatively successful.

Stresemann's death in 1929 meant that his foreign policy was not tested by the economic adversity and international tension of the Depression. He was succeeded by Julius Curtius of the DVP, but Brüning himself took over the portfolio in his second administration. The tenor of the foreign policy pursued by the 'presidential cabinets' of the early 1930s was characterised by a much sharper political and economic nationalism. Brüning wanted to be free of the constraints of Versailles and of reparations payments, and his deflationary economic policy has been interpreted as a means of demonstrating Germany's inability to pay. For the Nazis the Depression demonstrated only too well the short-comings of economic liberalism, and in the context of an increasingly protectionist world market, German governments intervened directly to stimulate recovery and the idea of economic self-sufficiency (autarky) – within the framework of a supra-national, regional economy (*Grossraum-wirtschaft*) – gained acceptance as a desirable objective. Theories of autarky promoted by the 'reform' school complemented the geopolitical concept of *Lebensraum* and provided the Nazis with an alternative to the principle of free trade as a way of organising international economic relations. Hitler himself was sceptical of economic motives as the basis for foreign policy, but there was nevertheless a strong economic dimension to his foreign policy in that one of its central objectives was providing for Germany's material needs. Territorial expansion would be the means of providing the food and raw materials Germany needed, but this would in turn encourage population growth and further expansion, as befitted a 'master race' in Hitler's social Darwinist concept of international rela-tions. The alternative, in his view, was a degenerate commercialism which would sap Germany's lifeblood and deliver the economy into the hands of the Jews.[6]

Revisionism, Re-armament and the Restoration of German Greatness

When the Nazis came to power in 1933 they were necessarily constrained by the realities of the international situation: Germany was still weak, militarily and economically, and the new government could do little in the short term to improve the country's international position, although Hitler made very clear from the outset his intention to pursue a radical, aggressive foreign policy. He had the support of leading generals, including Werner von Blomberg (whom Hindenburg had appointed defence minister on his own initiative on 30 January 1933) and Walther von Reichenau. The new government and the armed forces shared the goals of rearmament and the restoration of German greatness, but this did not mean that the relationship between the regime and the army was unproblematic. Senior army officers shared the nationalist objectives of the Nazis' conservative allies, but were suspicious of a mass party with its own armed formations. Tensions mounted as stormtroopers seemed increasingly reluctant to bring the 'national revolution' to an end, and conservative anxieties were expressed in Papen's speech at Marburg University on 17 June 1934. The purge that followed effectively removed the threat of the SA (and some conservative critics of the regime), but failed to resolve tensions between the regime and the armed forces. Steps were taken to extend the regime's control over the war economy with the launch of the four-year plan in 1936 and measures to regulate the labour market in the late 1930s.

Following the rapid stabilisation of the domestic political situation with the repressive measures of 1933, however, Hitler increasingly turned his attention to foreign policy. Steps were taken immediately to rearm Germany, to create what was called a 'defence economy' (*Wehrwirtschaft*), a peacetime economy fully geared for preparing for war, where the needs of the domestic economy, of consumer goods industries and exporters, were clearly subordinated to the requirements of the rearmament programme, for labour, capital and raw materials, giving rise to shortages and structural problems as production switched to arms-related industries. The regime's propaganda, which proclaimed Reich's peaceful intentions to all who would listen, also relentlessly reiterated the need for sacrifice if Germany's position as a great power was to be restored, and housewives in particular were targeted by propaganda promoting the idea of economic self-sufficiency. The injunction to economise, like later propaganda designed to bring more women into the workforce, fell largely on deaf ears and indeed the two messages contradicted each other: working women had *less* time to darn old clothes and make jam, especially during the war.[7] In fact, Nazi Germany maintained a working level of popular consent for its policies by avoiding excessive demands on the population.

After the experience of the First World War, anxiety about the possibility of another war was widespread in Germany, and reached a crescendo each time international tension peaked, only to subside and give way to relief as the crisis was passed, a process which accompanied all of Hitler's major foreign policy triumphs. 'Everybody is convinced that the Saar plebiscite will lead to war', a Sopade reporter from Silesia noted in 1934, and the subject dominated political discussion both before and after the event. The result of the plebiscite, an overwhelming victory for the regime on 13 January 1935, disappointed dissenters, strengthened Hitler's position and dispelled anxieties about war – a pattern that was repeated on several occasions throughout the 1930s.[8] In March 1935 conscription was reintroduced in violation of the Treaty of Versailles. Germany's neighbours had long been aware of the Reich's secret rearmament reactions abroad were subdued; at home, too, the move had long been expected, and the response was mixed. People were shocked and unsettled by the news, and feared the worst; but there were also reports of wild enthusiasm – from Munich, for example: ' you can make people sing, but you can't make them sing with such enthusiasm'. There were mixed feelings even among the Nazis themselves, and not least among the young stormtroopers most likely to be recruited for the coming war: 'They feel that it's all up now with their lording it, . . . and they'll soon be under Prussian discipline, where only Prussian officers count. The talk is everywhere [. . .]. We brought Hitler to power and now we're finished, he'll do everything to promote the interests of big business; he's betrayed socialism and above all the "brown battalions" '. Other young people, with labour service behind them, were equally sceptical, and many small business people suspected they would have to pay for all these military preparations one way or another. Workers in the Ruhr and Rhineland were resolutely unenthusiastic, while others (in south-western Germany and Bavaria, for example) expected the call-up to improve the unemployment situation at least, especially if it was matched by increased arms production. The regime itself was anxious to dampen anxiety and Kurt Jahnke, head of the press department at the propaganda ministry, explicitly warned the press not to talk up rumours of war.

The stakes were raised by a further violation of the Versailles Treaty: the reoccupation of the Rhineland by German troops on 7 March 1936. Again the international response was muted, and domestic opinion was first unsettled and then relieved. News of the move first of all fuelled fears of reprisals from the Western powers and the outbreak of another European war, but there was also some disappointment that Britain and France were so reluctant to act against Hitler, and that the League of Nations was too weak. Others, including many workers, were jubilant at the occupation. Hitler's triumphant announcement of the event was broadcast in public places across Germany, and observers of the crowd in Munich noted the strength of popular resentment against Versailles: 'Everybody felt that there was definitely some justification in Hitler's demands.' Across all sections of society, and regardless of political attitudes to the regime, there was now a widespread conviction that war was inevitable, and again the press was instructed to talk down anxieties.[9] Nevertheless the preoccupation with an imminent war persisted, and increased as the tone of the regime's own public statements on international relations became sharper during the late 1930s. 'Chief topic of conversation', according to a Sopade report from the Palatinate in August 1937, 'is still the approach of war. "They want war, you can see it everywhere. You hear and see nothing else now but military stuff; they won't rest till there's war." That's the sort of talk you hear, in all its variations'.[10] Although much of the preparation far the coming war was concealed from the public, some things, such as work on fortifications and troop movements near the border, became increasingly difficult to ignore.

War and Expansion

In November 1937 Hitler set out his foreign policy for the foreign minister the war minister and the commanders-in-chief of the armed forces, at a meeting ostensibly called to decide priorities in the allocation of resources for rearmament. A memorandum produced five days later by Colonel Hossbach was subsequently used at Nuremberg as evidence of Germany's plan to wage aggressive war.[11] Historians have been more sceptical about the existence of any detailed plan for war and conquest, and interpreted the meeting as an attempt by Hitler to avoid taking sides in the dispute over raw materials by diverting the attention of the squabbling parties to more general questions of foreign policy. He began in self-important vein by describing his thoughts as the summation of his thinking over a number of years, and requesting that what he had to say be regarded as his political testament in the event of his death. Germany's problems, he argued, could not be solved by increasing economic self-sufficiency within the country's present borders, and greater participation in the world economy was not a viable alternative. Within a number of years – by 1943–45 at the latest – military action would be necessary if the nation's decline was to be halted before the Reich lost its military advantage, and any one of a number of contingencies made it imperative that Germany move against Austria and Czechoslovakia. Convinced now that Britain was weak enough for her consent to be dispensable, Hitler sought to reassure the generals that German aggression in central Europe would not provoke a general war, but failed to convince them.

The meeting on 5 November 1937 has been seen as a fateful turning point in the history of the Nazi dictatorship, and of Germany.[12] The sense of urgency that Hitler brought to the November meeting was reflected in the subsequent purge of conservatives, beginning with Schacht's resignation from the economics ministry on 26 November, and culminating in the removal of Neurath, Blomberg and Fritsch on 4 February 1938. (Attempts by Ludwig Beck to organise residual military resistance to Hitler's plans were to be thwarted once and for all by Germany's foreign policy triumph at Munich.)[13] The way was now clear for a more active foreign policy and attention immediately turned to Austria when Hitler received the Austrian chancellor Kurt von Schuschnigg at Berchtesgaden a week later.

Many Austrians, as well as Germans, had felt after the First World War that the treaty clauses forbidding the union of Austria and Germany were unfair. With the collapse of the Habsburg Empire in 1918 the German crown lands had been reconstituted as an Austrian republic, which was roughly the size of Scotland, and was considered by many of its people and political leaders to be economically unviable. In both Berlin and Vienna the prohibition of 'Anschluss' was held to violate the principle of the self-determination of peoples which had been made so much of in relation to the political reorganisation of central and eastern Europe. Austrian enthusiasm for Anschluss ebbed during the 1920s, but became a contentious political issue again during the 1930s with the rise of the Nazis in Austria and the establishment of the Hitler regime in Germany. An initial attempt to force the pace of events in the summer of 1934 ended in disaster when the Austrian chancellor Engelbert Dollfuss, then busily consolidating his own authoritarian dictatorship, was assassinated by Nazis, and Mussolini demonstratively moved troops to the Austrian border. The 'reunion' of Germany and Austria remained very much on the agenda (just as it had done for revisionists during the Weimar republic), but Hitler remained cautious for fear of provoking a confrontation with Italy. The issue acquired increasing urgency, however, as war became more likely and Germany's economic bottlenecks multiplied: Göring, who was more impatient than Hitler, had long emphasised the strategic economic importance of Austria to the Reich in the event of war, and it was clear that Austrian resources would help resolve some of the Reich's short-term supply problems.[14]

Hitler used his meeting with Schuschnigg on 12 February to increase political pressure on the Austrian government to such an extent that Austria became a German puppet state. The Austrian Nazi leader Seyss-Inquart was appointed minister for the interior and took control of the police. A general political amnesty was announced, and the Austrian Nazis were jubilant, and the domestic political situation deteriorated rapidly. Schuschnigg's political authority had been undermined, and his response was to rally support for his own regime by inviting the Austrian electorate to affirm Austria's independence as a German and Christian state. The minimum voting age was set at 24, thereby excluding most of the young Nazis then rioting in Vienna.[15] The German leadership responded with an ultimatum and when the Austrian president, Wilhelm Miklas, refused to appoint Seyss-Inquart chancellor the order was given for the invasion.

German armed forces occupied Austria on 11 March. There was no military resistance; Schuschnigg was reluctant to order Austrian troops to fire on German soldiers and Hitler did not want to wage war on a 'fraternal nation' (although he was quite prepared to be brutal if necessary). In any case, Austria was isolated and international opinion indifferent (only the USSR, Mexico, Chile and China protested at the annexation). Austrians themselves were initially very enthusiastic, and endorsed the 're-unification' of Austria with the Reich in a plebiscite a month later with a larger majority than in Germany itself. It may be that this initial Anschluss euphoria influenced Hitler's decision to abandon plans for a personal union, and incorporate Austria directly into the Reich. Although initially the whole of Austria was designated a *Land* (comparable in size to Bavaria), and the term '*Ostmark*' persisted in everyday usage as a 'politically correct' term for Austria as a whole, the country was in fact rapidly dismembered, its internal administrative boundaries were adjusted and the resulting new *Reichshgaue* incorporated separately into Germany.[16] Austria was the first and most important of a number of territories in central Europe to be incorporated directly and wholly into a new Greater Germany (*Grossdeutschland*): German law was introduced, and the Austrian economy – which had continued to suffer from deflationary policies into the late 1930s – was absorbed into the over-heated economy of the Reich, with the result that German taxation, price levels and the drafting of labour to cover shortages in Germany helped dispel the initial euphoria. Enthusiasm gave way to a certain amount of grumbling and opposition, and even in the 'old Reich' itself there was criticism of the Anschluss as an 'economic burden' for Germany.[17]

Not all the Germans of the old Habsburg monarchy had found themselves in the new Austria of 1918, however. There was also a substantial German minority in Czechoslovakia, and the regime now turned its attention to bringing those Germans 'home into the Reich' too, using the local Sudeten German Party (*SudetendeutschePartei*, SdP) and its leader Konrad Henlein to destabilise Czechoslovakia from within. German propaganda was able to exploit the rhetoric of self-determination to draw attention to the allegedly oppressed German minority, and profited from the efforts of the Western democracies, led by the British Prime Minister Neville Chamberlain, to appease Hitler by conceding to his territorial demands in central Europe. There was no question that Hitler wanted to destroy Czechoslovakia, it was only a question of when and how, and that depended on the development of the international situation in Europe; but for the time being there was no pressure to act quickly. The situation was transformed, however, by a diplomatic incident in May.

German troop movements near the border prompted a partial mobilisation in Czechoslovakia and warnings from Paris and London. Hitler now recognised that a *Blitzkrieg* against Czechoslovakia might well bring intervention from the West, and changed plans accordingly, giving orders for accelerated naval rearmament (and thereby acknowledging the distinct possibility of war with Britain) and for the building of fortifications in the West.

The final crisis was initiated in September, however, when Prague agreed to make concessions to the Sudeten Germans, who in turn immediately raised the stakes. 'Herr Beneš wants to organise negotiations', Hitler observed in a speech at the party's Nuremberg rally in September, but added, employing the Allies' own rhetoric against them: 'Things cannot go on this way! This is not a question of empty diplomatic phrases. This is a question of a right not granted. What we Germans demand is the right to self-determination, a right every nation possesses, and not an empty phrase.' Should the democracies persist in colluding with the oppression of Germans, he warned, the consequences would be grave. After all, he was not seeking to oppress three and a half million Frenchmen or Englishmen.[18] The following day Chamberlain proposed negotiations as Henlein's followers staged rehearsed riots throughout the Sudetenland. The British journalist G. E. R. Gedye reported from the spa town of Karlovy Vary: 'The main streets of Karlsbad were a wreckage of broken glass and shattered plate-glass windows. Shop after shop bearing a Czech or Jewish name had great holes in the windows, many of which had been plundered of their contents.' With the arrival of the Czech police, Gedye observed, the 'Henleinist heroes' disappeared immediately. 'The trouble for the Czech police and gendarmerie was that British representations and pressure in Prague continually tied their hands behind their backs.'[19] Popular opinion in the Reich itself reflected the mixed feelings of many Germans. The grievances of the Sudeten Germans against their 'Hussite-Bolshevik' oppressors found little popular resonance. Although ordinary people knew nothing specific of the regime's plans for war, the temper of the agitation against Czechoslavakia was enough to unsettle the public, and the prospect of imminent war drove anxiety to a new pitch. A number of commentators, including Goebbels and General Beck, commented on the 'war psychosis' that gripped the nation.[20] The regime's own intelligence services were aware of the growing anxiety, mistrust and defeatism; but at the same time there were hopes, particularly after his meeting with Hitler at Godesberg on 22 September, that Chamberlain will resist Hitler after all, or – if it came to it – that a war would be the undoing of the Nazis.[21]

The Munich Conference put an end to the war fever. In return for the German annexation of the Sudetenland, Hitler agreed to accept an international guarantee of 'rump Czechoslovakia'. With further territorial adjustments in November a territory of some 30,000 square kilometres and 3.6 million people was incorporated into the Reich, largely as the new *Reichsgau Sudetenland*. (Some territory was incorporated into Bavarian or Austrian *Gaue*.) Poland and Hungary also had revisionist claims, on Slovak territory, and gained, respectively, Těšin and Olše in the north and the 'Feldivék' in the south under the terms of the first Vienna award of November 1938.

For the Czechs the consequences of Munich amounted to much more than ceding territory and population: the country also lost its strongest military fortifications and important sources of raw materials. There were domestic political consequences too. Slovakia was granted autonomy (22 November 1938); all but two political parties in Prague were suppressed, and a right-wing government of the 'Republican Party' was installed, strengthened by an 'enabling law' which effectively neutralised parliament, strengthened press censorship and introduced anti-Semitic legislation. Nevertheless, the outcome of the Munich agreement was something of a reverse for Hitler, who felt cheated of Czechoslovakia, and conscious that, in contrast to the annexation of Austria, this latest move had prompted western intervention. In March 1939 it became clear that Germany's expansionist plans went beyond revisionism and self-determination. Hitler exploited the tensions between Prague and the Slovak government (assisted by German agents in Vienna and Bratislava) and occupied Bohemia and Moravia. Hitler made it clear that he intended to incorporate the Czech lands into the Reich and only a policy of no resistance would guarantee even minimal autonomy. When the Czechs hesitated over formalities, Göring threatened to destroy Prague from the air.[22]

The political dimension had been less thoroughly planned than the invasion. Slovakia declared independence and became a nominally independent puppet state, but the new status of Bohemia and Moravia was less clear. There were initially rumours that two new *Gaue* were to be established, with Reich governors (*Reichsstatthalter*) in charge, before the formula of the 'Protectorate of Bohemia and Moravia' was announced. The new state of affairs was enshrined in a Führer Decree of 16 March, which established the basic legal framework for the relationship between the Protectorate and the Reich: Bohemia and Moravia were to be administered by Czech civil servants, but the Reich would intervene directly if necessary. The authority of the president was dependent on Hitler's continuing approval, and a Reich Protector, Konstantin von Neurath, was appointed to represent the interests of the Reich, and ministerial appointments were subject to his approval. Foreign policy was taken over by Berlin, and the Reich was able to issue laws and decrees which would have validity in the Protectorate.[23] Bohemia and Moravia – no less than the 'Ostmark' and the Sudetenland – were celebrated as 'homecoming borderlands', whose towns and cities were 'often much more German than Czech', above all Prague, which was reclaimed as a quintessentially German city.[24]

In Berlin attention rapidly shifted north-east. Memel (Klaipėda), which had been separated from Germany after the First World War and occupied by Lithuania since 1924, was annexed on 23 March;[25] Danzig (Gdansk), which had been similarly separated and established as a Free City, was more problematic. Germany's diplomatic attempts to persuade Warsaw to agree to the annexation of the city, and to give up the Polish Corridor, effectively making Poland a German satellite, had failed. The British guarantee to Poland that followed the annexation of Bohemia-Moravia made the Poles even less willing to accede to German demands, and prompted Hitler to order preparations for military action. Such a move implied a reconfiguration of international relations. German relations with Poland had been relatively good since the conclusion of a non-aggression pact several years earlier (26 January 1934) and Hitler had also sought to avoid conflict with Britain. Much now depended on the relations of either side with the Soviet Union. Moscow had been shunned by the Western powers during the Czech crisis and diplomatic relations remained at best lukewarm. Leading political figures in London were as hostile to Bolshevism politically as their military counterparts were sceptical of the military capability of the USSR; and Poland was suspicious of Russia. Hitler saw his chance and, responding quickly to signs of a change in the political weather in Moscow, concluded a non-aggression pact with the Soviet Union (23 August 1939).

As Hitler had calculated, without Stalin's support or benevolent neutrality Britain and France would find it impossible to fulfil their guarantee towards Poland, which in the event was partitioned between Germany and the Soviet Union. He was now disappointed that Britain and France were not deterred from declaring war (3 September 1939), even though there was nothing they could do to assist, still less save Poland. The conquest of Poland was concluded within a matter of weeks, and the country was rapidly dismembered in preparation for the separate integration of its constituent parts into the Nazis' new European political

order. The Soviet Union annexed eastern Poland.[26] Danzig, West
Prussia, the 'Wartheland' and other territory were incorporated directly
into the Reich, and the Polish population there was to be resettled in
the remaining territory to the south-east, a 'rump Poland', called the
Generalgouvernement. The manner of the occupation was accompanied by
the mass murder of Poland's elites. The intention of the Nazis was to
destroy Polish nationhood and reduce the Poles to a labour reserve in
the service of the Reich. Although Polish Jews were not killed systematically at this stage death in the massacres and in the ghettos was already
resulting in mass mortality.[27]

The victory in Poland did much to dispel popular anxiety and to
bolster the political authority of the regime. 'The return to barracks of
the troops deployed in the East has been celebrated almost everywhere
with great enthusiasm by the public', the SD reported in October: 'The
troops were often decked with flowers, and were given cigarettes, fruit
and so on.'[28] The euphoria soon gave way to material concerns about
the impact war might have on everyday life, as was demonstrated by the
opposition to the War Economy Decrees. But the swiftness of the victory,
the minimal losses involved and its lack of real impact on the standard
of living of ordinary Germans served to reinforce the myth of Hitler as
statesman and military genius, and this in turn assisted the radicalisation of the regime: everything now seemed possible.[29] In this context
Hitler became convinced of the necessity of an early attack on the West,
preceded by the German occupation of Denmark and Norway for strategic reasons, and to secure the supply of raw materials from Scandinavia
on which Germany depended. Denmark was occupied in April 1940, and
then with more difficulty Norway, where military resistance, supported
by the British and French, persisted for 2 months. The campaign against
the West began before hostilities in the north had ceased and before
Norway had capitulated (10 June 1940). An occupation regime was established under Josef Terboven, *Gauleiter* of Essen, who was appointed Reich
Commissioner. All political parties were banned, other than the fascist
Nasjonal Samling, led by Vidkun Quisling, whose name became a generic
pejorative term for collaborators with the Nazis.

The '*Sitzkrieg*' – as the Germans called the 'phoney' war – came to an
end on 10 May with the German invasion and occupation of the neutral
Netherlands and Belgium. Within a matter of weeks this campaign too
had ended in victory, the Germans had entered Paris and the British
troops remaining on the continent had been evacuated from Dunkirk
by the RAF and Royal Navy, with the help of thousands of small civilian
boats responding to a government appeal for help. An armistice was

signed on 22 June, and northern France and the Atlantic coast were directly occupied by Germany. Alsace and Lorraine were annexed and incorporated into the Reich, and a further 'prohibited' zone in the north. A semi-autonomous French puppet state was set up in the south and governed from Vichy state under the leadership of Marshal Pétain. It was constituted along fascist lines: civil liberties were suppressed, political parties and trade unions were banned and government was by decree. Anti-Semitic legislation was passed very quickly (in October 1940), Jewish property was expropriated in 1941 and 350,000 French Jews were deported to the Reich and beyond between 1942 and 1944. The Germans demanded heavy reparations payments, charged burdensome occupation costs and undertook widespread requisitioning. In addition, the Germans drafted French workers for forced labour in the Reich. The so-called 'free zone' under the Vichy government was occupied by the Germans in November 1942 immediately after the Allied landings in North Africa.

The fall of France left Germany unquestionable master of continental Europe. With France defeated and the Soviet Union an ally, Britain remained Hitler's only remaining enemy. (The United States would not enter the war for another year and a half.) The prospect of an Axis victory seemed imminent, and with it the establishment of a new European political and economic order under the Nazis. Both the Germans themselves and the Allies took this prospect seriously. In Germany, planning and policy-making for the political, economic and 'racial' re-organisation of the continent were undertaken in earnest, albeit in the context of the ceaseless institutional rivalry and personal backstabbing that characterised the Nazi political system. There was a flurry of discussion in the German press about the new Europe that would follow Germany's 'victory peace'. Much of it was purely triumphalist, but it reflected broader and longer views among the country's political, business and academic circles about how Europe might look under German leadership. By the end of the year the 'New Order' was a mainstay of propaganda and public discussion, and variations on the theme remained topical until the end of the war, despite the vanishing hope of any possibility of victory. It also prompted a response from politicians, policy-makers and intellectuals in Britain and the Commonwealth. It would no longer do simply to assert the superiority of the British way of life, when it was clear that the Nazi critique of liberalism had found some resonance in those parts of Europe where parliamentarism had failed, free trade had damaged rather than helped fragile economies, and the free market was held responsible for Depression and unemployment.

In practice any real planning for the post-war future by either side was eclipsed by the urgency of the continuing war. Hitler was concerned with the building of strategic alliances and the urgency, in the absence of any real prospect of getting Britain out of the war, of launching a war for 'living space' in the East. Before the invasion of the Soviet Union could take place, however, German forces had to come to the aid of their Italian allies in North Africa and the Balkans. The *Afrikakorps* arrived in Tripoli in February, and in April German troops invaded Greece and Yugoslavia, which were quickly defeated and occupied. Yugoslavia was dismembered to create an 'independent' state of Croatia (incorporating much if Bosnia and Herzegovina) under a fascist puppet leader (*'Poglavnik'*) Ante Pavelić. Northern Slovenia was directly incorporated into the Reich and southern Slovenia into Italy. Part of Serbia was incorporated into Bulgaria (along with Macedonia), and the remainder was occupied by Germany. Greece suffered from the attentions of three occupying powers (Italy, Germany and Bulgaria). The disorder of the 'New Order' was as evident in the Balkans as anywhere in Europe. Existing political entities were sliced up and whole populations expropriated and displaced, ostensibly to rectify historical injustices and match ethnicity with statehood, but in practice to satisfy the revisionist demands and expansionist plans of the Axis states. Moreover, the institutional rivalry and administrative chaos of the Third Reich was exported to occupied Europe, so that beleaguered locals also had to contend with the conflicts between German business, military, police and diplomatic interests.[30]

Conflict of Ideologies: War with the Soviet Union

The invasion of the Soviet Union (22 June 1941) marked the beginning of a very different kind of war, one conceived as a war of annihilation, a battle to the death between two opposed and irreconcilable views of the world. It was the conflict with Bolshevism which had been central to Hitler's thinking throughout his career and it was supported to a greater or lesser extent by the armed forces, who under-estimated the military capacity of the USSR, and by Germany's anti-Bolshevik political elites.[31] The invasion took Stalin by surprise, and German forces advanced rapidly into Soviet territory as he struggled to come to terms with the situation and organise a military response, but if the Germans took their disarray as a sign of their inherent inferiority, they were mistaken. Germany enjoyed the advantage of surprise, and used it to destroy some 1200 Soviet aircraft and had penetrated some 300 miles into Soviet territory by the end of the month throwing Stalin into a leadership crisis which he spent in isolation in his *dacha* outside Moscow, returning on 1 July to rally the Soviet people to a 'total' war in defence of the 'fatherland'.[32]

The German public was also taken by surprise, and to some extent unsettled by the invasion; people had been expecting news of a closer rapprochement between the Reich and the USSR. But the regime was satisfied that, after the initial shock of the war, the public was more or less supportive. SD reports from the end of June recorded views that reflected those of the generals and politicians from the inferiority of the Russian soldiers and inadequacy of Soviet military capacity to a confidence in victory based on exaggerated rumours of Germany's military success. The rapid advance of German troops impressed the public and reinforced confidence in another *Blitzkrieg* victory, but the first doubts were registered within a couple of weeks, and there were 'occasional instances of surprise' that German forces had not already penetrated further into Russia.[33]

The invasion of the Soviet Union was to be a turning point in the war. The anticipated swift victory did not come, and the German armies stalled on the outskirts of Moscow as winter began to set in, and it became clear that the Germans had dramatically underestimated the Soviets' capacity for resistance, and that the Reich faced a protracted war on two fronts. To make matters worse, Hitler declared war on the United States on 11 December, in the wake of the Japanese attack on Pearl Harbour and the outbreak of hostilities between America and Japan. He was acknowledging, as he saw it, a state of hostilities which existed anyway except for the formalities; Japan on the other hand refused to enter the war against Russia in the Far East and concentrated her efforts on the war against the British empire in Asia and the United States in the Pacific.

Despite the military setback, however, the rapid initial German advance into the Soviet Union already placed an enormous territory at Germany's disposal. This was, at last, the *Lebensraum*, Hitler coveted for German expansion and settlement. He talked of exterminating Bolshevism and establishing a border at the Urals (by which, he later observed, he meant that no military power could be tolerated west of a line some 200–300 km *beyond* the Urals). Moscow would be wiped from the face of the earth. Hitler waxed lyrical about the development of the Crimea as a German tourist destination, and the role of the motor car in bringing people together and overcoming the frontiers of the new Europe even more effectively than the railways.[34] The reality of the German occupation of the western Soviet Union was far grimmer in reality. The savagery of the German forces knew no bounds: the scale of atrocities committed against the Jewish population escalated immediately from improvised killings and deportations to large-scale massacres such as that at Babi Yar near Kiev, and industrialised mass-murder at Auschwitz. All notions of 'civilised' warfare were abandoned in dealing with the enemy in the Soviet Union. International agreements on the treatment of POWs and civilians were deemed not to apply. The number of Soviet casualties was on a different scale to those of the other belligerents. Some 20 million lost their lives altogether, and almost a million died in the 900-day siege of Leningrad alone, often in the most appalling conditions: a ration of 'one hundred and twenty-five grams a day, water from a hole in the frozen Neva, the cold, which never let up, not during sleep, not at meal-times, not at work; . . . corpses in the gateways, corpses on sledges, lanky and thin – more like mummies than normal bodies'.[35]

Alfred Rosenberg was appointed Reich minister for the Occupied Eastern Territories on 17 July, and two Reich commissioners were appointed. Heinrich Lohse, *Gauleiter* of Schleswig Holstein, was to oversee the Reich Commissariat for the *Ostland,* a territory consisting of the Baltic republics and Belarus, and Erich Koch was put in charge of the Reich Commissariat for the Ukraine. If many among the local population initially saw the Germans as liberators from the Soviet system, and many collaborated in the persecution of the Jews, the German attitudes to the 'inferior people' (*Untermenschen*) in their charge and the mass deportations of slave labour to the Reich dispelled any remaining illusions and fuelled recruitment to the ranks of the growing resistance. By June 1943 four-fifths of the afforested area of the Ukraine and over half its arable land was under partisan control.[36]

By then the tide of the military conflict itself had turned. The defeat of the Axis forces at Stalingrad with 150,000 casualties and the surrender of some 90,000 men into Soviet captivity had an irreversible impact not only on Germany's military fortunes on the eastern front, but also on German civilian morale. The SD reported in detail on the sombre mood of the German public:

> The announcement of the *end of the battle in Stalingrad* has been a deep shock for the whole people. The speeches on 30 January and the proclamation of the Führer have been kicked into the background by this event and play a smaller part in national comrades' serious conversations than the many questions about the events in Stalingrad. The most common questions are about the number of blood sacrifices. Speculation ranges from 60,000 to 300,000. People estimate that the

majority of those fighting at Stalingrad have been killed. People waver between two points of view about those who have been taken prisoner. Some declare that being taken prisoner is worse than death because the Bolsheviks will treat those whom they have taken alive in an inhuman way. But others say that it is a good thing that not everybody has been killed, and that there is still a hope that some of them will later return. It is the relatives of those at the Battle of Stalingrad who suffer particularly from these conflicting responses and the uncertainty that arises from them.

It was also clear from the security intelligence that the public were asking serious questions about how the situation at Stalingrad had been dealt with, and whether the debacle could not have been avoided. This prompted people to think seriously about the significance of the battle for the course of the war itself. 'There is a general belief that *Stalingrad is a turning point in the war*', the SD report went on: 'While fighting spirits see Stalingrad as an obligation to concentrate all forces on the front and at home in a final struggle, and hope that such an effort will bring victory, weaker characters are inclined to see the beginning of the end in the fall of Stalingrad.'[37]

It was a turning point that was also acknowledged by the regime. On 3 February Goebbels announced a period of national remembrance and ordered the closure of theatres, restaurants and cinemas for three days. There was also an attempt to implement more practical measures aimed at regaining the initiative. In January Goebbels had pressed Hitler, with some success, to plan for 'total war' and on 20 January Lammers, Bormann and General Keitel – Hitler's closest collaborator in the Soviet campaign – met in the Reich Chancellery as the Committee for Total War. Then on 18 February Goebbels himself proclaimed the need for total war in a speech in the Berlin *Sportpalast* addressed not so much to a cross-section of the population (as he recorded it the following day in his diary), but to a carefully selected audience of 3000 devoted Nazis.[38]

If Stalingrad alone was not in itself an irretrievable turning point in the military fortunes of the Reich, it nevertheless came in the context of a series of several reverses for Germany. The victory at El Alemein in November of British forces led by General Montgomery was followed by Allied landings in Morocco, which created a second front in Africa, and rendered the Axis position hopeless. Although the Allies were still struggling to gain the upper hand in the Battle of the Atlantic, merchant shipping losses declined dramatically during 1943, while there was a sharp rise in U-Boat losses. On 10 July 1943 British and American forces landed in Sicily, and the first Allied bombardment of Rome began shortly afterwards. On 24 July the Fascist Grand Council overthrew Mussolini and he was arrested the next day. Although the *Duce* was subsequently sprung from prison by the Germans, who installed him as leader of a German puppet state based in Salò, in the north, Italy now changed sides and joined the Allies.

In the Reich itself, German cities were now subjected to constant aerial bombardment. From March 1943 cities in the Rhineland and Ruhr valley were subjected to heavy bombing raids, and much of Hamburg was destroyed in a devastating attack in July.[39] At Casablanca the Allies agreed on a bombing strategy designed to weaken Germany sufficiently to enable a successful invasion. The Americans bombed by day and the British by night, disrupting war production and communications, and – as recent research has shown – undermining civilian morale more effectively than was acknowledged at the time. Air raid defences were often inadequate, personnel inexperienced or untrained, and equipment faulty or lacking.[40] The 'community of fate' (*Schickalsgemeinschaft*), which propaganda sought to conjure up, was far from the reality of the experience of real communities shattered – literally – by the bombing, fragmented by homelessness and displacement, and unable to concentrate on anything other than personal survival.[41] One mayor reported in May 1944 that all the women employed in the council offices who had heard the radio report of increased attacks on north-western Germany had promptly dropped everything and headed home – even though the actual alarm was not sounded for another 2 hours – to look after their children and save what they could of their personal possessions. Even when employees were forbidden to go home, the cumulative nervous exhaustion brought about by the constant air raids meant that little or no useful work could be done.[42]

Disinclined to take the official news at face value, people listened to foreign radio stations, and passed on rumours they heard about the impact of the bombing and the course of the war in general. News of the Allied invasion of France in June 1944 was leaked from party and government offices before it was announced on the radio, and although the response was upbeat at first (at least according to the regime's own reports), and characterised by a release from the tension of expectation, it quickly became clear that the Allies were advancing rapidly, and that Germany was going to lose the war. In September 1944 all remaining men between 16 and 60, who were capable of bearing arms (although mostly untrained), were called up to join the *Volkssturm*, a last ditch attempt to avoid the inevitability of defeat. There was no longer any question of the outcome of the war, only of how long it would last.

Women and the War Effort

German women were increasingly called upon to play an active part in the defence of the Reich. Despite the ideological emphasis on domesticity, attempts were made to recruit more women into the workforce. Young women were drafted into the Reich Labour Service (*Reichsarbeitsdienst der weiblichen Jugend*, RADwJ) after the outbreak of war. Working-class women perceived such pressure as unfair, and complained about being pressed to take jobs when the better off still had one or more maids, sat around in bars and cafés, and still managed to frequent beaches, tennis courts and sports clubs. Women already in the workforce became increasingly disgruntled, and increasingly felt that a general labour service should be introduced for all women.[43] The 'Decree concerning the Registration of Men and Women for Work for the Defence of the Reich' of 13 January 1943 required all women between the ages of 17 and 45 to register for work at labour offices, unless they had a child under school age (or two children under the age of 14). The measure was initially greeted with enthusiasm, and in some cases – at the general Post Office in Saarbrücken, for example – volunteers had to be turned away. As the initial enthusiasm ebbed, however, attempts to recruit women into the workforce ran into the sands, and the same problems cropped up again and again – 'training, accommodation and domestic circumstances'. Child care in particular was problematic, even for mothers of schoolchildren, if a job involved travelling any distance from home to work, and shortages, queues and bombing raids made mere survival more time-consuming. Women cited the provisions of the decree against the authorities in order to resist recruitment, and of those who did register for work and take up jobs few remained in employment for long. When women did work they were often unused to industrial discipline and frequently subordinated the demands of their employers to their more pressing domestic concerns, which often gave rise to unpredictable and disruptive absenteeism. The number of women in industrial employment remained lower throughout the war than in 1939 and the female proportion of the industrial workforce fell from 25.9 per cent in 1942 to 25.5 per cent in 1943 and 24.6 per cent in 1944.[44]

Nazi women's organisations were expected to co-ordinate the contribution of women to the war effort not only cajoling them into work, but also organising voluntary work, which was increasingly important in the context of bombing raids and other emergencies on the home front.[45] Other women were more directly involved in the war and the occupation of Europe, supporting the armed forces, the police and the civilian administration both at the front and in the occupied territories. Womanly duties continued even here, as in the case of German kindergarten teachers recruited to assist in the Germanisation of Poland, as missionaries in the wake of the onslaught of Nazi imperialism.[46]

Demoralisation and Defeat

Unlike the defeat in 1918, that in 1945 was total and was preceded by desperation and resignation as shortages of food, clothing and fuel took their toll and air raids increased in regularity and intensity, culminating in the raid on Dresden in February 1945. Rumours of the damage caused by the bombing raids spread across the country in the absence of reliable or credible news reporting, as did rumours that Germany would be saved at the last minute by 'miracle weapons'.[47] The progress of the Red Army through eastern Europe was followed with particular anxiety as first Romania and then Bulgaria fell to the Soviets, and German propaganda increasingly presented the war as a crusade to save Christian Europe and its civilisation from the barbarity of the Bolshevik hordes. The fear generated by the Germans' own propaganda, combined with the actual experience of the Soviet occupation when it came, prompted a mass exodus of refugees from east to west as the war approached its end.

In 1918 many people had continued to believe the government's reassuring propaganda about inevitable victory, and the defeat had come as a shock, creating fertile ground for the myth of betrayal. In 1945 there were no such illusions. A summary of popular opinion from the end of March 1945 reported that although nobody wanted to lose the war, nobody believed any more that Germany could win. The last spark of hope was being extinguished; people were no longer capable of imagining how the war could still be won now, especially now that important industrial regions such as Upper Silesia and the Ruhr had been occupied by foreign troops. Thousands had been recruited into factories and workshops for crucial war work, but as the total war effort was shattered by constant bombardment there was nowhere left for them to go, and as the Germans themselves now wandered around unemployed they were joined by thousands of the foreign workers, all of them competing for the same scarce food.

Furthermore it was generally felt that if the war was lost, then it was Germany's own fault, and not so much that of ordinary people as the leadership. There was a widespread belief that the defeat could have been avoided, and there was a great deal of popular criticism of military leadership, foreign policy and above all occupation policies, especially in the East. There was no longer any faith in the country's leaders, in the party or in its propaganda. The Führer, even now, remained the last hope for many people; but now even he was increasingly subject to criticism. Finally, the will to fight itself was being eroded by the belief that further conflict was pointless.[48]

Within weeks Soviet troops had taken Berlin and Hitler had committed suicide (on 30 April 1945).[49] His designated successor, Admiral Karl Dönitz, hoped even now to make a separate peace with West and continue the war against the Soviet Union. In the event, however, he was compelled to confront the reality of defeat and oversee Germany's total capitulation to the Allies within a week. Germany's human, territorial and capital losses were much greater than they had been after the First World War. Almost 4 million German soldiers had been killed or were missing, a figure which was dwarfed by the 14 million Soviet losses, but which was twice the military death toll of the First World War. In addition over one and a half million civilians were killed, over a quarter of them through the effects of enemy bombing. German cities had been reduced to rubble, and a fifth of the country's housing stock had been destroyed. The situation was exacerbated by the flight of Germans from eastern Europe as the Red Army advanced. Some 9 million refugees left their homes in the eastern provinces of the Reich and headed west to the Allied occupation zones, and the exodus continued after the end of the war as Germans were expelled from eastern Europe.

No agreement on the future of Germany had been reached by the end of the war, so that the provisional arrangements agreed by the allies at the Yalta Conference in February 1945 became the basis for the occupation of Germany. All German territory east of the Oder-Neisse line was lost to Poland or the Soviet Union, along with all other territorial gains from Nazi expansionism. The Soviet Union took control of an occupation zone between the Elbe-Werra and Oder-Neisse lines. The United States took control of Bavaria, Württemberg and Hesse in the south, and a smaller territory based on Bremen and Bremerhaven in the north. Britain occupied the rest of northern Germany, including the Ruhr valley, and France took control of an occupation zone based on the southern Rhineland, including the Saarland, the Palatinate, Baden and Württemberg-Hohenzollern. Military governors assumed governmental powers in each of the zones. Similar arrangements came into force in Austria, which was re-established as an independent state. The Wehrmacht was disarmed and German soldiers interned.

Leading Nazis were arrested, in so far as they had not committed suicide (Hitler and Goebbels) or disappeared (Bormann), and put on trial as major war criminals before an international military tribunal in Nuremberg.[50] A further twelve trials were organised for industrialists, the SS, the armed forces, doctors and civil servants. For the rest of the population a process of 'denazification' and re-education was planned, but the programme was unevenly implemented, and quickly ran into the bureaucratic sands, especially as those most likely to have been involved with the Nazis were also more likely to be better educated, skilled or experienced in administration. Eventually the project was eclipsed by the emergence of the two German states and the new political agendas of the Cold War.

Violence had been the defining characteristic of Nazism from its rowdy beginnings in Munich, and war had been the central objective of the Nazi state from its establishment in 1933. Nazi ideology glorified violence in the struggle for survival and supremacy, extolled military combat as a rite of passage into manhood, and saw war as the test of a nation – which Hitler himself finally deemed the Germans to have failed. The uncompromising nature of this conflict, however, and the total defeat it entailed meant that 1945, while it was not the 'year zero' that some claimed, saw a far more fundamental break in the course of German history than 1918, and one which laid the foundations for the development of a stable German democracy in the second half of the twentieth century.

Conclusion

The defeat and unconditional surrender of Germany in May 1945 was also the definitive defeat of Nazism. Although there had been little resistance within Germany, even up to the final days there was little effective resistance to the Allied occupation that now followed. In 1945 the Allies took control of Germany far more completely than in 1918, dividing Germany into four zones of occupation (British, French, Soviet and American), and Berlin into four sectors. Similar arrangements were put in place in Austria, which was separated from Germany and re-established as an independent state. All other territory acquired during the war was restored, and Germany's own territorial losses were greater than in 1919. Most leading Nazis were either dead or had disappeared, and those that remained were arrested and tried for war crimes by a military tribunal at Nuremberg.[1] In addition a more prolonged process of 'denazification' was inaugurated, although its success was limited. Above all, the shaping of post-war politics was in the hands of the Allies: there could be no myth-making about betrayal from within as there had been after the First World War.[2]

Hitler's thousand-year Reich had lasted barely twelve, but it was enough to inflict on Germany the greatest disaster in its history. The country's armed forces were defeated and disarmed, and although Germany's military and civilian losses were only a fraction of the total (and were far outnumbered by those of the Soviet Union), almost 4 million soldiers and two million civilians had been killed. Some three million soldiers had been taken prisoners of war by the Soviet Union during the course of the war, and many of those who survived imprisonment remained there long after the end of the war. Germans in eastern Europe were reviled and mistreated both by local civilians and by the Red Army (which Hitler's anti-Bolshevik crusade had brought to the River Elbe) and thousands were expelled from Poland, Czechoslovakia, and the Baltic, in some cases from towns and districts which had been settled by Germans for centuries. German cities were in ruins, the economy had collapsed, and the economic infrastructure had suffered immense damage.[3] There is little wonder that 1945 came to be referred to as 'year zero' (*Stunde Null*).

Yet the impression of a total break with the Nazi past – in Germany and in Europe – is misleading. The NSDAP was – and remains – banned in Germany, along with Mein Kampf; and despite the emergence of neo-Nazi groups in the Federal Republic there has been no clear organizational continuity, as there has been, for example, in the case of Italy. Nevertheless the 'old right' regrouped after the war. The *Sozialistische Reichspartei* thought of itself as a successor party to the NSDAP and its leaders were overwhelmingly former Nazis. It won 11 per cent of the votes in *Landtag* elections in Lower Saxony in 1951, and was banned the following year. Former DNVP members also regrouped, and allied themselves with anti-Semites and monarchists in a *Deutsche Konservative Partei* which mutated several times between 1945 and 1949 before winning 8 per cent of the vote in Lower Saxony in the first federal elections of 1949.[4] Ultimately the political achievements and phenomenal electoral success of Konrad Adenauer's Christian Democratic Union eclipsed the radical right for a generation. If the 'Bonn Republic' differed from the Weimar Republic immediately in one very important respect it was that it had a united and successful conservative party which was also committed to liberal democratic political institutions.

Political stabilisation and, perhaps above all, the 'economic miracle' of the 1950s helped to keep radical right-wing politics off the agenda, but initially Nazism was suppressed at the behest of the Allies. This was clearest in the Soviet Zone (and later in the German Democratic Republic), where adherence to an official ideology of anti-fascism was more or less obligatory in public life; but it was also the case in West Germany and Austria, where explicitly neo-fascist parties were banned. (Some former Nazis became submerged in more mainstream politics: In Austria the so-called 'League of Independents', predecessor of the Freedom Party, absorbed large numbers, as did the German Free Democratic Party during the early 1950s; and several members of Adenauer's cabinet had Nazi connections.

Denazification proved difficult, and generated enormous resentment in Germany, where it was often felt that the major culprits were getting away, while those who had been 'merely followers' were being disproportionately punished. This reinforced the increasingly widespread impression that many – perhaps most – Germans themselves were also victims.

Most Germans were happy to move on when the Cold War made it expedient for the Allies to draw a line under the denazification process; and many politicians, professionals, public servants and business people who had been deeply implicated in the dictatorship and its crimes were readily rehabilitated during the 1950s, while allegations of corporate complicity with the Nazis in slave labour and arms profiteering were contested by cleverly constructed apologias.[5] In any case the demands of reconstruction required the expertise of educated classes from among whom the Nazis had disproportionately recruited support – and, of course, with the advent of the Cold War it could be assumed that former Nazis would make some of the most reliable anti-Communists.

All this raises the question of the place of the Nazi dictatorship in German history – or for that matter the history of Europe. In the West, theories of 'totalitarianism' removed Hitler and the Nazis from the mainstream development of German history: as a 'breakdown in the works' (*Betriebsunfall*) of German political development. (Similarly, Fascism, in the Italian variant of this approach, was a 'parenthesis'.) If, as this approach, implied, the 12 years between 'seizure of power' and 'year zero' were a deviation from 'normal' political development, then there was no need to scrutinise Germany's institutions or the actions of the country's governing elites to explain the demise of constitutional government in the 1930s. To argue on the other hand that the origins of the Third Reich were rooted in German exceptionalism (a '*Sonderweg*') is unconvincing: Germany was not so much an under-developed society beleaguered by the persistence of feudalism as a modern industrial society undergoing a political crisis of a very modern kind, and the response cannot be seen as merely a retreat into 'medieval' barbarism.[6]

Although many Nazis affected a backward-looking nostalgia for a lost world of guilds and gabled houses, the success of the movement is unthinkable without modern technology and modes of thought. Nazi leaders understood the importance of popular politics as the basis for a 'plebiscitary democracy' in which political participation was expected but limited to acclamation. In power the Nazis also recognised that the suppression of opposition through coercion alone was not enough, and sought to elicit not only support but collusion and complicity as well. The 'national community' was to be founded on a consensus manufactured in the Propaganda Ministry and managed by a mixture of promise and exhortation, discipline and threat. This is not to detract from the brutal reality of the police state, or understate the sufferings of the Nazis' victims; the terror was very real, affected large numbers of Germans for different reasons, and increased in intensity after the outbreak of war.

The regime's worst crimes were committed outside Germany, above all in the occupied territories of eastern Europe where national political elites and those deemed racially undesirable were massacred in the wake of German expansion, while others were shipped back to the Reich as slave labour. It was here too, away from Germany itself, that plans were implemented for the systematic mass murder of all Europe's Jews, genocide on an unprecedented scale in European history. Much of what the Nazis undertook in Germany itself, from factory canteens and hiking holidays to the sterilisation and euthanasia programmes for the unfit, was inextricably connected with the more savage racial policies practised in eastern Europe. The unique enormity of the Holocaust should not prompt us to see it as the Nazis' murderous anti-Semitism as somehow separate from other aspects of the regime.

This is particularly important in the context of interpretations of Nazi Germany as one 'modernising' society among many, where neither the war for *Lebensraum* nor the mass-murder of the Jews was an 'overriding' objective, but a temporary expedient necessary for the implementation of modernising reforms akin to those of other industrial societies in the democratic West.[7] With the hindsight of 50 years it may be tempting to see the catastrophe of Nazi Germany as the temporary by-product of a crisis of modernisation, but that would be to ignore not only the persistent and periodic recrudescence of racism, bigotry and intolerance in industrial societies; but also the many ways in which individuals rights and freedoms are eroded in the name of a notional collective good. For these reasons too the history of Nazi Germany remains a 'past that will not pass away'.[8]

Notes

Introduction

1. Dieter Bossmann (ed.), '*Was ich über Adolf Hitler gehört habe...*'. *Folgen eines Tabus: Auszüge aus Schüler-Aufsätzen von Heute* (Frankfurt, 1977).
2. Pierre Ayçoberry, *The Nazi Question: An Essay on the Interpretations of National Socialism (1922–1975)* (London, 1981) was first published in 1979; Hiden and Farquharson, *Explaining Hitler's Germany. Historians and the Third Reich* (London, 1983); Ian Kershaw, *The Nazi Dictatorship. Problems and Perspectives of Interpretation* (London, 1985; 4th edition, London, 2005).
3. On the *Historikerstreit* see Charles Maier, *The Unmasterable Past: History, Holocaust and German National Identity* (Cambridge, Mass., 1988); Richard Evans, *In Hitler's Shadow. West German Historians and the Attempt to Escape from the Nazi Past* (London, 1989).
4. See for example, Marcus Kreuzer, 'Parliamentarization and the Question of German Exceptionalism: 1867–1918', *Central European History* 36/3 (2003) and the accompanying commentaries by Jonathan Sperber and Kenneth Ledford.
5. David Blackbourn and Geoff Eley, *The Peculiarities of German History: Bourgeois Society and Politics in Nineteenth-Century Germany* (Oxford, 1984) is the definitive critique.
6. Michael Mann, *Fascists* (Cambridge, 2004), pp. 1–13. Here p. 1.
7. See David Beetham, *Marxists in the Face of Fascism* (Manchester, 1983).
8. *Monologe im Führerhauptquartier*, p. 43 (21/22 July 1941).
9. The classic statements of the theory of totalitarianism were Carl Friedrich and Zbigniew Brzezinski, *Totalitarian Dictatorship and Autocracy* (Cambridge, Mass., 1956) and Leonard Schapiro, *Totalitarianism* (London, 1973).
10. For a summary of the shifting perspectives during these years see Ian Kershaw, *The Nazi Dictatorship. Problems and Perspectives of Interpretation* (4th edition, London, 2000), pp. 20–46.
11. See for example, F. L. Carsten, *The Rise of Fascism* (London, 1967); Walter Laqueur (ed.), *Fascism. A Reader's Guide. Analyses, Interpretations, Bibliography* (Hardmondsworth, 1979).

12. See for example, Kevin Passmore (ed.), *Women, Gender and Fascism in Europe 1919–1945* (Manchester, 2003); Robert Paxton, *The Anatomy of Fascism* (London, 2004); Michael Mann, *Fascists* (Cambridge, 2004).

13. T. W. Mason, 'Intention and Explanation. A Current Controversy about the Interpretation of National Socialism', in Gerhard Hirschfeld and Lothar Kettenacker (eds), *Der 'Führerstaat'. Mythos und Realität./The 'Führer State'. Myth and Reality* (Stuttgart, 1981), pp. 23–42.

14. Kershaw, *Nazi Dictatorship*, pp. 69–92. Here especially pp. 91–92.

15. See Maier, *Unmasterable Past*, and Richard Evans, *In Hitler's Shadow*.

16. Alf Lüdtke (ed.), 'What is the History of Everyday Life and who are its Practitioners', *The History Everyday of Everyday Life. Reeconstructing Historical Experiences and Ways of Life* (Princeton, 1995), pp. 3–40.

17. Martin Broszat, 'Resistenz und Widerstand', in Martin Broszat, Elke Fröhlich and Anton Grossmann (eds), *Bayern in der NS-Zeit* (IV) *Herrschaft und Gesellschaft im Konflikt* (Munich, 1981), pp. 691–709. Here p. 692.

18. Michael Burleigh, *Germany Turns Eastwards. A Study of* Ostforschung *in the Third Reich* (Cambridge, 1988); Michael Burleigh and Wolfgang Wippermann, *The Racial State: Germany 1933–1945* (Cambridge, 1991).

19. Gisela Bock, *Zwangssterilisation im Nationalsozialismus: Studien zur Rassenpolitik* (Opladen, 1986); Michael Burleigh, *Death and Deliverance. Euthanasia in Germany c.1900–1945* (Cambridge, 1994); Lisa Pine, *Nazi Family Policy 1933–1945* (Oxford and New York, 1997).

20. See for example, Jonathan Petropoulos, *Art as Politics in the Third Reich* (Chapel Hill and London, 1996).

21. See for example, Bosworth, *The Italian Dictatorship* (London, 1998), pp. 23–32.

22. Peter Baldwin, 'Social Interpretations of Nazism: Renewing a Tradition', *Journal of Contemporary History* 25/1 (1990), pp. 5–37. Here p. 28.

23. *Deutschland-Berichte der Sopade* (7 volumes, Salzhausen Frankfurt, 1980).

Chapter 1: The Origins and Development of Nazism

1. David Blackbourn, 'The Politics of Demagogy in Imperial Germany', *Past and Present*, 113 (1986), pp. 152–184; Stanley Suval, *Electoral Politics in Imperial Germany* (Chapel Hill and London, 1985).

2. Peter Pulzer, *The Rise of Political Anti-Semitism in Germany and Austria* (2nd edition, London, 1988), pp. 83–97.

3. Geoff Eley, *Reshaping the German Right. Radical Nationalism and Political Change After Bismarck* (2nd edition, Ann Arbor, 1991); Marilyn Shevin Coetzee, *The German Army League. Popular Nationalism in Wilhelmine Germany* (Oxford, 1990); Roger Chickering, *We Men Who Feel Most German. A Cultural Study of the Pan-German League 1886–1914* (London, 1984).

4. Hans-Jürgen Puhle, 'Conservatism in Modern German History', *JCH*, 13 (1978), pp. 689–720. Here p. 689.

5. Fritz Stern, *The Politics of Cultural Despair* (Berkeley and Los Angeles, 1961); George Mosse, *The Crisis of German Ideology: Intellectual Origins of the Third Reich* (New York, 1964).

6. Geoff Eley, 'Anti-Semitism, Agrarian Mobilization and the Conservative Party. Radicalism and Containment in the Founding of the Agrarian League, 1890–93', in Larry Eugene Jones and James N. Retallack (eds), *Between Reform, Reaction and Resistance. Studies in the History of German Conservatism from 1789 to 1945* (Providence RI and Oxford, 1993), pp. 187–227. Here pp. 190–191. Eley also argues that the concept of 'prefascism' is not adequately explained and that Puhle's 'new right' simplifies the realignments in German conservatism, and conceals contradictions between the interests of the rural and urban right.

7. Paul Weindling, *Health Race and German Politics Between National Unification and Nazism 1870–1945*, pp. 36–59 on 'Darwinian demagogues' and 'scientizing race'.

8. Gerhard Sandner and Mechtild Rössler, 'Geography and Empire in Germany, 1871–1945' in Anne Godlewska and Neil Smith, *Geography and Empire* (Oxford, 1994), pp. 115–127; Bettina Arnold, 'The Past as Propaganda: Totalitarian Archaeology in Nazi Germany', *Antiquity*, 64 (1990), reproduced in Robert Preucel and Ian Hodder (eds), *Contemporary Archaeology in Theory* (Oxford, 1996), pp. 549–569; Ulrich Veit, 'Gustaf Kossina and His Concept of a National Archaeology', in Heinrich Härke (ed.), *Archaeology, Ideology and Society. The German Experience* (2nd edition, Frankfurt, 2002), pp. 41–66; Frank Fetten, 'Archaeology and Anthropology in Germany before 1945', in Heinvich Härke, pp. 143–182.

9. See Hermann Graml, *Antisemitism in the Third Reich* (Oxford, 1992), pp. 58–65.

10. John Boyer, *Politcal Radicalism in Late Imperial Vienna* (Chicago, 1981).

11. Adolf Hitler, *Main Kampf*, translated by Ralph Mannheim (London, 1992), pp. 90–93.

12. Brigitte Hamann, *Hitler's Vienna: A Dictator's Apprenticeship* (Oxford, 1999); Ian Kershaw, *Hitler 1889–1936: Hubris* (London, 1998), pp. 60–69.

13. Bruce Pauley, *Hitler and the Forgotten Nazis. A History of Austrian National Socialism* (London, 1981), pp. 19–21.

14. Mark Cornwall, 'The Struggle on the Czech-German Language Border 1880–1940', *English Historical Review*, 109/433 (1994), pp. 914–951.

15. Francis Carsten, *Fascist Movements in Austria from Schönerer to Hitler* (London, 1977).

16. Heinz Hagenlücke, *Deutsche Vaterlandspartei. Die nationale Rechte am Ende des Kaiserreichs* (Düsseldorf, 1997).

17. Belinda J. Davis, *Home Fires Burning. Food, Politics and Everyday Life in World War I Berlin* (Chapel Hill and London, 2000), pp. 190–236; Jürgen Kocka, *Facing Total War: German Society 1914–1918* (Leamington Spa, 1984), pp. 155–161; Francis Carsten, *Revolution in Central Europe* (London, 1972).

18. Helmut Heiber, *The Weimar Republic* (Oxford, 1993), p. 46.

19. Thomas Mergel, 'Das Schietern des deutschen Tory-Konservatismus. Die Umformung der DNVP zu einer rechtsradikalen Partei 1928–1932', *Historische Zeitschrift*, 276 (2003), pp. 322–368.

20. U. Lohalm, *Völkischer Radikalismus. Die Geschichte des Deutschvölkischer Schutz- und Trutzbundes 1918–1923* (Hamburg, 1970), p. 19.

21. Ibid., pp. 89–90, 110–111; Jeremy Noakes, *The Rise of the Nazi Party in Lower Saxony* (Oxford, 1971), pp. 9–10.

22. Michael Wildt, *Generation des Unbedingten. Das Führungskorps des Reichssicherheitshauptamtes* (Hamburg, 2003), pp. 53–60. On the *Freikorps* see Robert G. L. Waite, *Vanguard of Nazism. The Free Corps Movement in Postwar Germany 1918–1923* (Cambridge, Mass., 1952).

23. Richard M. Watt, *The Kings Depart. The German Revolution and the Treaty of Versailles 1918–19* (Harmondsworth, 1973), pp. 363–381.

24. Ian Kershaw, *Hitler 1889–1936: Hubris* (London, 1998), pp. 121–125.

25. Dietrich Orlow, *The History of the Nazi Party 1919–1933* (Pittsburgh, 1969), pp. 11–36.

26. Rainer Zitelmann, 'Adolf Hitler: The Führer', in Ronald Selser and Rainer Zitelmann (eds), *The Nazi Elite* (London, 1993), pp. 113–132. Here p. 117; Kershaw, *Hubris*, pp. 160–165. See also William Carr, *Hitler. A Study in Personality and Politcs* (London, 1978), pp. 15–16.

27. M. Kater, 'Zur Soziographie der frühen NSDAP', *Vierteljahreshefte für Zeitgeschichte*, 19 (1971), pp. 124–159.

28. Jeremy Noakes, 'Nazism and High Society', in Michael Burleigh (ed.), *Confronting the Nazi Past. New Debates on German History* (London, 1996), pp. 51–65.

29. Orlow, *Nazi Party 1919–1933*, p. 19.

30. Ian Kershaw, *Hitler* (Harlow, 1991), pp. 22–29; Michael Kellog, *The Russian Roots of Nazism. White Emigrés and the Making of National Socialism, 1917–1945* (Cambridge, 2005).

31. Carr, *Hitler*, pp. 23–26.

32. See Jeremy Noakes, ' "Viceroys of the Reich"? *Gauleiters* 1925–45', in Anthony McElligott and Tim Kirk (eds), *Working Towards the Führer* (Manchester, 2003), pp. 118–152.

33. Ian Kershaw, *The Hitler Myth. Image and Reality in the Third Reich* (Oxford, 1987), pp. 19–21.

34. Henry Ashby Turner, *Big Business and the Rise of Hitler* (Oxford, 1985), pp. 83–99.

35. Orlow, *Nazi Party 1919–1933*, pp. 119–120.

36. Conan Fischer, *Stormtroopers* (London, 1983); Peter Longerich, *Die braunen Bataillone. Geschichte der SA* (Munich, 1989).

37. See Detlef Mühlberger, *The Social Bases of Nazism 1919–1933* (Cambridge, 2003) for a summary of the changing perspectives.

38. The liberal German Democratic Party (*Deutsche Demokratische Partei*, DDP) and the conservative, business-orientated German People's Party (*Deutsche Volkspartei*, DVP), along with the DNVP.

39. Orlow, *Nazi Party 1919–1933*, pp. 76–184.

40. Dietmar Petzina, Werner Abelshauser and Anselm Fest (eds), *Sozilgeschicht-liches Arbeitsbuch III. Materialien zur Statistik des deutschen Reiches 1914–1945* (Munich, 1978), p. 130; J. Noakes and G. Pridham, *Nazism. A Documentary Reader 1919–1945: The Rise to Power 1919–1934* (Exeter, 1983), p. 86 has slightly different figures, as the figures for the working German popula-tion are based on a later census, but the profile of the party is broadly similar.

41. Richard F. Hamilton, *Who Voted for Hitler?* (Princeton, 1982); *Statistik des deutschen Reichs (Neue Folge)*, Vol. 434; Dick Geary, 'Employers, Workers and the Collapse of Weimar', in Ian Kershaw (ed.), *Weimar. Why did German Democrarcy Fail?* (London, 1990), pp. 92–190. Here p. 109.

42. F. L. Carsten, *The German Workers and the Nazis* (Aldershot, 1995), p. 6.

43. Helen Boak, 'Women in Weimar Germany: The "Frauenfrage" and the Female Vote', in Richard Bessel and E. J. Feuchtwanger (eds), *Social Change and Political Development in Weimar Germany* (London, 1981), pp. 6–173; Julia Sneeringer, *Winning Women's Votes: Propaganda and Politics in Weimar Germany* (Chapel Hill and London, 2002).

44. Jill Stephenson, *The Nazi Organisation of Women* (London, 1981). Elizabeth Harvey, 'Visions of the Volk: German Women and the Far Right from Kais-erreich to Third Reich', *Journal of Women's History* 16/3 (2004), pp. 152–167.

45. Jürgen W. Falter, 'The National Socialist Mobilisation of New Voters: 1928–1933', in Thomas Childers (ed.), *The Formation of the Nazi Constituency 1919–1933* (Totowa, NJ, 1986), pp. 202–231.

46. Eberhard Kolb, *The Weimar Republic* (London, 1988), pp. 81–82.

47. 'The Constitution of the German Republic', in Anton Kaes, Martin Jay and Edward Dimdenberg (eds), *The Weimar Republic Sourcebook* (Berkeley, 1994), pp. 46–51. Here p. 48.

48. William L. Patch Jr, *Heinrich Brüning and the Dissolution of the Weimar Republic* (Cambridge, 1998), pp. 72–89; Andreas Dorpalen, *Hindenburg and the Weimar Republic* (Princeton, 1964), pp. 179–194.

49. William Mc Neil, *American Money and the Weimar Republic. Economics and Politics on the Eve of the Great Depression* (New York, 1986), p. 277; Ian Kershaw (ed.), *Weimar: Why did German Democracy Fail?* (London, 1990), pp. 30–91.

50. See Henry Ashby Turner, *German Big Business and the Rise of Hitler* (Oxford, 1985).

51. Much of the gain in Hamburg had come in an earlier election the year before.

52. Martin Broszat, *Hitler and the Collapse of Weimar Germany* (Providence, RI and Oxford, 1987), pp. 108–115; Patch, *Brüning*, pp. 265–271.

53. See Anthony McElligott, *Contested City: Municipal Politics and the Rise of Nazism in Altona, 1917–1937* (Ann Arbor, 1998).

54. Friedrich Karl von Plehwe, *Reichskanzler Kurt von Schleicher. Weimars letzte Chance gegen Hitler* (Munich, 1983); Peter Hayes, 'A Question Mark with Epaulettes? Kurt von Schleicher and Weimar Politics', *JMH* 52/1 (1980), pp. 35–65.

Chapter 2: The Nazi Dictatorship

1. Richard Overy, *Göring. The Iron Man* (London, 1984).

2. Minutes of Conference of Ministers, 31 January 1933, in *Documents on German Foreign Policy* (London: HMSO, 1957) C1, No. 3, pp. 5–7.

3. See Martin Broszat, *The Hitler State. The Foundation and Development of the Internal Structure of the Third Reich* (London, 1981), p. 62.

4. Kolb, *Weimar Republic*, pp. 194–95, citing *Statistisches Jahrbuch für das deutsche Reich*, 52 (Berlin, 1933), p. 539.

5. Count Harry Kessler, *The Diaries of a Cosmopolitan 1918–1937* (London, 2000), p. 449.

6. Karl Dietrich Bracher, Wolfgang Sauer and Gerhard Schulz (eds), *Die nationalsozialistische Machtergreifung. Studien zur Errichtung des totalitären Herrschaftssystems* (Cologne and Opladen, 1962), pp. 88–136.

7. George K. Glaser, *Geheimnis und Gewalt. Ein Bericht* (Frankfurt, 1956), pp. 51–52, cited in Eve Rosenhaft, *Beating the Fascists. The German Communists and Political Violence 1929–1933* (Cambridge, 1983), p. 214.

8. Jeremy Noakes, 'The Nazi Party and the Third Reich: The Myth and Reality of the One-Party State', in Jeremy Noakes (ed.), *Government Party and People in Nazi Germany* (Exeter, 1980), pp. 16–17; Dietrich Orlow, *The History of the Nazi Party: 1933–1945* (Pittsburgh, 1973).

9. Broszat, *Hitler State*, pp. 242–243.

10. Ibid., pp. 98–132; Joseph W. Bendersky, *Carl Schmitt: Theorist for the Reich* (Princeton, 1983), pp. 196–201.

11. Jane Caplan, 'Recreating the Civil Service: Issues and Ideas in the Nazi Regime', in Noakes (ed.), *Government, Party and People*, pp. 34–56. Here p. 37.

12. Hans Mommsen, 'State and Bureaucracy in the Brüning Era' in Hans Mommsen, *From Weimar to Auschwitz. Essays in German History* (Cambridge, 1991), pp. 79–118.

13. J. Noakes and G. Pridham, *Nazism. A Documentary Reader 1919–1945: State, Economy and Society, 1933–1939* (Exeter, 1984), pp. 223–225.

14. Jane Caplan, *Government without Administration. State and Civil Service in Weimar and Nazi Germany* (Oxford, 1988), p. 141.

15. Michael Schneider, *Unterm Hakenkreuz. Arbeiter und Arbeiterbewegung 1933 bis 1939* (Bonn, 1999), pp. 62–63; Noakes and Pridham, *Rise to Power*, pp. 148–150.

16. Helmut Krausnick and Martin Broszat, *Anatomy of the SS State* (St Albans, 1973), pp. 144–150. *Völkischer Beobachter* 21 March 1933, in Wolfgang Michalka

(ed.), *Deutsche Geschichte 1933–1945. Dokumente zur Innen- und Aussenpolitik* (Frankfurt, 1993), p. 23.

17. This excerpt is in Wolfgang Michalka (ed.), *Deutsche Geschichte 1933–1945. Dokumente zur Innen- und Aussenpolitik* (Frankfurt, 1993) pp. 23–24.

18. Norbert Frei, *National Socialist Rule in Germany The Führer State 1933–1945* (Oxford, 1993), p. 24; Carl Schmitt, 'Der Führer schützt das Recht', in Michalka, *Deutsche Geschichte*, p. 41.

19. Kershaw, *Hitler Myth*, pp. 84–95.

20. *Deutschland-Bericht der Sopade*, 1934 (Frankfurt, 1980), pp. 197–203.

21. Erlass Hitlers über die Erhebung der SS zueiner selsbstständign Organisation, in Michalka, *Deutsche Geschichte*, p. 42.

22. Broszat, *Hitler State*, p. 280.

23. Richard Overy, *The Dictators. Hitler's Germany and Stalin's Russia* (London, 2004), pp. 70–71.

24. Broszat, pp. 263–270.

25. Caplan, *Government Without Administration*, pp. 137–138.

26. On the establishment of the RMVP see Jonathan Petropoulos, *Art as Politics in the Third Reich* (Chapel Hill and London, 1996), pp. 19–50.

27. Richard Overy, *Goering. The 'Iron Man'* (London, 1984), pp. 22–75.

28. Hans Mommsen, 'Cumulative Radicalisation and Progressive Self-destruction as Structural Determinants of the Nazi Dictatorship' in Ian Kershaw and Moshe Lewin (eds), *Stalinsim and Nazism: Dictatorships in Comparison* (Cambridge, 1997), pp. 75–87; Ian Kershaw ' "Cumulative Radicalisation" and the Uniqueness of National Socialism', in Christian Jansen, Lutz Niethammer and Bernd Weisbrod (eds), *Von der Aufgabe zur Freiheit. Politische Verantwortung und bürgerliche Gesellschaft im 19. und 20. Jahrhundert. Festschrift für Hans Mommsen zum*, 5 November 1995 (Berlin, 1995?), pp. 323–336.

29. See Ian Kershaw, *The Nazi Dictatorship. Problems and Perspectives of Interpretation* (4th edition, London, 1993), pp. 69–92.

30. See Tim Mason, 'Intention and Explanation: A Current Controversy about the Interpretation of National Socialism', in Gerhard Hirschfeld and Lothar Kettenacker (eds), *Der "Führerstaat": Mythos und Realität. Studien zur Struktur und Politik des Dritten Reiches* (Stuttgart, 1981), pp. 23–42. Here pp. 27–28.

31. William Carr, *Hitler. A Study in Personality and Politics* (London, 1993), p. 40; Ian Kershaw, ' "Working towards the Führer": Reflections on the Nature of the Hitler Dictatorship', in Kershaw and Lewin (eds), *Stalinism and Nazism. Dictatorships in Comparison*, pp. 88–106. Here pp. 91–92.

32. Ian Kershaw, *The Hitler Myth. Image and Reality in the Third Reich* (Oxford, 1987); Kershaw, 'Working towards the Führer', pp. 97–98.

33. Noakes, 'The Nazi Party and the Third Reich', pp. 14–22.

34. Caplan, *Government without Administration*, p. 136.

35. Broszat, *Hitler State*, pp. 112–113.

36. Gesetz über das Staatsoberhaupt des Deutschen Reichs, 1.8.1934, Michalka (ed.), *Deutsche Geschichte*, p. 42; Broszat, *Hitler State*, p. 282.

37. *Deutschland-Berichte*, 1934, p. 356.
38. Broszat, *Führer State*, pp. 286–287.
39. *Deutschland-Berichte*, 1937, p. 1238.
40. Ulrich Herbert, 'Good Times, Bad Times: Memories of the Third Reich', in Richard Bessel (ed.), *Life in the Third Reich* (Oxford, 1987), pp. 97–110.
41. 'Rheinlandbesetzung und Kriegs-Angst', *Deutschland-Berichte* (1936), pp. 460–478.
42. R. Griffiths, *Fellow Travellers of the Right.*
43. Tim Mason, *Social Policy in the Third Reich* (Oxford, 1993), pp. 71–72.
44. Ian Kershaw, *Hitler 1936–1945: Nemesis* (New York, 2000), pp. 43–46.
45. Cf., Pierre Ayçoberry, *The Social History of the Third Reich* (New York, 1999), p. 191.
46. Broszat, *Hitler State*, pp. 294–299.
47. *Deutschland-Berichte*, 1939, p. 267, pp. 543–562.
48. Broszat, *Hitler State*, p. 308; Nikolaus Wachsmann, *Hitler's Prisons. Legal Terror in Nazi Germany* (New Haven and London, 2004), pp. 191–194.
49. Kershaw, *Nemesis*, p. 219; Noakes, *Home Front*, pp. 4–7; Broszat, *Hitler State*, pp. 308–310.
50. Dietrich Orlow, *The History of the Nazi Party 1933–1945* (Pittsburgh, 1973), pp. 333ff.; Jochen Long, Martin Bormann: Hitler's Secretary', in Ronald Smelser and Rainer Zitelmann (eds), *The Nazi Elite* (Basingstoke, 1993), pp. 7–17.
51. Martin Kitchen, *Nazi Germany at War* (Harlow, 1995), pp. 28–38; Noakes, *Home Front*, pp. 31–53.

Chapter 3: Nazism and the Economy

1. Italy; Gerhard Senft, *Im Vorfeld der Katastrophe. Die Wirtschaftspolitik des Ständestaates: Österreich 1934–1938* (Vienna, 2002); Charles Delzell, *Mediterranean Fascism 1919–1945* (New York and London, 1970), pp. 337–437.
2. See Tim Mason, 'The Primacy of Politics. Politics and Economics in National Socialist Germany' in Tim Mason, *Nazism, Fascism and the Working Class*, edited by Jane Caplan (Cambridge, 1995), pp. 53–76; Ian Kershaw, *The Nazi Dictatorship. Problems and Perspectives of Interpretation* (4th edition, London, 2000), pp. 49–51.
3. See William Carr, *Arms, Autarky and Aggression. A Study in German Foreign Policy* (London, 1972).
4. Reinhard Opitz (ed.), *Europastrategien des deutschen Kapitals 1900–1945* (Bonn, 1994); Volker Berghahn (ed.), 'German Big Business and the Quest for a European Economic Empire in the Twentieth Century' *Quest for Economic Empire. European Strategies of German Big Business in the Twentieth Century* (Providence and Oxford, 1996), pp. 1–35. Here particularly pp. 5–10. See also Henry Cord Meyer, *Mitteleuropa in German Thought and Action* (The

Hague, 1955); see also Jörg Brechtefeld, *Mitteleuropa and German Politics. 1848 to the Present* (Basingstoke, 1996), pp. 31–38.

5. Fritz Fischer, *Germany's Aims in the First World War* (London, 1967), pp. 103–106.

6. 'Dcnkschrift Hermann Röchlings an den Statthalter von Elsass-Lothringen v. Dallwitz, betr. Französische Erzgebiete', in Opitz (ed.), *Europastrategien*, pp. 211–212; *Kriegszieldenkschrift Walther Rathenaus an Bethmann Hollweg*, 7 September 1914, ibid., pp. 212–215.

7. See for example, Vejas Gabriel Liulevicius, *War Land on the Eastern Front. Culture, National Identity, and German Occupation in World War I* (Cambridge, 2000).

8. See Alf Lüdtke, 'The "Honor" of Labor: Industrial Workers and the Power of Symbols under National Socialism', in David Crew (ed.), *Nazism and German Society 1933–1945* (London, 1994), pp. 67–109.

9. Here the Social Democrats won 61 per cent, the Communists 34 per cent, and the Nazis 4 per cent. F. L. Carsten, *The German Workers and the Nazis* (Aldershot, 1995), pp. 5–9; Schneider, *Unterm Hakenkreuz*, p. 74.

10. See Tim Mason, 'The Origins of the Law on the Organization of National Labour of 20 January 1934. An investigation into the relationship between "modern" and "archaic" elements in recent German history', in Mason, *Nazism Fascism and the Working Class*, pp. 77–103.

11. Rüdiger Hachtmann, *Industriearbeit im "Dritten Reich": Untersuchungen über den Lohn- und Arbeitsbedingungen in Deutschland 1933–1945* (Göttingen, 1989), pp. 30–31.

12. Frei, *Führer State*, p. 54; *Deutschland-Berichte*, pp. 36–40.

13. Arthur Schweitzer, *Big Business in the Third Reich* (Bloomington, 1964), pp. 246–249.

14. See Tim Mason, 'The Primacy of Politics. Politics and Economics in National Socialist Germany', in Mason, *Nazism, Fascism and the Working Class*, pp. 53–76.

15. Thomas Childers, 'The Middle Classes and National Socialism', in David Blackbourn and Richard J. Evans (eds), *The German Bourgeoisie. Essays on the Social History of the German Middle Class from the Late Eighteenth to the Early Nineteenth Century* (London, 1993), pp. 318–337. Here pp. 330–332.

16. See Oded Heilbronner, 'Der verlassene Stammtisch. Vom Verfall der bürgerlichen Infrastruktur und dem Aufstieg der NSDAP am Beispiel der Region Schwarzwald', *Geschichte und Gesellschaft* 19 (1993), No. 2, pp. 178–201.

17. Adalheid von Saldern, *Mittelstand in "Dritten Reich". Handwerker – Enzelhändler –Bauern* (Frankfurt, 1979) is the standard work on the subject and gives details of policies and measures.

18. *Deutschland-Berichte*, 1934, p. 426.

19. Von Saldern, *Mittelstand*, pp. 171–174; See also, Ian Kershaw, *Popular Opinion and Political Dissent in the Third Reich. Bavaria 1933–1945* (Oxford, 1984), pp. 111–155, on 'petty bourgeois complaint and compliance'.

20. *Deutschland-Berichte*, 1934, pp. 110–112; 131–133; 425–428. See also, Ian Kershaw, *Popular Opinion and Political Dissent* (Oxford, 1984), pp. 111–155, on 'petty bourgeois complaint and compliance'.

21. *Deutschland-Berichte*, 1935, pp. 453–465, 1335.

22. *Deutschland-Berichte*, 1939, pp. 868–891.

23. Von Saldern, *Mittelstand*, pp. 173–174; see for example *Meldungen*, 14, 5320–5324 (31 May 1943).

24. See J. E. Farquharson, *The Plough and the Swastika. The NSDAP and Agriculture in Germany 1928–45* (London, 1976), pp. 71–85. On Darré see Gustavo Corni, 'Richard Walther Darré: The Blood and Soil Ideologue', in Smelser and Zitelmann, *The Nazi Elite*, pp. 18–27.

25. *Deutschland-Berichte*, 1934, pp. 230–234.

26. Von Saldern, *Mittelstand*, pp. 72–74.

27. Kershaw, *Bavaria*, p. 43.

28. *Deutschland-Berichte*, 1934, p. 52; Corni, 'Darré', p. 53.

29. Von Saldern, *Mittelstand*, pp. 174–176; see also Kershaw, *Bavaria*, pp. 33–65 on 'Peasant Opinion and the "Coercive Economy"'.

30. Farquharson, *The Plough and the Swastika*, p. 75.

31. *Deutschland-Berichte*, 1934, pp. 53, 114, 233.

32. See Richard Overy, *The Nazi Economic Recovery 1932–1938* (London, 1982), pp. 13–21.

33. Harold James, 'Innovation and Conservatism in Economic Recovery: The Alleged "Nazi Recovery" of the 1930s', in Caplan and Childers (eds), *Reevaluating the Third Reich* (New York and London, 1993), pp. 114–138.

34. Overy, *Economic Recovery*, pp. 39–41.

35. James, 'Innovation and Conservatism', pp. 116–117.

36. *Deutschland-Berichte*, 1934, pp. 22–24.

37. Carr, *Arms, Autarky and Aggression* (London, 1972), pp. 40–41.

38. See for example Lagebericht der Staatspolisei, *Hannover, 4 May 1935 and 18 August 1935 in Klaus Mlynek*, Gestapo Hannover meldet . . . *Polizei- und Regierungsberichte für das mittlere und südliche Niedersachsen zwischen 1933 und 1937* (Hildesheim, 1986), pp. 335, 412. See also Ian Kershaw, 'Social Unrest and the Responses of the Nazi Regime, 1934–1936', in Francis R. Nicosia and Lawrence D. Stokes (eds), *Germans Against Hitler: Nonconformity, Opposition and Resistance in the Third Reich: Essays in Honour of Peter C. Hoffmann* (New York, 1990), pp. 157–174. *Deutschland-Berichte*, 1935, pp. 951–959.

39. *Deutschland-Berichte*, 1935, pp. 1138–1157.

40. Ibid., pp. 1393–1394.

41. Kershaw, 'Social Unrest', pp. 161–162.

42. James, 'Innovation and Conservatism', p. 132.

43. Carr, *Arms, Autarky and Aggression*, pp. 45–65; Overy, *Goering*, pp. 39–47.

44. Peter Hayes, *Industry and Ideology. IG Farben in the Nazi Era* (Cambridge, 1987), pp. 165–169.

45. *Deutschland-Berichte*, 1935, pp. 454–455.

46. David E. Kaiser, *Economic Diplomacy and the Origins of the Second World War. Germany, Britain, France and Eastern Europe* (Princeton, 1980), p. 268. On the economic dimension of the Anschluss see Norbert Schausberger, *Der Griff nach Österreich. Der Anschluss* (Vienna, 1978).

47. Tim Kirk, *Nazism and the Working Class in Austria. Industrial Unrest and Political Dissent in the 'National Community'* (Cambridge, 1996), pp. 56–61.

48. Schreiben des Reichs- und Preussischen Arbeitsministers an den Chef der Reichskanzlei, Dr Lammers vom 28 August 1936', in Timothy W. Mason, *Arbeiterklasse und Volksgemeinschaft. Dokumenteund Materialien zur deutschen Arbeiterpolitik 1936–1939* (Opladen, 1975), pp. 194–196.

49. Schneider, *Unterm Hakenkreuz*, pp. 290–346.

50. Stephen Salter, 'Class Harmony or Class Conflict? The Industrial Working Class and the National Socialist Regime, 1933–1945', in Noakes (ed.), *Government, Party and People in Nazi Germany* (Exeter, 1980), pp. 76–97. Here pp. 84–85.

51. Josef Moser, *Oberösterreichs Wirtschaft 1938 bis 1945* (Vienna, 1995); Helmut Fiereder, *Reichswerke "Hermann Göring" in Österreich (1938–1945)* (Vienna and Salzburg, 1983); Evan Burr Bukey, *Hitler' Home Town. Linz, Austria, 1908–1945* (Bloomington, 1986), pp. 201–207; Richard Overy, 'The Reichswerke Hermann Göring': A Study in German Economic Imperialism', in R. J. Overy, *War and Economy* (Oxford, 1994), pp. 144–174.

52. Salter, 'Class Harmony or Class Conflict', p. 85.

53. Hans-Erich Volkmann, 'The National Socialist Economy in Preparation for War', in Wilhelm Deist *et al.* (eds), *Germany and the Second World War,* Vol. 1, *The Build up of German Aggression* (Oxford, 1990), pp. 157–372. Here pp. 365–366.

54. Timothy W. Mason, 'Labour in the Third Reich', *Past and Present,* 33 (1966); 'The Legacy of 918 for National Socialism', in Anthony Nicholls and Erich Matthias (eds), *German Democracy and the Triumph of Hitler* (London, 1971); 'Internal Crisis and War of Aggression, 1938–1939', in Tim Mason, *Nazism, Fascism and the Working Class,* pp. 104–130.

55. Ludolf Herbst, 'Die Krise des nationalsozialistischen Regimes am Vorabend des zweiten Weltkriegs und die forcierte Aufrüstung', *Vierteljahreshefte für Zeitgeschichte,* 26 (1978), pp. 347–392; Richard Overy, 'Domestic Crisis and War in 1939', *Past and Present,* 116 (1987), pp. 138–168; Kershaw, *Nazi Dictatorship,* pp. 88–91; Tim Mason, 'The Domestic Dynamics of Nazi Conquests: A Response to Critics', in Childers and Caplan (eds), *Reevaluating the Nazi Past,* pp. 161–189.

56. Mason, *Arbeiterklasse,* pp. 1043ff.

57. Mason, *Social Policy,* pp. 252–255; Wolfgang Werner, '*Bleib übrig!' Deutsche Arbeiter in der nationalsozialistischen Kriegswirtschaft*' (Düsseldorf, 1983), pp. 34–40; Kirk, *Nazism and the Working Class in Austria,* pp. 88–93; Ulrich Herbert, 'Arbeiterschaft im Dritten Reich. Zwischenbilanz und offene

Fragen', in *Geschichte und Gesellschaft*, 15 (1989), pp. 320–360. Here pp. 345–346.

58. Jill Stephenson, *Women in Nazi Germany* (Harlow, 2001), pp. 53–58; Matthew Stibbe, *Women in the Third Reich* (London, 2003), pp. 91–96.

59. Ulrich Herbert, *Fremdarbeiter. Politik und Praxis des Ausländer-Einsatzes in der Kriegswirtschaft des Dritten Reiches* (Berlin, 1986), pp. 46–49, 64.

60. See Czeslaw Łuczak, 'Polnische Arbeiter im nationalsozialistischen Deutschland während des Zweiten Weltkriegs', in Ulrich Herbert (ed.), *Europa und der Reichseinsatz. Ausländische Zivilarbeiter, Kriegsgefangene und KZ-Häftlinge in Deutschland 1938–1945* (Essen, 1991), pp. 90–105.

61. Herbert, *Fremdarbeiter*, p. 77.

62. Herbert, *Einleitung*, in Herbert (ed.), *Reichseinsatz*, pp. 7–25. Here pp. 7–8.

63. Alan Milward, *The German Economy at War* (London, 1965), p. 8.

64. R. J. Overy, 'Hitler's War and the German Economy: A Reinterpretation', in R. J. Overy, *War and Economy* (Oxford, 1994).

65. Rolf-Dieter Müller, 'The Mobilization of the German Economy for Hitler's War Aims', in Bernhard R. Kroener, Rolf-Dieter Müller and Hans Umbreit, *Germany and the Second World War*, Vol. V, *Organization and Mobilization of the German Sphere of Power*, Part 1, *Wartime Administration, Economy and Manpower Resources 1939–1941* (Oxford, 2000), pp. 407–786. Here pp. 409–411. Noakes, *German Home Front*, pp. 186–187; Deist *et al.*, *Build up of Aggression*, p. 350.

66. Müller, 'Mobilization', pp. 474–495.

67. Franz W. Seidler, 'Fritz Todt: From Motorway Builder to Minister of State', in Smelser and Zitelman, *Nazi Elite*, pp. 245–256.

68. R. J. Overy, 'Mobilization for Total War in Germany 1939–1941', *English Historical Review* (1988), pp. 613–639; and Overy, 'Rationalization and the "Production Miracle" in Germany during the Second World War', in Overy, *War and Economy*, pp. 342–375.

69. Müller, 'Mobilization', pp. 773–786, and particularly p. 786, where he cites General Thomas' evidence to British interrogators.

Chapter 4: The Myth of the 'National Community': German Society under Nazism

1. Pierre Ayçoberry, *The Social History of the Third Reich 1933–1945* (New York, 1999), p. 65.

2. Jeffrey Herf, *Reactionary Modernism. Technology, Culture and Politics in Weimar and the Third Reich* (Cambridge, 1984), pp. 18–69; Anthony McElligott, *The German Urban Experience. Modernity and Crisis* (London, 2001), pp. 28–30.

3. Ferdinand Tönnies, *Community and Civil Society* edited by Jose Harris and translated by Margaret Hollis (Cambridge, 2001).

4. David Schoenbaum, *Hitler's Social Revolution. Class and Status in Nazi Germany 1933–1939* (New York, 1990; originally published in 1966), p. 71, pp. 285–288.

5. Herbert, 'Arbeiterschaft im Dritten Reich', pp. 320–321; Peter Hüttenberger, 'Heimtückefälle vor dem Sondergericht München 1933–1939', in Broszat et al., *Bayern IV*, pp. 435–526.

6. Günter Morsch, *Arbeit und Brot. Studein zu Lage, Stimmung, Einstellung und Verhalten der deutschen Arbeiterschaft 1933–1936/7* (Frankfurt, 1993), pp. 81ff.

7. *Deutschland-Berichte*, 1934, p. 108.

8. Alf Lüdtke, 'The "honor of Labor". Industrial workers and the power of symbols under National Socialism', in David Crew (ed.), *Nazism and German Society 1933–1945* (London, 1994), pp. 67–109.

9. *Deutschland-Berichte*, 1934, p. 107; 1935, p. 1310.

10. Schneider, *Unterm Hakenkreuz*, pp. 556–568; Carola Sachse, *Betriebliche Sozialpolitik als Familienpolitik in der Weimarer Republik und im Nationalsozialismus: mit einer Fallstudie über die Firma Siemens* (Hamburg, 1987); Neil Gregor, *Daimler Benz in the Third Reich* (New Haven and London, 1988), p. 154.

11. See Shelley Baranowski, *Strength through Joy. Consumerism and Mass Tourism in the Third Reich* (Cambridge, 2004), pp. 75–117.

12. Peter Reichel, *Der schöne Schein des Dritten Reiches. Faszination und Gewalt des Faschismus* (Frankfurt, 1993), pp. 237–243; Schneider, *Unterm Hakenkreuz*, p. 566.

13. The examples here are selected from among many in the *Deutschland-Berichte* between 1934 and 1938. Here *Deutschland-Berichte*, 1935, p. 1462; 1936, pp. 886–887; 1938, pp. 173–175, 441.

14. *Deutschland-Berichte*, 1938, p. 163.

15. Reichel, *Der schöne Scheindes Dritten Reiches*, p. 242; *Deutschland-Berichte*, 1935, p. 1312.

16. Schneider, *Unterm Hakenkreuz*, pp. 596–600.

17. *Meldungen*, 7, pp. 2284–2285 (8 May 1941).

18. Schneider, *Unterm Hakenkreuz*, 609–630; Baranowski, *Strength through Joy*, pp. 98–99; Lisa Pine, 'Hashude: The Imprisonment of "Asocial" Families in the Third Reich', *German History* 13 (1995), pp. 182–197.

19. See Overy, *War and Economy*, pp. 68–89.

20. Schneider, *Unterm Hakenkreuz*, pp. 609–632.

21. *Meldungen*, 2, p. 130.

22. Adalheid von Saldern, 'The Old Mittelstand 1890–1939. How "Backward" were the Artisans?', *Central European History* 25/1 (1992), pp. 27–51 Kershaw, *Bavaria*, pp. 154–155.

23. Oded Heilbronner, 'Der verlassene Stammtisch. Vom Verfall der bürgerlichen Infrastruktur und dem Aufstieg der NSDAP am Beispiel der Region Schwarzwald', in *Geschichte und Gesellschaft* 19 (1993), pp. 179–201.

24. Franz Neumann, *Behemoth. The Structure and Practice of National Socialism* (London, 1942), p. 305.

25. *Deutschland-Berichte*, 1934, pp. 115–117: 'Die Stimmung unter den Gebildeten'.

26. Alison Owings, *Frauen. German Women Recall the Third Reich* (Harmondsworth, 1993), pp. 8–9.

27. Anthony McElligott. '"Sentencing towards the Führer"? The judiciary in the Third Reich', in McElligott and Kirk (eds), *Working towards the Führer'*, pp. 153–185; Diemut Majer, *"Non-Germans" under the Third Reich. The Nazi Judicial System in Germany and Occupied Eastern Europe, with special Regard to Occupied Poland 1939–1945* (Baltimore, 2003), pp. 18–34.

28. See Ernst Fraenkel, *The Dual State. A Contribution to the Theory of Dictatorship* (London, 1941); Michael Stolleis, *Die Verwaltungsgerichtsbarkeit im Nationalsozialismus'*, in Bernhard Diestelkamp and Michael Stolleis (eds), *Jutizalltag im Dritten Reich* (Frankfurt, 1988), pp. 26–38.

29. Margit Szöllösi-Janze, 'National Socialism and the Sciences', in Margit Szöllösi-Janze (ed.), *Science in the Third Reich* (Oxford and New York, 2001).

30. Michael Burleigh, *Germany Turns Eastwards* (Cambridge, 1988).

31. Guntram Heinrik Herb, *Under the Map of Germany. Nationalism and Propaganda 1918–1945* (London, 1997); Mechtild Rössler, 'Geography and Area Planning under National Socialism', in Szöllösi-Janze, *Science in the Third Reich* (Oxford, 2001), pp. 59–78.

32. Szöllösi-Janze, 'National Socialism and the Sciences', pp. 10–11; Majer, *'Non-Germans'* under the Third Reich. The Nazi Judicial and Administrative System in Germany and Occupied Europe, with special Regard to Occupied Poland, 1939–1945 (Baltimore and London, 2003), p. 4; Jeremy Noakes, 'The Ivory Tower under Siege: German Universities in the Third Reich', in *Journal of European Studies* 23/4 (1993) pp. 371–408; Bruno W. Reimann, 'The Defeat of the German Universities 1933', in *Historical Social Research* 39 (1986), pp. 101–105.

33. Bettina Arnold, 'The Past as Propaganda: Totalitarian Archaeology in Nazi Germany', *Antiquity* 64 (1990), reprinted in Robert Preucel and Ian Hodder (eds), *Contemporary Archaeology in Theory* (Oxford, 1996), pp. 549–567. Here pp. 553–554.

34. Sylvia Paletschek, 'The Invention of Humboldt and the Impact of National Socialism: The German University Idea in the First Half of the Twentieth Century', in Szöllösi-Janze, *Science in the Third Reich*, pp. 37–58.

35. See for example, Ute Deichmann, 'The Expulsion of Jewish Chemists and Bio-Chemists from Academia in Nazi Germany', in *Perspectives on Science* 7/1 (1999), pp. 1–86.

36. Thomas Ellwein, *Die Deutsche Universität vom Mittelalter bis zur Gegenwart* (Wiesbaden, 1997), pp. 230–231.

37. *Meldungen*, 15, pp. 5781–5782 (20 September 1943), Tim Kirk, *Longman Companion to Nazi Germany* (Harlow, 1995), p. 109, for the figures.

38. Ellwein, *Deutsche Universität*, p. 280.

39. Gregory Paul Wegner, *Anti-Semitism and Schooling under the Third Reich* (New York, 2002).

40. Lisa Pine, *Nazi Family Policy* (Oxford, 1997), pp. 58–72.

41. H. W. Koch, *The Hitler Youth. Origins and Development 1922–1945* (London, 1975), pp. 179–203; Dietrich Orlow, 'Die Adolf-Hitler Schulen',

Vierteljahreshefte für Zeitgeschichte 12/3 (1965), pp. 272–284; idem, *History of the Nazi Party*, pp. 187–192; Harald Scholz, 'Die "NS-Ordensburgen"', *Vierteljahreshefte für Zeitgeschichte* 15/3 (1967), pp. 269–298; Michael H. Kater, *Hitler Youth* (Cambridge Mass., and London, 2004), pp. 48–53, p. 104.

42. Kater, *Hitler Youth*, pp. 96–101.
43. Hellmut Stellrecht, *Neue Erziehung* (Berlin, 1942).
44. *Deutschland-Berihchte*, 1937, pp. 552–558, 843–845.
45. Detlev Peukert, *Inside the Third Reich: Conformity, Opposition and Racism in Everyday Life* (Harmondsworth, 1989), pp. 145–174; Kater, *Hitler Youth*, pp. 113–166.
46. Emilio Gentile, *The Sacralisation of Politics in Fascist Italy* (Cambridge, Mass., 1996), and 'Fascism as Political Religion', *Journal of Contemporary History* 25, 2/3 (May, 1990), pp. 229–251.
47. See Richard Steigmann-Gall, *The Holy Reich. Nazi Conceptions of Christianity 1919–1945* (Cambridge 2003).
48. Klaus Scholder, *The Churches and the Third Reich 1918–1934* (London, 1987); Guenter Lewy, *The Catholic Church and Nazi Germany* (Cambridge, Mass., and New York, 2000).
49. Peukert, *Inside the Third Reich*, (London, 1987), pp. 98–99; Jeremy Noakes, 'The Oldenburg Crucifix Struggle', in Stachura, *The Shaping of the Nazi State*, (London, 1978).
50. Christine King, 'Strategies for Survival: An Examination of the History of Five Christian Sects in Germany 1933–1945', in *Journal of Contemporary History* 14 (1979), pp. 211–234; Carsten, *German Workers*, pp. 114–121; Gerhard Hetzer, 'Ernste Bibelforscher in Augsburg', in Broszat, Elke Fröhlich and Anton Grossmann (eds), *Bayern in der NS-Zeit* (IV) *Herrschaft und Gesellschaft im Konflikt* (Munich, 1981), pp. 621–643.
51. Schoenbaum, *Hitler's Social Revolution*, pp. 283–287.

Chapter 5: Culture, Leisure and Propaganda

1. See Alan Steinweis, 'Conservatism, National Socialism and the Cultural Crisis of the Weimar Republic', in Jones and Retallack, *Between Reform and Resistance*, pp. 329–346.
2. Reinhard Bollmuss, 'Alfred Rosenberg: National Socialism's Chief Ideologue', in Ronald Smelser and Rainer Zitelmann, *The Nazi Elite* (Basingstoke, 1993), pp. 183–193.
3. Alan Steinweis, 'Weimar Culture and the Rise of National Socialism: The Kampfbund für deutsche Kultur', *Central European History* 24/4 (1991), pp. 401–423.
4. Jonathan Petropoulos, *Art and Politics in the Third Reich* (Chapel Hill and London, 1996).
5. David Welch, *The Third Reich. Politics and Propaganda* (London: Routledge, 1993), pp. 23–26; Jonathan Petropoulos, *Art as Politics in the Third Reich* (Chapel Hill and London: University of North Carolina Press, 1996), pp. 21–22.

6. Alan E. Steinweis, *Art, Ideology and Economics in Nazi Germany. The Reich Chambers of Music, Theater and the Visual Arts* (Chapel Hill, 1993).

7. He was appointed Beauftragter des Führers für die Überwachung der gesamten Schulung und Erziehung der Partei und gleichgeschalteten Verbande' on 24 January 1934. Petropolous, *Art as Politics*, p. 34.

8. Eckard Michels, *Das Deutsche Institut in Paris 1940–1944. Ein Beitrag zu den deutsch-französischen Kulturbeziehungen und zur auswärtigenKulturpolitik des Dritten Reiches* (Stuttgart, 1993), pp. 44–56.

9. This excerpt is in Herschel B. Chipp, *Theories of Modern Art. A Source Book by Artists and Critics* (Berkeley, Los Angeles and London, 1968), pp. 474–483. Here p. 479.

10. See Michael H. Kater, *The Twisted Muse. Musicians and Their Music in the Third Reich* (Oxford, 1997).

11. Welch, *Politics and Propaganda*, pp. 30–31.

12. *Deutschland-Berichte*, 1938, pp. 1326–1329; *Meldungen*, pp. 117–118.

13. *Meldungen*, 6, pp. 1849, 1980.

14. *Meldungen*, 7, p. 2357.

15. *Meldungen*, 6, p. 2179; 5, pp. 1637–1638.

16. *Meldungen*, 11, p. 4233.

17. *Meldungen*, 11, pp. 4385, 4847; 13, p. 4927

18. Verordnung über ausserordentliche Rundfunkmassnahmen vom 1., September 1939; *Meldungen*, 3, p. 636; 4, pp. 1172–1173.

19. *Meldungen*, 8, p. 3020.

20. Reinhard Mann, *Protest und Kontrolle im Dritten Reich. Nationalsozialistische Herrschaft im Alltag einer rheinischen Grossstadt* (Frankfurt, 1987), p. 262; *Meldungen*, 3, p. 636.

21. Welch, *Politics and Propaganda*, pp. 39–49.

22. *Meldungen*, 10, pp. 3758–3760.

23. *Meldungen*, 6, pp. 1917–1919.

24. *Meldungen*, 9, pp. 3175–3178.

25. *Meldungen*, 3, p. 829.

26. 'Der deutsche Film im Südosten. 38. Kulturbericht Südosteuropa, 19–25 May 1942. Österreichisches Staatsarchiv, Archiv der Republik, Statthalterie Wien 41a/VI.

27. Tim Kirk, 'Working Towards the Reich: The Reception of German Cultural Politics in South-Eastern Europe', in McElligott and Kirk (eds), *Working Towards the Führer*, pp. 205–223.

28. Oron J. Hale, *The Captive Press in the Third Reich* (Princeton, 1964).

29. The text of the law is reproduced in Welch, *Politics and Propaganda*, pp. 156–158.

30. Hale, *Captive Press*, pp. 131–151.

31. *Deutschland-Berichte*, 1936, pp. 777–825; Welch, *Politics and Propaganda*.

32. Baranowski, *Strength through Joy*, p. 40.

33. Schneider, *Unterm Hakenkreuz*, pp. 228–236.

34. Noakes and Pridham, *Nazism*, Vol. 2, pp. 348–349; Baranowski, *Strength through Joy*, 118–161; Reichel, *Der schöne Schein des Dritten Reiches*, pp. 255–272, 246; Schneider, *Unterm Hakenkreuz*, pp. 230–231.

35. *Deutschland-Berichte*, 1939, p. 490.

36. 'Aber die Autobahnen...!', Gudrun Brockhaus, *Schauder und Idylle: Faschismus als Erlebnisangebot* (Munich, 1997), pp. 68–117.

37. *Deutschland-Berichte*, 1938, p. 157.

38. On this issue see Mark Roseman, 'National Socialism and Modernisation', in Richard Bessel (ed.), *Fascist Italy and Nazi Germany. Comparisons and Contrasts* (Cambridge, 1996), pp. 197–229.

39. *Deutschland-Berichte*, 1938, p. 150.

Chapter 6: Consensus and Opposition in the Third Reich

1. See Wolfram Siemann, '*Deutschlands Ruhe, Sicherheit und Ordnung'. Die Anfänge der politischen Polizei 1806–1866* (Tübingen, 1985).

2. Christoph Graf, *Politische Polizei zwischen Demokratie und Diktatur die Entwicklung der preussischen Politischen Polizei vom Staatsschutzorgan der Weimarer Republik zum Geheimen Staatspolizeiamt des Dritten Reiches* (Berlin, 1983), pp. 93–108.

3. Robert Gellately, *The Gestapo and German Society. Enforcing Racial Policy 1933–1945* (Oxford, 1991), pp. 29–40; Graf. *Politische Polizei*, pp. 208–220; Noakes and Pridham, *State, Economy and Society*, pp. 506–515.

4. Boberach, *Meldungen aus dem Reich*, 1, pp. 12–13.

5. Graf, *Politische Polizei*, p. 177. Reinhard Mann, *Protest und Kontrolle*, pp. 147–176; Gellately, *Gestapo*, p. 45. Note that population figures refer to administrative divisions for which police forces were responsible, and that populations of cities were smaller. The city of Hanover, for example, had just over half the population of the administrative district of the same name.

6. Robert Gellately, *Backing Hitler* (Oxford, 2001), p. 4. Sheila Fitzpatrick and Robert Gellateley, 'Introduction to the Practices of Denunciation in Modern European History', in *Journal of Modern History* 68/4 (1996), pp. 747–767. Here p. 753.

7. Eric Johnson, *The Gestapo, Jews, and Ordinary Germans* (London, 1999), particularly pp. 253–375. Johnson takes issue with Gellatelly's perspective, arguing that the police acted on denunciations largely only in relation to minor cases, but were very 'proactive' against the main objects of persecution.

8. See Peter R. Black, *Ernst Kaltenbrunner: Ideological Soldier of the Third Reich* (Princeton, 1984).

9. Bernd Wegener, *The Waffen-SS. Organisation, Ideology and Function* (Oxford, 1990), pp. 14–57.

10. Wegener, *Waffen-SS*, pp. x–xii briefly summarises these developments and refers to the literature associated with them.

11. Krausnick and Broszat, *Anatomy of the SS State*, pp. 60–76.

12. See Robert L. Koehl, *RKFDV: German Resettlement and Population Policy 1939–1945. A History of the Reich Commission for the Strengthening of Germandom* (Cambridge Mass., 1957).

13. Krausnick and Broszat, *Anatomy of the SS State*, p. 154.

14. Frankl, *Dual State.*

15. See Florian Freund and Bertrand Perz, *Das KZ in der Serbenhalle. Zur Kriegsindustrie in Wiener Neustadt* (Vienna, 1987); Florian Freund, *Arbeitslager Zement. Das konzentrationslager Ebensee und die Raketenrüstung* (Vienna, 1989) and Bertrand Perz, *Projekt Quartz. Steyr-Daimler-Puch und das Konzentrationslager Melk* (Vienna, 1991).

16. Krausnick and Broszat, *Anatomy*, pp. 190–199; Lisa Pine, *Nazi Family Policy 1933–1945* (Oxford 1997), p. 119; Nikolaus Wachsmann, 'From indefinite confinement to extermination: "habitual criminals" in the Third Reich', in Robert Gellately and Nathan Stoltzfuss, Social Outsiders in Nazi Germany (Princeton, 2001), pp. 165–191.

17. F. L. Carsten, *The German Workers and the Nazis* (Aldershot, 1995), p. 117.

18. Yisrael Gutman, 'Auschwitz – An Overview', in Yisrael Gutman and Michael Berenbaum (eds), *Anatomy of the Auschwitz Death Camp* (Bloomington and Indianapolis, 1998), pp. 55–33. Here p. 16.

19. Kurt Klotzbach, *Gegen den Nationalsozialismus: Widerstand und Verfolgung in Dortmund 1930–1945. Eine historisch-politische Studie* (Hanover, 1969), p. 127.

20. Hermann Weber, 'Die Ambivalenz der kommunistischen Widerstandsstrategie bis zur "Brüsseler" Parteikonferez', in Jürgen Schmädeke and Peter Steinbach (eds), *Der Widerstand gegen den Nationalsozialismus. Die deutsche Gesellschaft und der Widerstand gegen Hitler* (Munich and Zurich, 1986), pp. 73–85.

21. *Deutschland-Berichte*, 1939, p. 988.

22. Kuno Bludau, *Gestapo-Geheim! Widerstand und Verfolgung in Duisburg 1933–1945* (Bonn-Bad Godesberg, 1973), pp. 4–35.

23. See Larry Eugene Jones, 'The Limits of Collaboration: Edgar Jung, Herbert von Bose, and the Origins of the Conservative Resistance to Hitler, 1933–34', in Jones and Retallack, *Between Reform, Reaction and Resistance*, pp. 465–501. Robert Gellately and Nathan Stoltzfuss (eds), *Social Outsiders in Nazi Germany* (Princeton and Oxford, 2001).

24. See Klaus-Jürgen Müller, *The Army, Politics and Society in Germany 1933–1945. Studies in the army's relation to Nazism* (Manchester, 1987); Gerd Überschär, 'Militäropposition gegen Hitlers Kriegspolitik 1939 bis 1941. Motive, Struktur und Alternativvorstellungen des entstehenden militärischen Widerstands, in Schmädeke and Steinbach, *Der Widerstand gegen den Nationalsozialismus* (Munich, 1986), pp. 345–367.

25. See Hans Mommsen, 'Beyond the Nation-state: The German Resistance Against Hitler, and the Future of Europe', in McElligott and Kirk (eds), *Working towards the Führer*, pp. 246–259; Winfried Heinemann, 'Aussenpolitische Illusionen des nationalkonservativen Widerstands in den

Monaten vor dem Attentat', in Schmädeke and Steinbach, *Der Widerstand gegen den Nationalsozialismus*, pp. 1061–1070.

26. Klemens von Klemperer, *German Resistance Against Hitler: The Search for Allies Abroad 1938–1945* (Oxford, 1992), pp. 386–387.

27. See Peter Hoffmann, *The History of the German Resistance 1933–1945* (Montreal, 1996); Ulrike Hett and Johannes Tuchel, 'Die Reaktionen des NS-Staates auf den Umsturzversuch vom 20. Juli 1944', in Peter Steinbach und Johannes Tuchel (eds), *Widerstand gegen den Nationalsozialismus* (Berlin, 1994), pp. 377–410.

28. Martin Broszat, 'Resistenz und Widerstand. Eine Zwischenbilanz des Forschungsprojekts', in Broszat, Fröhlich and Grossmann (eds), *Bayern in der NS-Zeit* (IV), pp. 691–709. A short extract in English is in Neil Gregor, *Nazism* (Oxford, 2000), pp. 241–244.

29. Detlev Peukert, 'Der deutsche Widerstand 1933–1945 in *Aus Politik und Zeitgeschichte. Beilage zur Wochenzeitung Das Parlament*, 14 July 1979, p. 22.

Chapter 7: Reproduction, the Family and Racial Hygiene

1. See Paul Weindling, *Health, Race and German Politics Between National Unification and Nazism, 1870–1945*, pp. 489–564 (Cambridge, 1989); Gabriele Czarnowski, ' "The Value of Marriage for the Volksgemeinschft": Policies Towards Women and Marriage Under National Socialism', in Richard Bessel (ed.), *Fascist Italy and Nazi Germany. Comparisons and Contrasts* (Cambridge, 1996), pp. 94–112.

2. Jill Stephenson, *The Nazi Organisation of Women* (London, 1981); Gertrud Scholtz-Klink, *Das weite Wirkungsfeld. Frauen schaffen in Deutschland* (Berlin, 1942), p. 104, cited in Ute Benz (ed.), *Frauen im Nationalsozialismus* (Munich, 1993), p. 14.

3. *Der Kongress zu Nürnberg vom 5. bis 10. September 1934. Offizieller Bericht über den Verlauf des Reichsparteitages mit samtlichen Reden* (Munich, 1935), pp. 169–172, cited ibid., p. 42.

4. Stellrecht, *Neue Erziehung*, pp. 160–165; Lisa Pine, *Nazi Family Policy 1933–1945* (Oxford, 1997), especially pp. 47–87.

5. These examples are from the quarterly magazine of the Faith and Beauty organisation in Baden and Alsace for the summer of 1943: *Führerinnendienst der Hitler-Jugend: BdM-Werk "Gluabe und Schönheit"*. BA, NSD 38–125.

6. Dagmar Herzog, *Sex After Fascism: Memory and Mortality in Twentieth-Century Germany* (Princeton, 2005).

7. Irmgard Weyrather, *Muttertag und Mutterkreuz. Der Kult um die "deutsche Mutter" im Nationalsozialismus* (Frankfurt, 1993), pp. 18, 55.

8. See Maria Sophia Quine, *Population Politics in Twentieth-Century Europe* (London, 1996).

9. Atina Grossmann, *Reforming Sex; The German Movement for Birth Control and Abortion Reform 1920–1950* (New York and Oxford, 1995), Cornelie Usborne,

'Rebellious Girls and Pitiable Women: Abortion Narratives in Weimar Popular Culture', *German History* 23/3 (2005), pp. 320–338.

10. Jill Stephenson, *Women in Nazi Germany*, pp. 37–39.

11. Georg Lilienthal, *Der "Lebensborn e.V". Ein Instrument nationalsozialistischer Rassenpolitik* (Frankfurt, 1993).

12. D. Petzina *et al.*, *Sozialgeschichtliches arbeitsbuch III*, p. 32

13. Czarnowski, 'Value of Marriage', pp. 98–99.

14. Gisela Bock, 'Antinatalism, Maternity and Paternity in National Socialist Racism', in David F. Crew (ed.), *Nazism and German Society 1933–1945* (London, 1994), pp. 110–140. Here p. 120.

15. Burleigh and Wippermann, *Racial State*, p. 34.

16. See Gisela Bock, *Zwangssterilisation im Nationalsozialismsus: Studien zurRassenpolitikund Frauenpolitik* (Opladen, 1986).

17. 'Zehn Gebote für die Gattenwahl', *NS-Warte. Die einzige parteiamtliche Frauenzeitschrift* 3 (1834), no. 10, p. 295, cited in Benz (ed.), *Frauen*, pp. 54–58.

18. Diemut Majer, *"Non-Germans" under the Third Reich* (Baltimore and London, 2003), pp. 98–108; Czarnowski, 'Value of Marriage', pp. 101–110.

19. Pine, *Family Policy*, pp. 88–94.

20. Bock, 'Antinatalism', p. 127.

21. Pine, *Family Policy*, pp. 112–146; idem, 'Hashude: The Imprisonment of "Asocial" Families in the Third Reich', *German History* 13/2, pp. 182–197.

22. Nikolaus Wachsmann, 'From Indefinite Confinement to Extermination: "Habitual Criminals" in the Third Reich', in Gellately and Stoltzfuss (eds), *Social Outsiders in Nazi Germany*, pp. 165–191.

23. See Edward R. Dickinson and Richard F. Wetzell, 'The Historiography of Sexuality in Modern Germany', *German History* 23/3 (2005), pp. 291–305, for an overview of recent developments in research.

24. Julia Roos, 'Backlash against Prostitutes' Rights: Origins and Dynamics of Nazi Prostitution Policies', *Journal of the History of Sexuality*, 11/1–2 (2002), pp. 67–94.

25. Annette F. Timm, 'The Ambivalent Outsider: Prostitution, Promiscuity and VD control in Nazi Berlin', in Gellately and Stoltzfuss (eds), *Social Outsiders in Nazi Germany*, pp. 192–211; idem, 'Sex with a Purpose: Prostitution, Venereal Disease, and Militarized Masculinity in the Third Reich', *Journal of the History of Sexuality*, 11/1–2 (2002), pp. 223–255.

26. Majer, *"Non-Germans" under the Third Reich*, p. 331.

27. Doris L Bergen, 'Sex, Blood and Vulnerability: Women Outsiders in German-Occupied Europe', in Gellately and Stoltzfuss (eds), *Social Outsiders in Nazi Germany*, pp. 273–293. Here p. 276.

28. *Meldungen*, p. 4518, 30 November 1942.

29. Birthe Kundrus, 'Forbidden Company: Romantic Relationships between Germans and Foreigners, 1939 to 1945', *Journal of the History of Sexuality*, 11/1–2 (2002), pp. 201–222.

30. See Jörg Hutter, *Die gesellschaftliche Kontrolle des homosexuellen Begehrens. Mediz-inische Definitionen und juristische Sanktionen im 19. Jahrhundert* (Frankfurt, 1992).

31. Michael Burleigh and Wofgang Wippermann, *The Racial State: Germany 1933–1945* (Cambridge, 1991), pp. 185–188.

32. E. Kraepelin, 'Geschlechtliche Verirrungen und Volksmehrung, in *Münchener Medizinische Wochenschrift* 65/5 (1918), pp. 117–120, cited in Günter Grau, *Homosexualität in der NS-Zeit. Dokumente einer Diskriminierung und Verfolgung* (Frankfurt, 1993), pp. 47–48.

33. Günter Grau (ed.) with Claudia Schoppmann, *Hidden Holocaust. Gay and Lesbian Persecution in Nazi Germany* (London, 1995), pp. 1–7. See also the personal account of his experience by Heinz Heger, *The Men with the Pink Triangle* (London, 1986).

34. Claudia Schoppmann, 'National Socialist policies towards female homosexu-ality', in Lynn Abrams and Elizabeth Harvey, *Gender Relations in German History: Power, Agency and Experience from the Sixteenth to the Twentieth Century* (London, 1996), pp. 177–187.

35. Burleigh, *Death and Deliverance*, pp. 11–42; Ernst Klee, *'Euthanasie im NS-Staat. Die Vernichtung lebensunwerten Lebens'* (Frankfurt, 2004), pp. 19–25.

36. Joseph Mayer, *Gesetzliche Unfruchtbarmachung Geisteskranker* (*Studien zur kath-olischen Sozial- und Wirtschaftsethik*, Vol. 3, Freiburg, 1927), cited in Ernst Klee (ed.), *Dokumente zur 'Euthanasie'* (Frankfurt, 2001), pp. 44–46; Burleigh, *Death and Deliverance*, pp. 174–175.

37. Ulf Schmidt, 'Der medizinische Forschungsfilm im "Dritten Reich": Insti-tutionalisierung, politische Funktion und ethische Dimension', *Zeitgeschichte* 28/4 (2001), pp. 200–213. In 1940 the Office became the Reich Institute for Film and Pictures in Science and Education (*Reichstelle für den Unterrichtsfilm/ Reichsinstitutfür Film und Bild in Wissenschaft und Unterricht*).

38. Cited in Burleigh, *Death and Deliverance*, pp. 45-46.

39. See Ulf Schmidt, 'Reassessing the Beginning of the "Euthanasia" programme', *German History* 17/4 (1999), pp. 543–550.

40. Kershaw, *Nemesis*, pp. 255–256.

41. Burleigh, *Death and Deliverance*, pp. 93–110.

42. Ibid., pp. 162–180.

43. Gitty Sereny, *Into that Darkness: From Mercy Killing to Mass Murder* (London, 1974).

44. Hartmut M. Hanauske-Abel, 'Not a Slippery Slope or Sudden Subversion: German medicine and National Socialism in 1933', *British Medical Journal*, 313, 7 December 1996, pp. 1453–1463.

Chapter 8: Anti-Semitism and the Holocaust

1. See Pulzer, *Anti-Semitism*, pp. 71ff., and Graml, *Antisemitism in Modern Germany*, pp. 33–86.

2. Weindling, *Health, Race and German Politics*, pp. 25–59.

3. Shulamit Volkov, 'Antisemitism as a Cultural Code. Reflections on the History and Historiography of Anti-Semitism in Imperial Germany', in Michael R. Marrus (ed.), *The Origins of the Holocaust* (Westport and London, 1989), pp. 307–328. Here pp. 316–317.

4. Frank Bajohr, *Unser Hotel ist judenfrei. Bäder-Antisemitismus im 19. und 20. Jahrhundert* (Frankfurt, 2003).

5. Pulzer, *Anti-Semitism*, p. 10. The proportion was smaller (3.6 per cent) for greater Berlin in 1910.

6. See W. E. Mosse, *The German Jewish Economic Elite 1820–1935* (Oxford, 1989).

7. See Steven E. Aschheim, *Culture and Catastrophe. German and Jewish Confrontations with National Socialism and Other Crises* (Basingstoke, 1996), pp. 45–68: '"The Jew Within": The Myth of "Judaization" in Germany'.

8. See Richard Bessel, 'The Nazi Capture of Power', *Journal of Contemporary History* 39/2 (2004), pp. 169–188.

9. Frank Bajohr, *'Aryanisation' in Hamburg. The Economic Exclusion of Jews and the Confiscation of Their Property in Nazi Germany* (New York and Oxford, 2002), pp. 16–28.

10. Avraham Barkai, *From Boycott to Annihilation. The Economic Struggle of German Jews 1933–1943* (Hanover, NH and London, 1989).

11. Cited in Graml, *Antisemitism*, p. 208.

12. See Graml, *Antisemitism*, pp. 86–105 on the 'reversal of emancipation'.

13. *Deutchland-Berichte*, 1935, pp. 800–804.

14. Kershaw, *Nazi Dictatorship*, pp. 109–110.

15. Majer, *'Non-Germans' Under the Third Reich*, p. 113.

16. Christopher Browning, *The Origins of the Final Solution. The Evolution of Nazi Jewish Policy, September 1939–March 1942* (London, 2004), p. 11.

17. Krausnick and Broszat, *Anatomy of the SS-State*, pp. 49–55; Graml, *Antisemitism*, pp. 106–125.

18. *Deutschland-Berichte*, 1935, pp. 811–813.

19. Cited in Graml, *Antisemitism*, p. 210.

20. Gerhard Botz, *Wien vom Anschluss zum Krieg. Nationalsozialistische Machtüberbahme und Politisch-Soziale Umgestaltung am Beispiel der Stadt Wien 1938/9* (Vienna, 1980), pp. 93–98.

21. G. E. R. Gedye, *Fallen Bastions* (London, 1939), p. 308.

22. Gerhard Botz, 'National Socialist Vienna: Antisemitism as a Housing Policy', in Michael R. Marrus (ed.), *The Nazi Holocaust. Historical Articles on the Destruction of European Jews vol 2: The Origins of the Holocaust* (West Port and London: Meckler, 1989), pp. 640–657.

23. Götz Aly and Susanne Heim, *Architects of Annihilation. Auschwitz and the Logic of Destruction* (London, 2002), pp. 16–27; Hans Safrian, Expediting Expropriation and Expulsion: the Impact of the 'Vienna Model' on Anti-Jewish Policies in Nazi Germany, 1938', in *Holocaust and Genocide Studies* 2000 14(3), pp. 390–414.

24. Kershaw, *Nazi Dictatorship*, p. 109.

25. Graml, *Antisemitism*, pp. 5–29.
26. For details of both the meeting and the decree, see Noakes and Pridham, *Nazism*, Vol. II, pp. 558–561.
27. Max Domarus, *Hitler. Speeches and Proclamations 1932–1945* (London, 1997), Vol. 3, p. 1449.
28. Christopher R. Browning, *Nazi Policy, Jewish Workers, German Killers* (Cambridge, 2000), pp. 26–30.
29. Browning, *Origins*, p. 16.
30. Krausnick and Broszat, *SS State*, pp. 67–68.
31. Note by Walter Rauff (27 September 1939) on a meeting chaired by Heydrich (21 September 1939), in Werner Röhr (ed.), with Elke Heckert, Bernd Gottberg, Jutta Wenzel, and Heide-Marie Grünthal, *Die Faschistische Okkupationspolitik in Polen* (Cologne, 1989), pp. 119–120.
32. Götz Aly, *Final Solution. Nazi Population Policy and the Murder of the European Jews* (London, 1999), pp. 23–87; Browning, *Nazi Policy*, pp. 10–12. See also Robert Koehl, *RKFDV: German Resettlement and Population Policy 1939–1945. A History of the Reich Commission for the Strengthening of Germandom* (Cambridge Mass., 1957).
33. See Philippe Burrin, *Hitler and the Jews. The Genesis of the Holocaust* (London, 1994), pp. 65–92.
34. Browning, *Origins*, pp. 54–63.
35. Goebbels, *Tagebücher*, I/8, p. 406, 5 November 1940.
36. Gustavo Corni, *Hitler's Ghettos. Voices from a Beleaguered Society 1939–1944* (London, 2002), pp. 23–25.
37. Browning, *Origins*, pp. 81–89. Aly, *Final Solution*, pp. 88–104, presents the emergence and demise of the Madagascar plan as a chronology of events during the summer of 1940.
38. Corni, *Hitler's Ghettos*, pp. 119–226; Browning, *Origins*, pp. 111–168; J. Noakes and G. Pridham, *Nazism. A Documentary Reader 1919–1945: Foreign Policy, War and Racial Extermination* (Exeter, 1988), pp. 1067–1071.
39. Browning, *Origins*, pp. 89–93.
40. Aly, *Final Solution*, pp. 134–135.
41. Reichsgesetzblatt 1939, pp. 2107ff., cited in Peter Klein (ed.), *Die Einsatzgruppen in der besetzten Sowjetunion 1941/42. Die Tätigkeits- und Lageberichte des Chefs der Sicherheitspolizei und des SD* (Berlin , 1997), p. 17.
42. Graml, *Antisemitism*, p. 168. The order is in Klein, *Einsatzgruppen*, pp. 324–328, and an English translation of this section in Noakes and Pridham, *Foreign Policy*, pp. 1091–1092.
43. Jürgen Matthäus. 'Operation Barbarossa and the Onset of the Holocaust', in Browning, *Origins*, pp. 244–308. Here p. 255.
44. Browning, *Nazi Policy*, pp. 26–57 gives an account of the different positions.
45. See the 'confidential information from the Nazi Party Chancellery' encouraging the denial of reports of atrocities in the East, Aly *Final Solution*, p. 269.
46. Kershaw, *Nemesis*, p. 487.

47. Mark Roseman, *The Villa, the Lake, the Meeting. Wannsee and the Final Solution* (London, 2003).

48. Raul Hilberg, *The Destruction of the European Jews*, Vol. II (3rd edition, New Haven and London, 2003).

49. Graml, *Antisemitism*, p. 193; Bob Moore, *Victims and Survivors – The Nazi Persecution of the Jews in the Netherlands, 1940–45* (London, 1997); Hilberg, *Destruction of the European Jews* II, pp. 584–599; Hans Kirchhoff, ' "Doing all that can be done" – The Swedish Foreign Ministry and the Persecution of Jews in Denmark in October 1943'. A Study in Humanitarian Aid and Realpolitik, *Journal of Scandinavian History* 24/1 (1999), pp. 1–43.

50. Julian Jackson, *France. The Dark Years 1940–1944* (Oxford, 2001), pp. 354–381; Michael Marrus and Robert Paxton, *Vichy France and the Jews* (Stanford, 1995).

51. Walter Manoschek, *Serbien ist judenfrei* (Munich, 1993) and 'The Extermination of the Jews in Serbia', in Ulrich Herbert (ed.), *National Socialist Extermination Policies. Contemporary German Perspectives and Controversies* (New York and Oxford, 2000), pp. 163–185.

52. The phrase was used by a camp doctor cited by Raul Hilberg, *The Destruction of the European Jews*, Vol. III (New Haven and London, 2003, 3rd edn), p. 922.

53. Francisezk Piper, 'Gas Chambers and Crematoria', in Gutman and Berenbaum, *Anatomy of the Auschwitz Death Camp*, pp. 157–182. There are innumerable published and unpublished accounts of this process based on the testimony of both victims and perpetrators.

54. Browning, *Ordinary Men* (London, 1998), pp. 71–77.

55. Gunter Lewy, *The Nazi Persecution of the Gypsies* (Oxford, 2001).

56. Michael Berenbaum (ed.), *A Mosaic of Victims: Non-Jews Persecuted and Murdered by the Nazis* (New York, 1990).

57. See for example, Martin Dean, *Collaboration in the Holocaust. Crimes of the Local Police in Belorussia and the Ukraine, 1941–44* (Basingstoke, 2000).

58. Michael Marrus (ed.), *The Nazi Holocaust. 5 Public Opinion and Relations to the Jews in Nazi Europe.* Vol. 1 (Westport and London, 1989).

Chapter 9: Foreign Policy and the Second World War

1. *StenographsicherBericht über die öffentlichen Handlungen des 15. Untersuchung-sauschusses der verfassungsgebenden Nationalversammlung* (Berlin, 1920), pp. 700–701 excerpted in Kaes *et al.*, *Weimar Republic Sourcebook*, pp. 15–16.

2. Geoffrey Stoakes, *Hitler and the Quest for World dominion. Nazi Ideology and Foreign Policy in the* 1920s (Leamington Spa, 1986), pp. 30–63. Radomir Luža, *Austro-German Relations in the Anschluss Era* (Princeton, 1975).

3. See Kellog, *Russian Roots of Nazism.*

4. See Liulevicius, *War Land in the East.*

5. Mannfred Messerschmidt, 'Foreign Policy and Preparation for War', in Wilhelm Deist *et al.*, *German and the Second World War*, Vol. 1, *The Build-up of German Aggression* (Oxford, 1990), pp. 541–717. Here p. 557.

6. Carr, *Arms, Autarky and Aggression*, pp. 13–20.

7. Wolfram Wette, 'Ideology, Propaganda, and Internal Politics as Preconditions of the War Policy of the Third Reich', in Wilhelm Deist *et al.*, *German and the Second World War*, Vol. 1, *The Build-up of German Aggression* (Oxford, 1990), pp. 9–155. Jill Stephenson, 'Propaganda, Autarky and the German Housewife', in David Welch (ed.), *Nazi Propaganda* (London, 1983), pp. 117–142.

8. *Deutschland-Berichte*, 1934, p. 500; 1935, pp. 9–15; Wette, 'Ideology, Propaganda, and Internal Politics', p. 120

9. *Deutschland-Berichte*, 1935, pp. 279–281; 409–412; 1936, pp. 300–315; Richard Bessel, *Nazism and War* (London, 2004), pp. 59–61; Wette, 'Ideology, Propaganda, and Internal Politics', p. 120.

10. *Deutschland-Berichte*, 1937, p. 1088.

11. *Documents on German Foreign Policy* D, I, No. 19; Noakes and Pridham, *Foreign Policy*, pp. 680–688.

12. Bernd-Jürgen Wendt, *Grossdeutschland. Aussenpolitik und Kriegsvorbereitungdes Hitler-Regimes* (Munich, 1939), pp. 11–37.

13. Carr, *Arms, Autarky and Aggression*, pp. 70–83; Overy *Goering* (London, 1984), pp. 68–75; Klaus-Jürgen Müller, *The Army, Politics and Society in Germany, 1933–1945. Studies in the Army's Relation to Nazism* (Manchester, 1987), pp. 35–38, 54–99 (on Beck).

14. Overy, *War and Economy*, p. 148.

15. Gedye, *The Fallen Bastions*, pp. 237–299 provides a contemporary account of the atmosphere and events in Vienna.

16. Gesetz vom 13 März 1938 über die 'Wiedervereinigung Österreichs mit dem deutschen Reich'. (RGBl, 1938, p. 237), in Helma Kaden (ed.), with Ludwig Nestler, Sonja Kleinschmidt and Kurt Fortscher, *Die faschistische Okkupationspolitik in Österreich und der Tschechoslowakei (1938–1945)* (Cologne: Pahl-Rugenstein, 1988), p. 4; Gerhard Botz, *Die Eingliederung Österreichs in das deutsche Reich. Planung und Verwirklichung des politisch-administrativen Anschlusses (1938–1940)* (Vienna, 1972), pp. 73–81.

17. Gerhard Botz, 'Der ambivalente Anschluss 1938–1939. Von der Begeisterung zur Ernüchterung', *Zeitgeschichte*, 6 (1978), pp. 91–109; Kirk, *Nazism and the Working Class*, pp. 48–67; *Meldungen*, p. 72.

18. Max Domarus, *Hitler. Speeches and Proclamations 1932–1945. The Chronicle of a Dictatorship*, Vol. 2 (London, 1992), p. 1159.

19. Gedye, *Fallen Bastions*, p. 443.

20. Kershaw, *Nemesis*, p. 107.

21. *Meldungen*, 2, pp. 72–73; *Deutschland-Berichte* 1938, pp. 913–919.

22. Detlef Brandes, *Die Tschechen unter deutschem Protektorat. Teil I: Besatzung-spolitik, Kollaboration und Widerstand im Protektorat bis Heydrichs Tod.* (Munich and Vienna: Oldenbourg, 1969), pp. 15–16.

23. Igor-Philip Matić, *Edmund Veesenmeyer. Agent und Diplomat der nationalsozi-alistischen Expansionspolitik* (Munich, 2002), pp. 61–79; Tatjana Tönsmeyer, *Das Dritte Reich und die Slowakei 1939–1945. Politischer Alltag zwischen Koopera-tion und Eigensinn* (Paderborn, 2003). Brandes, *Die Tschechen unter deutschem Protektorat*, pp. 20–26.

24. Adolf Helbok and Emil Lehmann, *Heimkehrende Grenzlande. Ostmark und Sude-tengau mit dem Protektorat Böhmen und Mähren* (Leipzig, 1939), pp. 325–326.

25. Mieczyslaw Nurek, 'Great Britain and the Baltic in the Last Months of Peace', in John Hiden and Thomas Lane (eds), *The Baltic and the Outbreak of the Second World War* (Cambridge, 1992), pp. 21–49. Here pp. 25–31.

26. See Jan T. Gross, *Revolution from Abroad. The Soviet Conquest of Poland's Western Ukraine and Western Belorussia* (Princeton, NJ, 1988).

27. Koehl, RKFDV; Hans-Christian Harten, *De-Kulturation und Germanisierung. Die Nationalsozialistische Rassen- und Erziehungspolitik in Polen 1939–1945* (Frankfurt, 1996).

28. *Meldungen*, Vol. 2, p. 331 (9 October 1939).

29. Kershaw, *Hitler Myth*, pp. 151–152; *Nemesis*, p. 234.

30. Anthony McElligott, 'Reforging Mitteleuropa in the Crucible of War: The Economic Impact of Integration under German Hegemony', in Peter M. R. Stirk, *Mitteleuropa. History and Prospects* (Edinburgh, 1994), pp. 129–158.

31. Kershaw, *Nemesis*, p. 388.

32. Richard Overy, *Russia's War* (London, 1997), pp. 73–80.

33. *Meldungen* 7, pp. 2240–2242 (26 June), pp. 2458–2459 (30 June) and pp. 2470–2471 (3 July 1941).

34. *Monologe im Führerhauptquartier*, p. 39 (5–6 July); p. 48 (27 July), p. 48; McElligott on traffic.

35. Lidiya Ginzburg, *Blockade Diary* (London, 1995), p. 28.

36. Arnold Toynbee and Veronica M. Toynbee, *Hitler's Europe* (Oxford, 1951), p. 632.

37. *Meldungen*, 12, pp. 4750–4751 (4 February 1943).

38. Goebbels, *Tagebücher*, 19 February 1943.

39. Earl R. Beck, *Under the Bombs. The German Home Front 1942–1945* (Lexington, Kentucky, 1986) Martin Middlebrook, *The Battle of Hamburg. The Firestorm Raid* (London, 1980).

40. Martin Kitchen, *Nazi Germany at War* (London, 1995), pp. 87–90.

41. Neil Gregor, 'A *Schicksalsgemeinschaft*'? Allied Bombing, Civilian Morale and Social Dissolution in Nuremberg 1942–1945', *Historical Journal* 43/4 (2000), pp. 1051–1070.

42. *Meldungen*, 17, p. 6526.

43. *Meldungen*, 5, p. 1411 (22 July 1940).

44. Rüdiger Hachtmann, 'Industriearbeiterinnen in der deutschen Kriegswirtschaft 1936–1944/45', *Geschichte und Gesellschaft* 19/3 (1993), pp. 332–361. Here p. 357; *Meldungen*, 12, p. 4576; BA/MA.
45. Stephenson, *Women in Nazi Germany*, p. 103.
46. Elizabeth Harvey, *Women and the Nazi East. Agents and Witnesses of Germanization* (New Haven and London, 2003).
47. See Tim Kirk, 'The Policing of Popular Opinion in Nazi Germany', in Dermot Cavanagh and the Tim Kirk, *Subversion and Scurrility: Popular Discourse in Europe from 1500 to the Present* (Aldershot, 2000).
48. *Meldungen*, 17, pp. 6734–6740.
49. Hitler's secretary recalled the events of the day in the bunker in her memoirs: Traudl Junge, *Until the Final Hour. Hitler's Last Secretary* (London, 2003), pp. 186–189.
50. See Michael R. Marrus, *The Nuremberg War Crimes Trial 1945–46* (Boston and New York, 1997).

Conclusion

1. See Michael R. Marrus, *The Nuremberg War Crimes Trial 1945–46. A Documentary History* (Boston and New York, 1997).
2. For a comparison of the impact of the two world wars see Richard Bessel, *Nazism and War* (London, 2004).
3. Karl Dietrich Erdmann, *Das Ende des Reiches und die Neubildung deutscher Staaten* (Stuttgart, 1976).
4. Thomas Assheuer and Hans Sarkowicz, *Rechtsradikale in Deutschland. Die alte und die neue Rechte* (Munich, 1992), pp. 12–14.
5. See for example, S. Jonathan Wiesen, *West German Industry and the Challenge of the Nazi Past 1945–1955* (Chapel Hill, 2001).
6. See Detlev Peukert, *The Weimar Republic: The Crisis of Classical Modernity* (London, 1991).
7. Rainer Zitelmann, *Hitler. The Politics of Seduction* (London, 1999), pp. 450–452; and Mark Roseman, 'National Socialism and Modernisation', in Bessel (ed.), *Fascist Italy and Nazi Germany*, pp. 197–229, for a careful consideration of the question as a whole.
8. The reference is to one of the newspaper articles that sparked the *Historikerstreit* of the 1980s: Ernst Nolte, 'Vergangenheit, die nicht vergehen will. Eeine Rede, die geschrieben, aber nicht gehalten werden konnte', *Frankfurter Allgemeine Zeitung*, 6 June 1986.

Glossary of Terms and Abbreviations

Agrarian League (*Reichs-Landbund*): Pressure group formed in 1921 from the merger of the pre-war organisations *Bund der Landwirte* (League of Farmers) and *Deutscher Landsbund* (German Agrarian League).

Aktion T4: Nazi euthanasia programme. Named after the organisation's Berlin headquarters at Tiergartenstrasse 4.

Alltagsgeschichte: The 'history of everyday life', an approach to 'history from below' which emerged during the 1970s and 1980s.

Alte Kämpfer: Literally 'old fighters'; Nazi party veterans, a term used to distinguish long-serving party members from late converts, especially those who joined the party for opportunistic reasons.

Altreich: German state within the borders of 1937.

Amt: Office.

Anschluss: Unification of Germany and Austria.

Asocial: Category of people deemed incapable of integrating into German society, or 'biologically criminal', including beggars, vagrants and the 'workshy' as well as 'habitual criminals'.

Axis: Germany's alliance with Italy (originally the 'Rome-Berlin Axis'), Japan (after the Anti-Comintern pact of 1936), Hungary, Romania and Bulgaria.

Berchtesgaden: Bavarian location of Hitler's 'Eagle's Nest' retreat.

Barbarossa: Code name for invasion of Soviet Union.

Bauhaus: State school of design and architecture associated with the avant-garde.

BdM: *Bund deutscher Mädel* (League of German Girls), Girls' equivalent of the Hitler Youth for girls aged 14–18.

Beamte (pl.): Officials, civil servants.

Beauftragter: Commissioner; official charged with specific task.

Bezirk: Administrative district.

Blitzkrieg: 'Lightning war'; rapid attacks on limited battle fronts.

Blubo: Abbreviation of '*Blut und Boden*' used to describe Nazi films idealising rural life.

Blut und Boden: 'Blood and Soil': propaganda slogan idealising and mytholgising the countryside.

Council of People's Deputies: (*Rat der Volksbeauftragten*) National assembly of workers' and soldiers' councils during the revolution of 1918–19.

DAF: **Deutsche Arbeitsfront**, German Labour Front. Corporatist organisation established to replace the trades unions in 1933.

DDP: *Deutsche Demokvatische Partei*, German Democrative Party.

Deutsches Frauenwerk: 'German Women's Enterprise'. Nazi organisation set up in 1933 as umbrella for all existing German women's organisations.

Deutsches Jungvolk: Pre-Hitler Youth organisation for small boys (aged 10–14).

Dolchstosslegende ('Stab-in-the-back myth'): widespread belief on the right that Germany was not militarily defeated in 1918, but betrayed by socialists and Jews.

DNVP: *Deutschnationale Volkspartei*, German National People's Party.

DVP: *Deutsche Volkspartei*, German People's Party.

Einsatzgruppen: Special task force of Security Police (Sipo), or SD in occupied territories.

Free Trades Unions: Unions associated with the Social Democratic labour movement as distinct from those sponsored by employers or Christian trades unions associated with the Catholic church.

Freikorps (Free Corps): Right-wing paramilitary organisations active in the early years of the Weimar Republic.

Führer (leader): Title adopted by Hitler during the early years of the Nazi Party, and used after the death of Hindenburg to describe his position following the fusion of the offices of Chancellor and President.

Fulfilment policy (*Erfüllungspolitik*): German foreign policy based on adherence to the Treaty of Versailles.

Gau (pl. *Gaue*): Region, principal territorial division of NSDAP.

Gauleiter: Regional leader.

Gefolgschaft ('retinue'): Medieval term used in Nazi ideology to describe industrial workforce, which was to follow the 'factory leader'.

Generalgouvernement: 'General Government'; that part of Poland not directly incorporated into the Reich, but governed as a satellite territory by a German civilian administration in Kraków.

Gestapo (Geheime Staatspolizei): Secret State Police.

Glaube und Schönheit: (Faith and Beauty). Youth organisation for 17–21 year old girls.

Gleichschaltung: Generally translated as 'co-ordination' this term refers to the process of political alignment that took place in Germany after 1933, and specifically, the Nazification of German institutions and society with Nazism.

Grossraumwirtschaft: 'Greater regional economy': a term used to describe the organisation of a supra-national region under the aegis of a regional economic superpower (and specifically continental Europe under the leadership of Nazi Germany).

Hitler Jugend (HJ) Hitler Youth: Established in 1926 and still insignificant in terms of membership by 1933, it expanded during the Third Reich. Membership became compulsory in 1939.

Historikerstreit: Debate among German historians in the 1980s which followed attempts to relativise the Holocaust.

IG Farben: Giant chemicals cartel involved in attempts to manufacture synthetic materials for Four Year Plan; the firm developed the Zyklon B gas used to murder Jews in Poland.

Jungmädel-Bund: Nazi girls' organisation for those aged between 10 and 14.

Kapp Putsch: Attempt by right wing conspiracy with support of army officers to seize power in Germany in March 1920.

KdF (*Kraft durch Freude*), Strength through Joy: Nazi leisure organisation, a division of the German Labour Front (DAF).

KPD (*Kommunistische Partei Deutschlands*): German Communist Party.

Kreis: Administrative district.

Kripo: Kriminalplizei, criminal police.

Land (pl. *Länder*): State within Germany (such as Prussia, Bavaria or Saxony). The *Länder* had far-reaching autonomy between 1871 and 1933. Prussia was further divided into provinces (*Provinzen*).

Landtag: regional parliament or 'diet'; the legislative assembly of the *Land* (e.g. Prussian or Bavarian regional parliament).

Lebensraum (living space): Term used to describe territory to be gained for German settlement in eastern Europe and Russia.

Mein Kampf (*My Struggle*): Hitler's autobiographical account of his political education.

Mittelstand (middle estate): Lower middle class of small farmers, small businessmen and white collar workers.

NSBO (*Nationalsozialistische Betriebszellenorganisation*): National Socialist Factory Cell Organisation set up in 1928 to organise support for the Nazis in factories.

NSDAP (*Nationalsozialistische Deutsche Arbeiterpartei*): National Socialist German Workers' Party – the official name of the Nazi Party from 1920.

NS Frauenschaft: Nazi women's organisation, intended to recruit an elite cadre of Nazi women.

Paragraph 175: Section of Reich legal code used by Nazis for the persecution of homosexuals, reinforced by the more draconian Paragraph 175a in 1935.

Papen coup: Term used to refer to the unconstitutional dismissal by Chancellor Franz von Papen of the elected government of Prussia in 1932.

Regierungsbezirk: Administrative district.

Reichsarbeitsdienst: State Labour service.

Reichsstatthalter: Reich governor of a *Land*, often the same person as the *Gauleiter*.

Reichstag: Parliament of German Reich. It was retained by the Nazis, but was functionally without power.

Reichswehr: German army. It became the *Wehrmacht* in 1935.

RSHA (*Reichssicherheitshauptamt*): Reich Security Head Office formed in 1939 with the merger of the head office of the SS and the head office of the Gestapo under Heydrich.

SA (Sturmabteilung, 'storm division'): Nazi stormtroopers' organisation: the party's paramilitary force, founded in 1921.

Schönheit der Arbeit: German Labour Front (DAF) organisation established by the Nazis to encourage German employers to improve working conditions.

SD (Sicherheitsdienst): Security Service of the SS. Founded in 1931 as an intelligence service internal to the SS, it became Nazi Party intelligence service in 1934.

Sipo (Sicherheitspolizei, Security Police): Comprising Gestapo and *Kripo*.

Sonderweg: Term used by some historians to describe Germany's supposedly 'peculiar' or 'exceptuional' process of modernisation.

Sopade: German Social Democratic Party in Exile.

SPD: *Sozialdmokratische Partei Deutschlands,* German Social Democratic Party.

SS (Schutzstaffeln): Literally, guard unit. Founded in 1925, to protect leading Nazis. Under Himmler (from 1929) it became the most powerful affiliated organisation of the NSDAP, establishing control over the entire police and security systems, and forming the basis of the Nazi police state, and the major instrument of racial policy in the camps and in occupied Europe.

Stahlhelm: Largest and most important Freikorps formation in Weimar Republic, closely associated with the DN.

USPD (*Unabhängige Sozialdemokratische Partei Deutschlands*): Independent Social Democratic Party of Germany. Radical splinter group from the SPD after 1917 (the latter was referred to as the Majority SPD or MSPD). The USPD split in October 1920 when the majority of its members joined the KPD. The rest returned to the SPD in 1922.

Vaterlandspartei: Right-wing party formed in 1917 to mobilise popular opposition to the Reichstag peace initiative. It disbanded in December 1918.

Volk: Lit. people, a term which also contains meaning of nation or race.

Völkisch (adj.): Term used to describe the radical right racist nationalist movement and its values.

Völkischer Beobachter: Nazi Party newspaper.

Volksgerichtshof: 'People's Court', set up after the Reichstag fire to deal with treason.

Volksgemeinschaft: 'National community': Nazi notion of a harmonious society which transcended class conflict and was founded on racial exclusivity.

Volksgenossen: 'National comrades' term used to describe members of the 'Volksgemeinschaft'.

Volkssturm: Militia of all able-bodied German males between the ages of 16 and 60, formed in September 1944 and deployed, without training or adequate arms.

Volkstum: Term denoting nationhood, ethnicity or national cultural identity.

Wehrmacht: Armed forces. The term refers to army, navy and air force.

Further Reading

References to the material used in this book are in the notes, and this bibliography is an inevitable selective guide to further reading. It is arranged thematically to reflect the structure of the book itself. Book chapters have not been included where the collection from which they are taken is listed, and references to journal articles have generally been avoided. Three works stand out as obvious starting points. First, Jeremy Noakes and Geoffrey Pridham (eds), *Nazism 1919–1945* (3 vols, 1983–1988), along with Jeremy Noakes, *Nazism 1919–1945 Volume 4: The German Home Front in World War II. A Documentary Reader* (Exeter, 1998), is not only the best comprehensive selection of primary sources in English, but provides explanatory commentary more helpful than many secondary works. Neil Gregor (ed.), *Nazism* (Oxford, 2000), in the Oxford Readers series, is a carefully chosen anthology of excerpts from secondary sources (including material otherwise unavailable in English), and makes an indispensable starting point to forays in to the vast secondary literature on Nazism. Ian Kershaw, *The Nazi Dictatorship. Problems and Perspectives of Interpretation* (4th edition, London, 2000) has, in successive editions, surveyed and summarised the most important debates about Nazism and, increasingly, set the historiographical agenda.

Two published collections of primary sources in German have proved extremely useful to historians of Nazi Germany over the last 25 years and have been used extensively in this book: *Deutschland-Berichte der Sopade 1934–1940* (7 vols, Salzhausen/Frankfurt, 1980). Heinz Boberach (ed.), *Meldungen aus dem Reich. Die Geheimen Lageberichte des Sicherheitsdienstes der SS 1938–1945* (17 vols, Herrsching, 1984).

Primary Sources, Diaries, Memoirs and Autobiographies

Ute Benz, *Frauen im Nationalsozialismus. Dokumente und Zeugnisse* (Munich, 1993).
Max Domarus, *Hitler. Speeches and Proclamations 1932–1945. The Chronicle of a Dictatorship* (London, 1990–1997).

Günter Grau, *Homosexulaität in der NS-Zeit. Dokumente einer Diskriminierung und Verfolgung* (Frankfurt, 1993).

Helmut Heiber (ed.), *The Early Goebbels Diaries.*

Adolf Hitler, *Mein Kampf* (London, 1992) *Hitler's Second Book.*

Traudl Junge, *Until the Final Hour. Hitler's Last Secretary* (London, 2003).

Harry Kessler, *The Diaries of a Cosmopolitan 1918–1937* (London, 1971).

Ernst Klee (ed.), *Dokumente zur 'Euthanasie'* (Frankfurt, 2001).

Victor Klemperer, *I Shall Bear Witness: The Diaries of Victor Klemperer* (London, 1998).

Timothy W. Mason, *Arbeiterklasse und Volksgemeinschaft. Dokumente und Materialien zur deutschen Arbeiterpolitik 1936–1939* (Opladen, 1975).

Wolfgang Michalka (ed.), *Deutsche Geschichte 1933–1945. Dokumente zur Innen- und Aussenpolitik* (Frankfurt, 1993).

Klaus Mlynek, *Gestapo Hannover meldet... Polizei- und Regierungsberichte für das mittlere und südliche Niedersachsen zwischen 1933 und 1937* (Hildesheim, 1986).

Reinhard Opitz (ed.), *Europastrategien des deutschen Kapitals 1900–1945* (Bonn, 1994).

Alison Owings, *Frauen. German Women Recall the Third Reich* (Harmondsworth, 1993).

Dietmar Petzina, Werner Abelshauser and Anselm Fest (eds), *Sozialgeschichtliches Arbeitsbuch III. Materialien zur Statistik des deutschen Reiches 1914–1945* (Munich, 1978).

F. Taylor (ed.), J *Goebbels, Diaries 1939–1941.*

H. R. Trevor Roper (ed.), *Hitler's Table Talk 1941–1944* (London, 1973).

Biographies

Peter R. Black, *Ernst Kaltenbrunner: Ideological Soldier of the Third Reich* (Princeton, 1984).

Richard Breitman, *The Architect of Genocide. Himmler and the Final Solution* (London, 1991).

Alan Bullock, *Hitler. A Study in Tyranny* (London, 1952).

William Carr, *Hitler. A Study in Personality and Politics* (London, 1993).

J. Fest, *The Face of the Third Reich* (London, 1970).

Ian Kershaw, *Hitler* (Harlow, 1991).

——, *Hitler 1889–1936: Hubris* (London, 1998).

——, *Hitler 1936–1945: Nemesis* (New York, 2000).

Jochen Lang, *Bormann: The Man Who Manipulated Hitler* (London, 1979).

Richard Overy, *Goering. The 'Iron Man'* (London, 1984).

Ronald Smelser and Rainer Zitelmann (eds), *The Nazi Elite* (Basingstoke, 1993).

General Books and Collections

Richard Bessel (ed.), *Fascist Italy and Nazi Germany. Comparisons and Contrasts* (Cambridge, 1996).

Karl Dietrich Bracher, *The German Dictatorship: The Origins, Structure and Consequences of National Socialism* (London, 1971).

Michael Burleigh (ed.), *Confronting the Nazi Past. New Debates on German History* (London, 1996).

Thomas Childers and Jane Caplan (eds), *Reevaluating the Third Reich* (New York and London, 1993).

Ernst Fraenkel, *The Dual State. A Contribution to the Theory of Dictatorship* (London, 1941).

Norbert Frei, *National Socialist Rule in Germany The Führer State 1933–1945* (Oxford, 1993).

Larry Eugene Jones and James N. Retallack (eds), *Between Reform, Reaction and Resistance. Studies in the History of German Conservatism from 1789 to 1945* (Providence RI and Oxford, 1993).

Ian Kershaw and Moshe Lewin (eds), *Stalinism and Nazism: Dictatorships in Comparison* (Cambridge, 1997), pp. 75–87.

Tim Kirk and Anthony McElligott (eds), *Opposing Fascism. Community, Authority and Resistance in Occupied Europe* (Cambridge, 1999).

Anthony McElligott and Tim Kirk (eds), *Working Towards the Führer. Essays in Honour of Sir Ian Kershaw* (Manchester, 2003).

Michael Mann, *Fascists* (Cambridge, 2004).

Hans Mommsen, *From Weimar to Auschwitz. Essays in German History* (Cambridge, 1991).

Jeremy Noakes (ed.), *Government Party and People in Nazi Germany* (Exeter, 1980).

Richard Overy, *The Dictators. Hitler's Germany and Stalin's Russia* (London, 2004).

Kevin Passmore (ed.), *Women, Gender and Fascism in Europe 1919–1945* (Manchester, 2003).

Robert Paxton, *The Anatomy of Fascism* (London, 2004).

H. A. Turner (ed.), *Nazism and the Third Reich* (New York, 1972).

Interpretations

P. Ayçoberry, *The Nazi Question. An Essay on the Interpretations of National Socialism (1922–1975)* (London, 1979).

Richard Evans, *In Hitler's Shadow. West German Historians and the Attempt to Escape from the Nazi Past* (London, 1989).

Carl Friedrich and Zbigniew Brzezinski, *Totalitarian Dictatorship and Autocracy* (Cambridge, Mass., 1956).

Ian Kershaw, *The Nazi Dictatorship. Problems and Perspectives of Interpretation* (London, 2000).

John Hiden and John Farquharson, *Explaining Hitler's Germany. Historians and the Third Reich* (London, 1983).

Alf Lüdtke (ed.), *The History of Everyday Life. Reconstructing Historical Experiences and Ways of Life* (Princeton, NJ, 1995).

Charles S. Maier *The Unmasterable Past: History, Holocaust, and German National Identity* (Cambridge, Mass., 1988).

Leonard Schapiro, *Totalitarianism* (London, 1973).

The Origins and Development of Nazism and the Politics of the Weimar Republic

Richard Bessel, *Political Violence and the Rise of Nazism* (New Haven, 1994).

——, 'The Nazi Capture of Power', *Journal of Contemporary History* 39/2 (2004), pp. 169–188.

Martin Broszat, *Hitler and the Collapse of the Weimar Republic* (Providence RI and Oxford, 1987).

Thomas Childers, *The Nazi Voter. The Social Foundations of Fascism in Germany 1919–1933* (Chapel Hill, 1983).

—— (ed.), *The Formation of the Nazi Constituency 1919–1933* (Totowa, NJ, 1986).

Andreas Dorpalen, *Hindenburg and the Weimar Republic* (Princeton, 1964).

Geoff Eley, *Reshaping the German Right. Radical Nationalism and Political Change After Bismarck* (2nd edition, Ann Arbor, 1991).

Richard Evans, *The Coming of the Third Reich* (London, 2003).

Conan Fischer, *Stormtroopers: A Social, Economic and Ideological Analysis 1929–1935* (London, 1983).

——, *The Rise of the Nazis* (Manchester, 1995).

Heinz Hagenlücke, *Deutsche Vaterlandspartei. Die nationale Rechte am Ende des Kaiserreichs* (Düsseldorf, 1997).

A. J. Nicholls, *Weimar and the Rise of Hitler* (London, 1979).

Detlev Peukert, *The Weimar Republic: The Crisis of Classical Modernity* (London, 1991).

Richard F. Hamilton, *Who Voted for Hitler?* (Princeton, 1982).

Michael Kellog, *The Russian Roots of Nazism. White Emigrés and the Making of National Socialism, 1917–1945* (Cambridge, 2005).

Ian Kershaw (ed.), *Weimar. Why did German Democrarcy Fail?* (London, 1990).

Eberhard Kolb, *The Weimar Republic* (London, 1988).

George Mosse, *The Crisis of German Ideology: Intellectual Origins of the Third Reich* (New York, 1964).

Detlef Mühlberger, *The Social Bases of Nazism 1919–1933* (Cambridge, 2003).

Julia Sneeringer, *Winning Women's Votes: Propaganda and Politics in Weimar Germany* (Chapel Hill and London 2002).

Robert G. L. Waite, *Vanguard of Nazism. The Free Corps Movement in Postwar Germany 1918–1923* (Cambridge, Mass., 1952).

The Nazi Dictatorship: Politics, the Party and the State

Karl Dietrich Bracher, Wolfgang Sauer and Gerhard Schulz (eds), *Die nationalsozialistische Machtergreifung. Studien zur Errichtung des totalitären Herrschaftssystems* (Cologne and Opladen, 1962).

Martin Broszat, *The Hitler State. The Foundation and Co-ordination of the Internal Structure of the Third Reich* (London and New York, 1981).

Jane Caplan, *Government Without Administration. State and Civil Service in Weimar and Nazi Germany* (Oxford, 1988).

Michael Kater, *The Nazi Party. A Social Profile of Members and Leaders, 1919–1945* (Oxford, 1983).

Ian Kershaw, *The Hitler Myth. Image and Reality in the Third Reich* (Oxford, 1987).

Dietrich Orlow, *The History of the Nazi Party 1919–1945*, 2 vols (Pittsburgh, 1969).

E. N. Peterson, *The Limits of Hitler's Power* (Princeton, 1969).

Peter Stachura (ed.), *The Shaping of the Nazi State* (London, 1978).

Nazism and the Economy

William Carr, *Arms, Autarky and Aggression* (London, 1972).

Gustavo Corni, *Hitler and the Peasants. Agrarian Policy in the Third Reich* (New York, 1990).

Peter Hayes, *Industry and Ideology. IG Farben in the Nazi Era* (Cambridge, 1987).

Ulrich Herbert, *Fremdarbeiter. Politik und Praxis des Ausländer-Einsatzes in derKriegswirtschaft des Dritten Reiches* (Berlin, 1986).

—— (ed.), *Europa und der Reichseinsatz. Ausländische Zivilarbeiter, Kriegsgefangene und KZ-Häftlinge in Deutschland 1938–1945* (Essen, 1991).

Alan Milward, *The German Economy at War* (London, 1965).

Franz Neumann, *Behemoth. The Structure and Practice of National Socialism* (London, 1942).

Richard Overy, *The Nazi Economic Recovery 1932–1938* (London, 1982).

——, *War and Economy in the Third Reich* (Oxford, 1994).

Arthur Schweitzer, *Big Business in the Third Reich* (Bloomington, 1964).

Henry Ashby Turner, *German Big Business and the Rise of Hitler* (Oxford, 1985).

German Society Under Nazism

Pierre Ayçoberry, *The Social History of the Third Reich 1933–1945* (New York, 1999).

Richard Bessel (ed.), *Life in the Third Reich* (Oxford, 1987).

F. L. Carsten, *The German Workers and the Nazis* (Aldershot, 1995).

David Crew (ed.), *Nazism and German Society 1933–1945* (London, 1994).

Bernhard Diestelkamp and Michael Stolleis (eds), *Justizalltag im Dritten Reich* (Frankfurt, 1988).

J. E. Farquharson, *The Plough and the Swastika. The NSDAP and Agriculture in Germany 1928–45* (London, 1976).

Robert Gellately and Nathan Stoltzfuss, *Social Outsiders in Nazi Germany* (Princeton, 2001).

Rüdiger Hachtmann, 'Industriearbeiterinnen in der deutschen Kriegswirtschaft 1936–1944/45', *Geschichte und Gesellschaft* 19/3 (1993), pp. 332–361.

Ulrich Herbert, 'Arbeiterschaft im Dritten Reich. Zwischenbilanz und offene Fragen', in *Geschichte und Gesellschaft* 15 (1989), 320–360.

Michael H. Kater, *Hitler Youth* (Cambridge Mass., and London, 2004).

Ian Kershaw, *Popular Opinion and Political Dissent in the Third Reich. Bavaria 1933–1945* (Oxford, 1984).

Martin Kitchen, *Nazi Germany at War* (London, 1995).

Hans Koch, *The Hitler Youth. Origins and Development 1922–1945* (London, 1975).

Tim Mason, *Social Policy in the Third Reich* (Oxford, 1993).

——, *Nazism, Fascism and the Working Class*, edited by Jane Caplan (Cambridge, 1995).

Günter Morsch, *Arbeit und Brot. Studien zu Lage, Stimmung, Einstellung und Verhalten der deutschen Arbeiterschaft 1933–1936/7* (Frankfurt, 1993).

Lisa Pine, 'Hashude: The Imprisonment of "Asocial" Families in the Third Reich', *German History* 13 (1995), 182–197.

Lisa Pine, *Nazi Family Policy* (Oxford and New York, 1997).

Detlev Peukert, *Inside the Third Reich: Conformity, Opposition and Racism in Everyday Life* (Harmondsworth, 1989).

Caroa Sachse, *Betriebliche Sozialpolitik als Familienpolitik in der Weimarer Republik und im Nationalsozialismus: mit einer Fallstudie über die Firma Siemens* (Hamburg, 1987).

Adalheid von Saldern, *Mittelstand in "Dritten Reich". Handwerker – Enzelhändler – Bauern* (Frankfurt, 1979).

Michael Schneider, *Unterm Hakenkreuz. Arbeiter und Arbeiterbewegung 1933 bis 1939* (Bonn, 1999).

David Schoenbaum, *Hitler's Social Revolution. Class and Status in Nazi Germany 1933–1939* (New York, 1990).

Culture, Leisure and Propaganda

Bettina Arnold, 'The Past as Propaganda: Totalitarian Archaeology in Nazi Germany', *Antiquity* 64 (1990), reprinted in Robert Preucel and Ian Hodder, *Contemporary Archaeology in Theory* (Oxford, 1996), 549–567.

Shelley Baranowski, *Strength through Joy. Consumerism and Mass Tourism in the Third Reich* (Cambridge, 2004).

Heinrich Härke (ed.), *Archaeology, Ideology and Society. The German Experience* (2nd edition, Frankfurt, 2002).

Guntram Heinrik Herb, *Under the Map of Germany. Nationalism and Propaganda 1918–1945* (London, 1997).

Jeffrey Herf, *Reactionary Modernism. Technology, Culture and Politics in Weimar and the Third Reich* (Cambridge, 1984).

Michael H. Kater, *The Twisted Muse. Musicians and Their Music in the Third Reich* (Oxford, 1997).

Rudy Koshar, *From Monuments to Traces: Artifacts of German Memory 1870–1990* (Berkeley, 2000).

Jeremy Noakes, 'The Ivory Tower Under Siege: German Universities in the Third Reich', in *Journal of European Studies* 23/4 (1993), pp. 371–408.

Jonathan Petropoulos, *Art as Politics in the Third Reich* (Chapel Hill and London, 1996).

Peter Reichel, *Der schöne Schein des Dritten Reiches. Faszination und Gewalt des Faschismus* (Frankfurt, 1993).

Klaus Scholder, *The Churches and the Third Reich* (2 vols, London, 187).

Alan E. Steinweis, *Art, Ideology and Economics in Nazi Germany. The Reich Chambers of Music, Theater and the Visual Arts* (Chapel Hill, 1993).

Margit Szöllösi-Janze (ed.), *Science in the Third Reich* (Oxford and New York, 2001).

David Welch (ed.), *Nazi Propaganda* (London, 1983).

——, *The Third Reich. Politics and Propaganda* (London, 1993).

Consensus and Opposition and the Police State

J. S. Conway, *The Nazi Persecution of the Churches* (London, 1968).

G. C. Browder, *Foundations of the Nazi Police State. The Formation of Sipo and SD* (Lexington, 1990).

Robert Gellately, *The Gestapo and German Society. Enforcing Racial Policy 1933–1945* (Oxford, 1991).

——, *Backing Hitler* (Oxford, 2001).

Oron J. Hale, *The Captive Press in the Third Reich* (Princeton, 1964).

Peter Hoffmann, *The History of the German Resistance 1933–1945* (Montreal, 1996).

Eric Johnson, *Nazi Terror: The Gestapo, Jews, and Ordinary Germans* (London, 1999).

Klemens von Klemperer, *German Resistance Against Hitler: The Search for Allies Abroad 1938–1945* (Oxford, 1992).

David Clay Large, *Contending with Hitler. Varieties of German Resistance in the Third Reich* (Cambridge, 1991).

Reinhard Mann, *Protest und Kontrolle im Dritten Reich. Nationalsozialistische Herrschaft im Alltag einer rheinischen Grossstadt* (Frankfurt, 1987).

Francis R. Nicosia and Lawrence D. Stokes (eds), *Germans Against Hitler: Nonconformity, Opposition and Resistance in the Third Reich: Essays in Honour of Peter C. Hoffmann* (New York, 1990).

Jürgen Schmädeke and Peter Steinbach (eds), *Der Widerstand gegen den Nationalsozialismus. Die deutsche Gesellschaft und der Widerstand gegen Hitler* (Munich 1986), pp. 73–85.

Peter Steinbach and Johannes Tuchel (eds), *Widerstand gegen den Nationalsozialismus* (Berlin, 1994).

W. Sweet, 'The Volksgerichtshof 1934–45', *Journal of Modern History* (1974).

Nikolaus Wachsmann, *Hitler's Prisons. Legal Terror in Nazi Germany* (New Haven and London, 2004).

Michael Wildt, *Generation des Unbedingten. Das Führungskorps des Reichssicherheitshauptamtes* (Hamburg, 2003), pp. 53–60.

Reproduction, the Family and Racial Hygiene

Lynn Abrams and Elizabeth Harvey, *Gender Relations in German History: Power, Agency and Experience from the Sixteenth to the Twentieth Century* (London, 1996).

Doris L. Bergen, 'Sex, Blood and Vulnerability: Women Outsiders in German-Occupied Europe', in Gellately and Stoltzfuss (eds), *Social Outsiders in Nazi Germany*, pp. 273–293.

Gisela Bock, *Zwangssterilisation im Nationalsozialismsus: Studien zurRassenpolitikund Frauenpolitik* (Opladen, 1986).

R. Bridenthal *et al.* (eds), *When Biology Became Destiny* (New York, 1984).

Michael Burleigh, *Germany Turns Eastwards. A Study of Ostforschung in the Third Reich* (Cambridge, 1988).

——, *Death and Deliverance. Euthanasia in Nazi Germany 1900–1945* (Cambridge, 1994).

Michael Burleigh and Wofgang Wippermann, *The Racial State: Germany 1933–1945* (Cambridge, 1991).

Edward R. Dickinson and Richard F. Wetzell, 'The Historiography of Sexuality in Modern Germany', *German History* 23/3 2005, pp. 291–305.

Günter Grau (ed.) with Claudia Schoppmann, *Hidden Holocaust. Gay and Lesbian Persecution in Nazi Germany* (London, 1995).

Atina Grossmann, *Reforming Sex; the German Movement for Birth Control and Abortion Reform 1920–1950* (New York and Oxford, 1995).

Elizabeth Harvey, 'Visions of the Volk: German Women and the Far Right from Kaiserreich to Third Reich', *Journal of Women's History* 16/3 (2004), pp. 152–167.

Heinz Heger, *The Men with the Pink Triangle* (London, 1986).

Birthe Kundrus, 'Forbidden Company: Romantic Relationships Between Germans and Foreigners, 1939 to 1945', *Journal of the History of Sexuality* 11/1–2 (2002), pp. 201–222.

Georg Lilienthal, *Der 'Lebensborn e.V'. Ein Instrument nationalsozialistischer Rassenpolitik* (Frankfurt, 1993).

Diemut Majer, *'Non-Germans' Under the Third Reich. The Nazi Judicial System in Germany and Occupied Eastern Europe, with Special Regard to Occupied Poland 1939–1945* (Baltimore, 2003).

Robert N. Proctor, *Racial Hygiene: Medicine Under the Nazis* (Cambridge, Mass., 1988).

Maria Sophia Quine, *Population Politics in Twentieth-Century Europe* (London, 1996).

Julia Roos, 'Backlash against Prostitutes' Rights: Origins and Dynamics of Nazi Prostitution Policies', *Journal of the History of Sexuality* 11/1–2 (2002), pp. 67–94.

Jill Stephenson, *The Nazi Organisation of Women* (London, 1981).

——, *Women in Nazi Germany* (Harlow, 2001).

Matthew Stibbe, *Women in the Third Reich* (London, 2003).

Annette F. Timm, 'The Ambivalent Outsider: Prostitution, Promiscuity and VD control in Nazi Berlin', in Gellately and Stoltzfuss (eds), *Social Outsiders in Nazi Germany*, pp. 192–211.

Annette F. Timm, 'Sex with a Purpose: Prostitution, Venereal Disease, and Militarized Masculinity in the Third Reich', *Journal of the History of Sexuality* 11/1–2 (2002), pp. 223–255.

Paul Weindling, *Health, Race and German Politics Between National Unification and Nazism, 1870–1945* (Cambridge, 1989).

Irmgard Weyrather, *Muttertag und Mutterkreuz. Der Kult um die 'deutsche Mutter' im Nationalsozialismus* (Frankfurt, 1993).

Anti-Semitism and the Holocaust

Götz Aly, *Final Solution. Nazi Population Policy and the Murder of the European Jew* (London, 1999), pp. 23–26.

Götz Aly and Susanne Heim, *Architects of Annihilation. Auschwitz and the Logic of Destruction.*

Frank Bajohr, *'Aryanisation' in Hamburg. The Economic Exclusion of Jews and the Confiscation of their Property in Nazi Germany* (New York and Oxford, 2002).

Frank Bajohr, *Unser Hotel ist judenfrei. Bäder-Antisemitismus im 19. und 20. Jahrhundert* (Frankfurt, 2003).

Avraham Barkai, *From Boycott to Annihilation. The Economic Struggle of German Jews 1933–1943* (Hanover, NH and London, 1989).

Michael Berenbaum (ed.), *A Mosaic of Victims: Non-Jews Persecuted and Murdered by the Nazis* (New York, 1990).

Christopher R. Browning, *Ordinary Men* (New York, 1992).

——, *Nazi Policy, Jewish Workers, German Killers* (Cambridge, 2000).

——, *The Origins of the Final Solution. The Evolution of Nazi Jewish Policy, September 1939–March 1942* (London, 2004).

Gustavo Corni, *Hitler's Ghettos. Voices from a Beleaguered Society 1939–1944* (London, 2002).

L. S. Dawidowicz, *The War Against the Jews 1933–1945* (London, 1975).

Martin Dean, *Collaboration in the Holocaust. Crimes of the Local Police in Belorussia and the Ukraine, 1941–44* (Basingstoke, 2000).

Hermann Graml, *Antisemitism in the Third Reich* (Oxford, 1992).

Yisrael Gutman and Michael Berenbaum, *Anatomy of the Auschwitz Death Camp* (Bloomington, 1998).

Ulrich Herbert, *National Socialist Extermination Policies. Contemporary German Perspectives and Controversies* (New York and Oxford, 2000), pp. 163–185.

Raul Hilberg, *The Destruction of the European Jews*, 3 vols (Third edition, New Haven and London, 2003).

Helmut Krausnick and Martin Broszat, *Anatomy of the SS State* (St Albans, 1973).

Gunter Lewy, *The Nazi Persecution of the Gypsies* (Oxford, 2001).

Bob Moore, *Victims and Survivors – The Nazi Persecution of the Jews in the Netherlands, 1940–45* (London, 1997).

Peter Pulzer, *The Rise of Political Anti-Semitism in Germany and Austria* (2nd edition, London, 1988).

Mark Roseman, *The Villa, the Lake, the Meeting: Wannsee and the Final Solution* (London, 2002).

Karl A. Schleunes, *The Twisted Road to Auschwitz. Nazi Policy Toward German Jews 1933–39* (London, 1972).

Gitta Sereny, *Into That Darkness* (London, 1977).

Foreign Policy, War and Occupation

Omer Bartov, *The Eastern Front 1941–45: German Troops and the Barbarisation of Warfare* (London, 1985).

Richard Bessel, *Nazism and War* (London, 2004).

Phillipe Burin, *Living with Defeat. France under German Occupation 1940–1944* (London, 1996).

W. Deist, *The Wehrmacht and German Re-armament* (London, 1981).

Elizabeth Harvey, *Women and the Nazi East. Agents and Witnesses of Germanization* (New Haven and London, 2003).

Klaus Hildebrand, *The Foreign Policy of the Third Reich* (Berkeley, 1973).

A. Hillgruber, *Germany and the Two World Wars* (Cambridge, Mass., 1981).

David E. Kaiser, *Economic Diplomacy and the Origins of the Second World War. Germany, Britain, France and Eastern Europe* (Princeton, 1980).

Robert Koehl, *RKFDV: German Resettlement and Population Policy 1939–1945. A History of the Reich Commission for the Strengthening of Germandom* (Cambridge Mass., 1957).

Christian Leitz, *Nazi Germany and Neutral Europe During the Second World War* (Manchester, 2000).

Valdis O. Lumans, *Himmler's Auxiliaries. The Volksdeutsche Mittelstelle and the German National Minorities of Europe 1033–1945* (Chapel Hill, 1993).

Militärgeschichtliches Forschungsamt, *Germany and the Second World War* (6 vols, Oxford, 1990–).

Bob Moore (ed.), *Resistance in Western Europe* (New York, 2000).

Klaus-Jürgen Müller, *The Army, Politics and Society in Germany 1933–1945. Studies in the Army's Relation to Nazism* (Manchester, 1987).

Richard Overy, *Russia's War* (London, 1997).

Norman Rich, *Hitler's War Aims* (2 vols, New York, 1973).

Woodruff D. Smith, *The Ideological Origins of Nazi Imperialism* (New York and Oxford, 1986).

G. Stoakes, *Hitler and the Quest for World Dominion: Nazi Ideology and Foreign Policy in the 1920s* (Leamington Spa, 1986).

Arnold Toynbee and Veronica M. Toynbee, *Hitler's Europe* (Oxford, 1951).

Bernd Wegener, *The Waffen-SS. Organisation, Ideology and Function* (Oxford, 1990).

Index